Acting Is Believing

Acting Is Believing
A Basic Method
FOURTH EDITION

Charles McGaw
Late of the Goodman School of Drama
A School of the Art Institute of Chicago

Fourth Edition Prepared by
Gary Blake

Holt, Rinehart and Winston
New York Chicago San Francisco Atlanta Dallas Montreal Toronto London Sydney

To Fern and Mary

EDITOR
Roth Wilkofsky

DEVELOPMENTAL EDITOR
Lester A. Sheinis

COPY EDITOR
Kristin Camitta Zimet

PRODUCTION MANAGER
Nancy Myers

ART DIRECTOR
Louis Scardino

TEXT DESIGN
Arthur Ritter

ILLUSTRATIONS
Dana Rasmussen

COVER DESIGN
Doug Fornuff

PAGE MAKEUP
Marion Feigl

Library of Congress Cataloging in Publication Data

McGaw, Charles J., date
Acting is believing.

Bibliography: p.
Includes index.
1. Acting. I. Blake, Gary. II. Title.
PN2061.M18   1980   792'.028   79–21527
ISBN 0–03–021671–0

Preface to the Fourth Edition

This revision of *Acting Is Believing* maintains the structure of earlier editions. It is organized into three parts—"The Actor Alone," "The Actor and the Play," and "The Actor and the Production." *Acting Is Believing* continues to give primary emphasis to those aspects of actor training that develop internal and interpretative skills.

In this revision, every effort has been made to add only concepts and phrases that sustain the spirit of Charles McGaw's work. The changes reflect a careful refinement of the comments obtained from acting teachers, scholars, and actors. The changes also take into account the plays produced in the past five years, as well as recent trends in acting theory and play production. The bibliography has been substantially enlarged to include a wide assortment of actor biographies and autobiographies and major books about acting.

I wish to thank the following reviewers for their helpful comments: Robert Baca, University of Utah; Marya Bednerik, University of Oregon; Harold Dixon, University of Arizona; Sara Daspin, Seminole Community College; David Emmes, Long Beach City College; Lonny Fraze, Ohio University; Joseph Garry, Cleveland State University; Phillip A. Graneto, Glassboro State College; Howard Jensen, Indiana University; Jan M. Kirschner, Tufts University; Dale Luciano, University of Arizona; Robert A. McDonald, University of Connecticut; Susan Miller, University of Illinois; Susan Murray, University of Illinois; Geoffrey Newman, Howard University; Dale Rott, Bethel College; Donald W. Seay, University of Wyoming; and Errol Segal, University of Georgia. I also wish to thank Joe Fishback, actor, teacher, and director.

GARY BLAKE

New York, New York
December 1979

Preface to the Third Edition

Each part of *Acting Is Believing* has been revised thoroughly in light of changing attitudes toward theatre during the last ten years, and two new chapters have been added. The book recognizes that today's actor must be prepared to take part in a theatre of infinite variety in which no single style prevails, and in which no single approach to acting is adequate. Today's theatre has demonstrated that the psychological technique, so fiercely championed a few years ago, is by no means mistaken, but that it is insufficient. This technique must be practiced in conjunction with other skills to provide an external form through which actors can make clear their intentions. There is an ever-increasing need for the actor to develop simultaneously both an inner and an outer technique in order to achieve complete mastery of the craft.

A basic premise of the book is that there is no essential contradiction between inner technique and theatrical effectiveness. Acting involves both a personal improvisational process and a formal structuring requiring good movement, good speech, and a good voice. Further, it is an interpretative process requiring that actors discover the playwright's meaning and communicate it to an audience, a principal means of communication being speaking the words the playwright has "set down for them." Acting is also a cooperative process in which a group of individuals work together to accomplish a common purpose.

The book maintains that, while a not quite definable something called talent is necessary for success, basic acting consists in performing a number of specific tasks about which there is no mystique. These tasks are likely to demand a good deal of hard work. *Acting Is Believing* is intended to serve talented students who are willing and able to work hard.

CHARLES McGAW

Chicago, Illinois
December 1974

Contents

PART 1
THE ACTOR ALONE

A scene from the New York Shakespeare Festival production of *A Chorus Line*, book by James Kirkwood and Nicholas Dante; setting by Robin Wagner, costumes by Theoni V. Aldredge; lighting by Tharon Musser. (Photo—Martha Swope.) In this internationally acclaimed musical, dancers compete in a grueling audition in order to secure a place in the chorus line of a Broadway musical. As with most creative endeavors, acting, for many people, is rewarding in almost every way—except monetarily. To succeed as a professional actor requires training, talent, perseverance, and a knack for being in the right place at the right time.

Training Your Talent

1

Acting is at one and the same time the simplest and the most complex of the arts. It is one of the simplest because everybody does it more or less instinctively from early childhood to the end of his life.[1] It is one of the most complex because it involves every cell and organ of the human body—the most complicated of all mechanisms. There is no single satisfactorily comprehensive definition of acting. In fact, throughout this book we will be trying to understand what acting is. At one level we can say that acting is behaving as if things that are *not* real *are* real, and we can readily see that the make-believe games of childhood are covered by this definition. At this level, depending to a degree, of course, upon the quality of his imagination, almost every child is a good actor. That is he is good provided he acts, as most children do, only for the benefit of himself and for others who are participating in the make-believe game. When he performs for the benefit of spectators, he is usually said to be "showing off." He becomes self-conscious and demonstrates his inability to solve one of the basic problems confronting anyone who professes to act in the professional sense of the word—the problem of establishing the proper relationship between the actor and the audience.[2]

A little later in life, everyone begins to gather experience in acting in another context and for another purpose. This perhaps may suitably be termed "social acting." Its practice, depending upon the circumstances and the intention of the actor, may be described at times as good manners, at times as "little white

[1] Wherever the generic "he" appears in this book, it is naturally to be taken to mean "he or she." Women and men make equally gifted actors, directors, playwrights, and producers.

[2] Throughout this book the term *professional* should be understood to mean a highly developed level of competence, not necessarily an actor who makes his living in the theatre.

lies," and at other times as downright deception. It can vary from cordially receiving guests whom one has no desire to see, to disguising a splitting headache so a companion's pleasure won't be ruined, to pretending ignorance that a surprise party is being planned, to the proverbial story of having had to work late at the office when one has actually been out on the town. This social acting involves a dimension that is not present in childhood games. The actor performs for the benefit of someone else (in many cases for an audience of only one), and the success of his performance consists in *convincing* someone else that what is not real is real. Although some people's behavior in such situations is so transparent that no one is ever "taken in," almost everyone develops some degree of skill at this level. Many wife-deceivers are known to have had long and very successful runs.

Further evidence that everyone acts is the fact that we all can relate events that we have observed, or participated in, so that our listeners share to some extent the quality of the original experience, which is to say we can tell these stories with some degree of dramatic effectiveness. And most of us attempt on occasion to mimic the speech and behavior patterns of others—even the sounds and movements of animals and machines.

This natural aptitude and these rudimentary experiences are frequently all the training the actors bring to school, college, or community theatre productions; and it must be recognized that, along with a general intelligence, they provide the basis for a certain level of success, especially when the actors have the advantage of working with a director of some skill and imagination. Indeed, repeated experiences under such conditions can produce actors of some overall ability. But the person who aims at professional competence needs a more thorough and demanding preparation. He must be made aware that the process of acting is highly complex, that the performance of a major role requires talent and technical skills fully as great as those necessary for the performance of a major concerto. This talent can be developed and these skills acquired only through long and intensive training.

Today, more than ever before, such training is necessary. A very informative handbook for the serious student of acting says:

> In the old days . . . actors without formal training were the rule. Now they are definitely the exception. Training in the art and craft of acting is a virtual necessity for a successful career, and if you *are* hired at first without it, you will need it thereafter.[3]

The "old days" were a time when fledgling actors received their training by beginning as walk-ons and bit players in stock companies or touring road shows, learning their skills in a school of very hard knocks; or a time somewhat later when young aspirants descended upon Broadway or Hollywood depending entirely upon charm, physical attractiveness, or an individual personal quality.

[3] Robert Cohen, *Acting Professionally* (National Press Books, 1972), pp. 18–19.

Those days are over. Stock companies have practically ceased to exist. The number of touring shows has been reduced greatly, especially those offering opportunities to untrained actors. Contracting horizons both in New York and in the centers for producing motion pictures have created a competitive market in which thorough training is necessary for even moderate success. Furthermore, the best opportunities today are in the regional theatre with permanent or semipermanent companies in which range and versatility are required. In the past decade, the growth of regional theatre, street theatre, and children's theatre has given both actors and playwrights a place to practice their craft away from the boom-or-bust syndrome of Broadway.

Today it has become commonplace for acting teachers to announce to their students that "there are no jobs" in acting. It is true that even within Actor's Equity, members earn, on the average, less than $4000 a year (and included within that average are several actors who make more than $2,000,000 annually!). Yet the skills a student acquires in an acting class have many applications beyond the perimeters of professional theatre. First, studying drama gives a better understanding of oneself and others. Second, creative dramatics, theatre for the aged, and the application of acting skills to the "human potential" movement in psychology provide new opportunities, and the recent emphasis on fitness, healthy diet, and meditation opens interesting employment opportunities to trained actors willing to put their skills to other than theatrical use.

Acting with Professional Competence

By now it has been clearly inferred that, while everyone acts and in a simple way achieves some measure of success, game playing and social acting fall far short of professional accomplishment. How does the behavior of a child who attains belief in an imaginary situation, or the conduct of a hostess who convinces her guests that she is unconcerned about the coffee spilt on her new sofa differ from a performance onstage?

The successful stage performance is a feat of artistry that has been carefully planned for the purpose of communicating with the greatest possible effectiveness the meaning of a particular play to an audience. The stage is not a casual world in which the actors behave impulsively and with self-determination. It is a world of careful design in which all the parts of the pattern serve to illuminate the purpose of a playwright. There is, of course, a place for inspiration and spontaneous responses, and we will talk about it later. It is quite necessary, however, to realize from the very beginning that acting is not doing what "feels natural," that spontaneous responses are most valid after careful preparation, and that inspiration comes as a result of hard work, not as the stimulus for it. Tyrone Guthrie, one of the most eminent of twentieth-century directors, wrote:

A performance at the Delacorte Theatre in Central Park. (Photo—George E. Joseph.) Free Shakespeare in the park is a tradition in New York City as well as in other cities across America. Actors performing outdoors must contend with wind, rain, and the noise of airplanes passing overhead. At the Delacorte, Shakespeare fits naturally into the pleasant "picnic" setting of the park, and enthusiastic audiences line up for their tickets hours before the play begins.

. . . drama is absolutely and elaborately prescribed, and the greatest acting contains a minimum of spontaneous invention and a maximum of carefully calculated effect repeated with only minute variations at every performance of the same part. Dramatic performance, therefore, is concerned with repeating a series of intelligibly prescribed actions in order to form an intelligibly prescribed design.[4]

To list some of the more important characteristics of good acting we may say that it is:

1. *analytical* requiring careful study so that the actor understands and appreciates the playwright's meaning

[4] Tyrone Guthrie, *The New York Times*, August 28, 1966.

2. *interpretative* requiring a faithful expression of this meaning in terms of the actor's experience and imagination

3. *formalized* having a visual and oral form that will make the meaning comprehensible to others and which has in itself artistic value

4. *projectable* having dimension, energy, and clarity that can communicate the meaning to an audience of certain size occupying a certain space

5. *repeatable* having enough permanence that the actor can effectively repeat this performance as required over a period of time.

Before going further it will be helpful to name the requisites for success in this exacting art. We can state them quite simply, the two "t's":

talent, and
training.

Talent has to be talked about rather than defined because, again, there is no satisfactory definition. Not only is talent undefinable, frequently it is also unrecognizable in an undeveloped state. Theatre history tells of many instances in which actors of great prominence were advised early in their careers that they had no potential for success. And talent must not be confused with being stagestruck or "screenstruck" because many such people are absolutely without it. They are attracted only by the most superficial elements of theatre.

The theatre can have both an artistic and a therapeutic effect when plays are presented in prisons, hospitals, and at demonstrations. In this scene, prison serves as the theatre, and each of the actors is an inmate. (Photo— Thomas J. Moran, reprinted by permission of Cell Block Theatre.)

A talented person has a body and a voice that can be trained to achieve dramatic effectiveness. He is a person who has a great desire, perhaps a great need, to share his experiences with others. He is perceptive to the world about him to the extent that his sensory and emotional responses are more intense than those of the average person. He is sensitive enough to other people that he can appreciate and understand their modes of behavior even though they may be quite different from his own. He has enough imagination that he can project himself into other periods and other places. He has enough intelligence to comprehend a playwright's purpose and to understand how the character he is playing relates to it. He has enough courage and self-confidence that he is not afraid to reveal his inmost thoughts and feelings on a public stage. He has a histrionic sense that tells him what is and what is not interesting to an audience.

A person with these talents probably can learn to act. Without them, he probably cannot.

Training, the second "t," is the method by which talent is developed. It requires time, patience, hard work, and self-discipline, and it is a process that is never finished. There is no such thing as the completely trained actor. Anyone who starts his training with the idea that acting is just fun and games will soon become discouraged. Enthusiasm, a striving for perfection (although it can never be achieved), a willingness to work cooperatively with others are all important. Abundant talent, necessary as talent is, can be a trap because it sometimes makes it possible to get along with a minimum of effort. A person of lesser talent with more discipline and a better attitude may ultimately accomplish more.

To arrive at an understanding of what an actor's training involves we can divide the process into six parts:

1. *cultural development*, an important and inadequately emphasized aspect of the training process. The material on which the actor draws is the entire realm of human knowledge and experience. He cannot afford to be ignorant of either historical or contemporary events, nor of the related arts of literature, music, and painting. An actor without access to such accumulated knowledge is deprived of one of his richest sources.
2. *external training*, the development of his body and his voice as a responsive and expressive instrument. Speech and movement are the actor's principal tools.
3. *internal training*, learning how to control and to make effective use onstage of his sensory and emotional responses
4. *interpretative training*, learning how to read a play, to analyze its structure, and to discover its total meaning
5. *rehearsal techniques*, learning how the actor prepares for rehearsals at home; how he works at rehearsals during the various stages in the preparation of a play for public presentation; how he relates to the other actors,

the director, the stage manager, the production staff; how he observes the principles of rehearsal ethics and discipline

6. *performance skills*, learning how to prepare before a performance; how to relate to the audience, how to share the play with them; how to maintain energy, tempo, and rhythm; how to keep repeating a performance without losing its original effectiveness.

This training cannot be accomplished only from study of a book. It requires the guidance of able teachers, coaches, and directors. Since theatre is a highly cooperative endeavor, training must provide the opportunity to work with others in exercises and in scene study. *After basic skills have been acquired*, it must make provision for the student to work before an audience, preferably first in a laboratory situation and later under conditions that approximate those existing in the professional theatre.

Acting is not, as it may once have been believed to be, a God-given gift that enabled some special people to go onstage without training or experience and perform instinctively. Good acting results from the practice of certain skills that can be learned if one has the aptitude and the determination to do so. These skills provide an external and an internal technique enabling the actor at each performance to execute a series of specific tasks that taken together create a design that reveals the purpose of the play. It is true that great actors have about them an aura, a personal magnetism, sometimes described as "star quality." It is another of these indefinable terms. Possibly more than anything else it is a quality that compels attention, that makes an audience want to watch them and listen to them. At this time, however, we should not be thinking about astral heights. We should be concentrating upon developing basic skills.

While a book cannot do the entire job, it can point directions and organize the training process into a logical progression. It can create an awareness of the problems and suggest solutions, thus guiding the student toward technical proficiency. It can provide exercises both for the individual and for a group. No book can be comprehensive in this area. This one, while not ignoring any aspects of the process, is concerned primarily with the development of internal and interpretative skills.

Where does the student actor begin his training? It is a matter of self-exploration. He begins with himself.

Exploring Your Resources

There is an essential difference between acting and other arts. The painter works with pigments and canvas, the sculptor with clay and stone, the pianist with keys that control hammers on strings, but the actor is his own instrument. He communicates with an audience by playing upon his own voice and his own body.

These truths are obvious. The actor's need for a well-trained voice and body is equally obvious. A musician is at a disadvantage if he has to perform on an inferior instrument. An actor is at a similar disadvantage if his muscular and vocal control are not all that they could be. Such training is necessary for effective achievement upon the stage. It was in this direction—the training of the actor's voice and body as an instrument—that writers and teachers, until well into the present century, turned their almost exclusive attention.

This essential training must be carried on in conjunction with other disciplines which are also fundamental to the actor's development. A fine speaking voice and a well-coordinated body in themselves do not make an actor, any more than possessing a Stradivarius makes a violinist. While the importance of the instrument, the *how* by which the artist reaches his audience, cannot be minimized, along with the *how* must come the *what*. Essential also to an actor's training is the development of a technique for using his inner resources to create a character conceived by the playwright. Creation of an imaginary character behaving logically in circumstances given by the playwright is the primary task of the actor, and his inner resources are a vital consideration as he begins his study.

What inner resources? What does the actor have within him that is so important?

Let us suppose you have been cast in a play and your part requires an enactment of the funeral rites for a native of Bandjarmasin. Like most untrained actors, you go to the rehearsal without having given any thought to what you will do when you get there. Your preparation has consisted of visualizing yourself in a storm of applause on opening night, receiving the recognition of hundreds of spectators that you "have it in you."

Now what exactly is "in you" that will help in bringing to life upon the stage a native of Bandjarmasin engaged in the solemn ritual of disposing of his dead? The chances are ten to one against your ever having heard of the place, to say nothing of your having a familiarity with its customs. Yet here you are at a rehearsal, and your job is to create a definite character in given circumstances. In all probability you are temporarily defeated. You have never been to Bandjarmasin. You have never read about its funeral customs. You don't know what attitude prevails toward death—whether this occasion would be a time of lamentation or one of joy and thanksgiving that the dead has finally been released from the burdens of life. In other words, you neither *know*, nor can you *imagine* anything you might do that you are certain would be truthful to this situation.

What the actor has "in him" is the accumulation of his own experience. His *inner resources* are everything that he has done, seen, thought, or imagined. His actions onstage are limited to these resources—to what he understands about life. As he is dependent upon his voice and body to carry out his actions, he is dependent upon his inner resources to tell him *what* actions to carry out.

His life experience is not derived solely from what he has personally gone through; it comes also from reading, observation, seeing plays—from many other ways. And all experience may be deepened and extended in the imagination.

The need for inner resources in the circumstances just described is so apparent that no young actor can fail to be aware of it. The need in many other circumstances, although no less great, is much less obvious.

Let us suppose you have been cast as Romeo or as Juliet, two famous parts in dramatic literature. Here you certainly have a splendid chance to prove you "have it in you." Perhaps this time you will begin less naïvely by taking stock of how your inner resources can help you in creating one of these challenging characters.

Suppose further that the scene for rehearsal is Act III, Scene 5, sometimes called the second Balcony Scene. Romeo and Juliet are the son and daughter of two powerful and wealthy families who have long been bitter enemies. Having met by chance, they have fallen deeply in love and have married secretly. Within an hour after their marriage, Romeo, involved in an outbreak of the ancient enmity, has killed Juliet's cousin and has been banished from his native city of Verona. There appears to be no hope of happiness together as the young couple say farewell in the dawning light.

You are excited at the prospect of playing one of these famous lovers. But you must also be aware of the responsibility you have assumed, and perhaps you may be somewhat frightened at the thought of your possible inadequacy. Of course you want to make a brilliant success; so foremost in your mind is the desire to create a character in whose behavior you, the other actors, and the audience can *believe*. Only in this way can such an opportunity help you to develop the talent you are sure you have. Only in this way can you learn to become a fine actor—a creative artist in your own right.

The first step in your preparation is discovering the physical actions. It is the subject of our next chapter.

Discovering the
Physical Actions

2

Begin your preparation by discovering the physical life of the character you are playing. Ask yourself what Romeo or Juliet would *do*. What specific actions would they carry out? What logical sequence would these actions follow from the beginning to the end of the scene?

The answers to these questions are derived from a careful study of the given circumstances. You need to discover what actions are stated and what are implied, and what further actions may have to be provided from the actor's imagination to make the sequence logical. Without exception, the greater the actor's inner resources, the more the circumstances will stimulate him to logical and meaningful behavior. Stanislavski's advice here is clear and specific:

> Let each actor give an honest reply to the question of what physical action he would undertake, how he would act (not feel, there should for heaven's sake be no question of feeling at this point) in the circumstances given by the playwright. . . . When these physical actions have been clearly defined, all that remains for the actor to do is to execute them.[1]

This quotation brings up two important matters which should be clarified. The first is "to act in the circumstances given by the playwright." The second is "there should be no question of feeling at this point."

The "given circumstances" include the dramatic elements of character, plot, dialogue, and locale. The playwright tells the actor *who* the character is, what he *says*, what he *does*, and *where* and *when* he does it.

[1] Constantin Stanislavski, *Creating a Role* (New York: Theatre Arts Books, 1961), p. 201.

Who?
What?
Where?
When?

Four "w's," asking questions to which the actor *must* find specific answers. We will add an essential fifth "w" in the next chapter. The answers constitute the given circumstances that the actor must observe and without which any acting, from the simplest exercises to the most complex characterizations, has no meaning. These answers generate physical actions, and these actions clearly performed communicate the circumstances of the play to the audience. *Never embark on an acting assignment until you have specific answers to these questions.* In some cases the playwright provides a fully developed character giving the actor the necessary information. Often the answers are only suggested in the play, and the actor must supply a great deal from his imagination.

Romeo is a specific character drawn by a master dramatist. He is neither you, some movie actor, a popular singer, nor the boy next door. To act in the given circumstances places a clear injunction on you to play the character the playwright has prescribed to the fullest extent that your experience and imagination enable you to understand the prescription. You must play with your own body, your own voice, your own live responses; and in seeking to discover the physical life of a character, you must always find a logical sequence of actions which you can understand and which you can believe is necessary in the situation. So the vital question always is, "What would I do *if I were this character* in these circumstances?" To ask only "What would I do in these circumstances?" would probably mean that you would not play the character the playwright has drawn.

The four "w's" trigger the imagination, whether the actor is beginning to prepare a role or just about to step onstage. It is not enough to answer them with vague, general responses. It is not very helpful for an actor in *When You Comin Back, Red Ryder?* to answer the question, "Where am I?" by saying, "In a restaurant." The actor must think in greater detail: "In a small, grimy, dusty diner in the New Mexican desert." It is not enough for the actors playing Jerry and Peter in *The Zoo Story* to imagine themselves "in a park." Instead, they should concentrate on being "in Central Park, near 75th Street and Fifth Avenue in New York, about nine blocks north of the Central Park Zoo."

An actor answers the question "What?" (What has happened previously? What is happening in the play right now?) with the same specificity. In *The Zoo Story*, Jerry is coming from the zoo and looking for someone to kill him. To answer "When?" it also helps to be specific: Is the scene in the afternoon? Does that mean twilight? Noon? Mid-afternoon? To answer "Who?" it is not enough for an actor merely to think of a saleswoman, a prince, or a second baseman. No two princes are alike. Do you imagine yourself like Prince Hamlet, Prince Valiant, or Prince Charles? You use the reply to build a character's specific, consistent behavior and to make the actions your own.

The problems of "making actions your own" and of "playing with your own live responses" will be considered in a later chapter as will the actor's use of emotion. For the present we must adhere strictly to Stanislavski's warning "there should be no question of feeling at this point."

It is true, of course, that feeling is an important part of acting. But feelings are unpredictable. You cannot directly act an emotion, nor can you call forth an emotional response *at will*. You must learn to begin with physical actions because they are tangible, controllable, actable. You can carry out a series of actions whenever you *will* to do so. What is more, carrying out the needed actions in the given circumstances may bring forth the desired feeling. Stanislavski continues the passage quoted above:

> Note that I say execute physical actions, not feel them, because if they are properly carried out the feelings will be generated spontaneously. If you work the other way and begin by thinking about your feelings and try to squeeze them out of yourself, the result will be distortion and force. . . .

But whether or not the physical actions generate an emotional response, the careful playing of them will realize the intention of the scene and accomplish the actor's primary responsibility. Success is not to be judged by whether or not emotion is aroused in the actor.

Committing Yourself to Action

The references in the preceding paragraph to the actor's *will* introduce one of his most valuable inner resources. In attempting to solve his many, and sometimes complex problems, the actor must search always for solutions which are subject to his will. He must find things to do which he can repeat whenever he wants to, and which he can control.

The will to action is one of his most powerful inner motive forces, both on the stage and off. What he *wills* to do in his search for the physical life of the character determines what he creates onstage. The strength of his desire to do these things determines how interesting his performance will be to himself and, to a large extent, how interesting it will be to his audience. The will to action is effectual to the degree that it is directed toward logical and meaningful activity, and to the degree that it is motivated by strong desire. An essential part of acting talent is strength of determination. There is no place either on the stage or in the rehearsal room for half-hearted or indifferent action. The actor must learn, without reservation, to commit himself to what he does. This personal commitment is one of the principal generators of feeling. But the actor must also be made to recognize that, through lack of knowledge, or taste, or imagination, he can will, sometimes tenaciously, to do the wrong thing—the thing that his character would not do in the given circumstances.

There are many parallels between the actor's life onstage and off. Commitment to proper action is as vital to his training as to his performance. Many would-be actors do not possess the will to do the work necessary to fine achievement. To learn how to work and how to keep working also takes talent.

To illustrate what is meant by "exploring your inner resources" and "discovering physical actions" we have talked about playing a native of Bandjarmasin or Romeo or Juliet. These problems involving a knowledge of exotic customs or an inderstanding of what you would do in a scene of emotional crisis are too complex for the beginning of actual practice. We will start with a simpler exercise.

EXERCISE

In Act II of *The Sea Gull*, by Anton Chekhov, Masha has sat for a long time listening to the conversation of others. She finally rises and hobbles offstage with the line, "Oh, my foot's gone to sleep."

Here is an acting problem providing opportunity to explore your inner resources for the purpose of finding the logical sequence of actions demanded by the given circumstances. If your foot had never gone to sleep, or if you had never observed the behavior of anyone whose foot had gone to sleep, it would be impossible for you to solve this problem until you had enlarged your experience. You would have to investigate the nature of this occurrence to find out what actions would be truthful. Fortunately, this is a common happening. It is relatively easy for you to find in your own experience what you would do if you were Masha in this situation. You would rise from the chair, discover your foot is asleep as you put your weight down on it, and take five or six uncomfortable steps to eliminate the numbness.

This is a simple, but very real acting problem. Work on it until you can *believe your actions.* Here, as in all succeeding exercises, choose your actions so they constitute a definite dramatic structure. This means there should be a *beginning* (acquainting the audience with the problem), a *middle* (developing the problem), and an *end* (resolving the problem). Each of these three structural elements should be played clearly and precisely. In the early exercises the structure will be simple. In this exercise the beginning is Masha's discovery that her foot is asleep. The middle is the painful steps she takes to restore the circulation. The end is her exit after her recovery, after she has solved her problem.

Believing Your Actions Onstage

There have been several references to "believing your actions" or to "creating a character in which you can believe." It is necessary to the actor to believe what he is doing, and his first responsibility to his audience is to induce their belief in his actions. So the objective of this exercise from *The Sea Gull* is not to pretend your foot is asleep. It is to make yourself *believe* your foot is asleep through the actions you take to ease the numbing sensation. Acting is literally a matter of "make-believe." We have already mentioned that a child in his make-believe games is acting in a rudimentary way; and his attitude is almost identical with the attitude of the actor onstage.

Children with their mud pies, their kings and queens, their cowboy-and-Indian games give themselves a set of circumstances very similar to those given to the actor by the dramatist. Then they proceed to behave in whatever fashion their experience or imagination leads them to think is true to the imposed conditions. The pleasure they receive from the game is in direct proportion to their ability to give themselves over to what they are doing—in other words, to the extent they are able to believe their actions. As the game wears thin and their belief decreases, they invent new circumstances to stimulate further action. An imaginative child proposes: "Let's make believe the king wasn't really hurt when he fell off his horse, but was only pretending. He did it so the prince would feel sorry for him and help him fight the Black Knight." Immediately a whole new sequence of actions is suggested, and every child continues the game with renewed belief.

Of course the throne is not real. It is only Father's dining chair. The king's crown is cardboard. The swords are sticks ("Mother won't let us sharpen the ends because then they would be dangerous"). The child never thinks these things are real. When the game is over, the precious crown that has been guarded so carefully is kicked to one side of the living-room floor. But while the game is on he believes these "props" are true, and it is a pretty dull adult who can pick up the throne as if it were an ordinary chair and carry it back to the dining room.

It is the same for the actor. During the day King Lear's robes hang limply on a hook in the dressing room, and the imperial crown lies unguarded on the prop table. But when the performance begins, if Lear is to convince us that he is every inch a king, the actor must believe in the circumstances given him by Shakespeare, by the costumer, and by the scene designer as thoroughly as he believes in the actual world around him. "No half-belief," as Michael Redgrave says. "Belief . . . does not begin and end by an intellectual process, but is so deep-rooted that it fires each moment, echoes in each silence, and penetrates beyond 'the threshold of the subconscious,' where it becomes creative. . . ." [2]

None of this means that the actor is subject to a kind of hallucination which makes him unconscious of the surrounding reality and induces him to accept the glass in the crown as diamonds. He knows there is no such thing as actuality in the imaginative life of the character he is playing. Like the child he knows that the crown and the robes are not real. He knows, too, that the situation is not real and that he is not actually King Lear. Toward all of these he maintains the same attitude. Toward all of them he says: "*I will act as if they were real.*" And this conviction in the truth of his actions enables him to believe also in the truth (not the reality) of the cardboard crown. If he loses his sense of truth, it is not because the crown is not real. It is because he cannot believe his own actions in relation to it.

The best way an actor can evoke a feeling of belief in what he is doing is to concentrate on simple physical actions. Stanislavski frequently emphasized that "small physical actions, small physical truths and the moments of belief in them . . . acquire a great significance on the stage. . . ." [3]

Sustaining Belief

Sustaining belief is a difficult and ever-present problem. The actor must work in front of an audience and in the midst of all the inevitable distractions of a theatrical production. He must be able to summon his belief whenever he is required to perform. Any doubt as to the rightness or truth of what he or the other actors are doing is likely to upset him immediately. An actor who treats his crown like the cardboard that it really is can destroy the belief of a stageful of others, just as a cynical child can destroy the magic of the game by protesting he can't fight with "an old stick."

The actor may renew a wavering belief, just as the child does, by discovering new circumstances that will excite new actions. When, for instance, you need further stimulation in the problem from *The Sea Gull*, try introducing circumstances such as these:

Masha is deeply (and futilely) in love with Trepleff. She does not want her movements to make her appear clumsy.

[2] Michael Redgrave, "The Stanislavski Myth" (London: *New Theatre*, Volume III, Number 1, June 1946), pp. 16–18. "Copyright, 1946." Quoted in *Actors on Acting*, ed. by Toby Cole and Helen Krich Chinoy (New York: Crown Publishers, 1949), p. 387.

[3] David Magarshack, Introduction to *Stanislavsky on the Art of the Stage* (New York: Hill and Wang, 1961), p. 49.

Masha drinks a great deal, mostly by herself. This speech and action are a ruse to conceal the fact that she is tipsy.

Masha wants others to know that their long tiresome conversation has put her foot to sleep.

Discovering additional circumstances helps to renew the actor's belief. When he asks the vital question, *"What* would I do if I were this character in this situation?"* and finds the true answer, he is provided with fresh reasons for action.

EXERCISE   Continue to work on the problem from *The Sea Gull*; carry out the actions in each of the circumstances given above. Study the play to find suggestions for other circumstances in which Masha might repeat these actions.

Making a Score of Physical Actions

Before taking up the final point in this chapter, let us summarize the points made so far:

1. The actor must develop simultaneously his inner and outer techniques. His outer technique trains his voice and body to provide an effective instrument for communicating the meaning of a play to an audience. His inner technique trains him to use his own life experience as a means of finding and understanding what that meaning is.
2. The actor's first step to understanding is to discover what logical sequence of physical actions the character he is playing would carry out in the circumstances given by the dramatist. He begins with physical actions because they are tangible, subject to his will.
3. The actor must find strong reasons for these actions. He must commit himself to carrying them out.
4. To make these actions personal and, at the same time, to satisfy the intention of the dramatist, the actor asks: "What would *I do if I were this character* in these given circumstances?"
5. Finding the answer to this question induces the actor to *believe the truth* of his actions, even though nothing in the imaginary world of the character is *real*.
6. The actor's belief is sustained by finding additional circumstances that stimulate fresh action.
7. Carefully chosen and clearly performed physical actions are one of the surest ways of communicating the play to the audience, which you must always remember is the actor's primary function.

To accomplish these objectives (as well as others that will follow) the actor must develop a method of work consisting of specific devices that will yield practical results. Some would-be actors have a notion that practical effort, especially if it involves the use of pencil and paper, will dampen spontaneity and hamper creativity. This notion is ill-founded. Inspiration comes from conscious technical effort, and a talent that cannot survive hard practical work is not very robust.

You know now how to discover the physical actions for your character in a given scene. Your first practical device (and it does require pencil and paper) is to list them. Your list of actions (and don't be afraid to number them) should form a sequence that is logical and appropriate for the character in the situation; and each action should be such that you are psychologically and physically capable of carrying it out. Your list for each of the problems in the exercise that follows should be short and not excessively detailed. It will not be practical unless you can keep it easily in mind. It should, on the other hand, be complete—no gaps which make it difficult for you to go from one action to the next. Your imagination, stimulated by the given circumstances, will provide the necessary strong desire to accomplish the sequence.

This list will be the beginning of a practical technique which Stanislavski called "making a score of the role." [4] It is just a beginning because throughout the book we will be finding ways of expanding and deepening the score. It will become ultimately a comprehensive working design of your role. It will include your physical and psychological actions, your major and minor objectives, relations, images, subtext, line readings. This score provides three advantages:

1. The preparation of it forces you to dig deeply into the play, and into yourself. You will be pleased and surprised how much both of these sources have to offer.
2. Augmenting it during rehearsal keeps you alert to the stimulation of the director and the other actors. You will miss or forget much otherwise.
3. The existence of the score makes it possible for you to review your creative effort whenever you need to; and you will need to review it often to keep it clearly and freshly in mind.

But we are anticipating a later stage of development. The score begins with simple lists of actions for the problems at the end of the chapter. Here is an example of a problem and a sample list:

In *The Wild Duck*, by Henrik Ibsen, Hjalmar (pronounced Yalmar) becomes aware that his young daughter, Hedvig, is not carrying on her customary activities in her usual place. He searches for her in great concern. He hears a shot from an adjoining room. He goes hurriedly to investigate, and returns carrying Hedvig's dead body.

---

[4] See Stanislavski, *Creating a Role*, pp. 56–62.

The Beginning: "Coffee and Comfort"

1. Enter living room reading a magazine and carrying a cup of coffee.
2. Place coffee on a table, settle comfortably in a chair beside it, and continue reading.
3. Drink coffee.
4. Settle feet on a hassock.
5. Untie one shoe and kick it off.
6. Untie the other shoe and kick it off.
7. Glance around room for slippers.
8. Call Hedvig to bring slippers (speech is an action).
9. Call again. She is an obedient child and usually comes running.

The Middle: "Comfort Disrupted"

10. Get out of comfortable position and go to door of Hedvig's room.
11. Call again at the door.
12. Exit into her room to see if she may be asleep.
13. Enter, cross living room to window, open it and call outside.
14. Hear shot. Exit into adjoining room to investigate.
15. Return carrying Hedvig.

The End: "Increasing Concern"

16. Place Hedvig's body on sofa.
17. Loosen her clothing to determine the extent of the wound.
18. Call for help.

Note carefully two elements of this score in addition to the listing of the physical actions. It has been divided into structural units—a beginning, a middle, and an end—that will give the exercise form, clarity, and dramatic interest. Also each of the units has been given a name suggestive of the essential quality and the basic reason for the series of actions. Choosing a right name for each part of the structure is an extremely helpful technique. It unifies the actions and helps the actor to understand the attitude of the character toward what he is doing. It helps also to establish proper relationships toward the objects he is handling and toward other characters in the exercise or scene.

While the parts of the structure should be closely related progressing logically and inevitably from one to the other, a *transition* from one part to the next should be clearly made. A clear transition is accomplished by bringing each unit of the structure to a definite *terminal point* and starting the new unit with a firmly positive *attack*, a new impulse manifesting itself in movement, gesture, or speech. Terminal points and new attacks are necessary to make the structure evident, and to give both actor and audience a sense that the play is moving forward.

The beginning, middle, and end of a score of physical actions are not arbitrary. They represent distinct components of the overall action. For example, it is important for the acting student to understand and eventually sense that the "routine of coffee and comfort" must come to a complete and in this case abrupt end (terminal point) before the action of searching can begin. The conclusion of an action like "getting comfortable" results in an instant of "stasis," a momentary vacuum, a transition from which comes a strong impulse toward new action—searching and calling for Hedvig. Recognizing the terminal point of an action is essential to building a score of actions, and pushing off or attacking a new task is necessary to reproducing human actions.

Distinguishing the parts is further accomplished by giving each unit its own pace or tempo and its own rhythm. Because the two are so closely related, Stanislavski used the term *tempo-rhythm* to designate the combination of the basic rhythmic flow and the speed of execution of the physical action (including speech) in a given scene. Tempo-rhythms have a natural appeal to both actor and audience, an almost magic power to affect an inner mood. This power is, of course, most evident in music. Recall the different moods created by your responses to a waltz, a military march, a funeral march. The popularity of rock is due primarily to the effect of its pervasive tempo-rhythm.

In their own way, the tempo-rhythms of physical actions can create like responses. Establishing suitable tempo-rhythms is a subtle process. If an actor is intuitively right in sensing what is being done and said onstage, a correct tempo-rhythm is likely to come without conscious effort. In learning a technique, however, it is usually necessary to make a *conscious* effort before mastery of the technique produces *unconscious* results. Since tempo-rhythm is of such significance in acting, it is not too early to give attention to it. In this exercise from *The Wild Duck*, make clear transitions between the units by using the technique of terminal points and new attacks. Attempt to sense an effective and distinct tempo-rhythm for each part. Consciously change it as you move from one part to the next.

Within a scene there are usually variations in tempo-rhythm from unit to unit. Tempo-rhythm even may change within a single passage. For example, the way Hjalmar (in *The Wild Duck*) sits in his chair is affected by the circumstances of the scene—he settles down to relax.

Tempo-rhythm is the basic flow and speed of execution in each unit of the play, not in whole scenes of a play. In a sense, the various tempo-rhythms of a scene add up to a scene's overall pace. Scenes tend to have a pace that remains constant. The term *pace* refers to the speed at which the actors speak their lines, pick up their cues, and perform their actions.

To *pick up cues* does not imply that actors should race through a passage or scene. Usually, a director asks actors to pick up their cues to avoid the constant "line-pause-line" syndrome so common among new actors. In "real life" our communication with each other has a flow, and our pauses have a significance that a dramatist can only hint at in translating the spoken word to the written page. Actors translate the playwright's words back into the sound of real "speech."

Before proceeding to the exercises, here is a second score of actions, taken from *The Effect of Gamma Rays on Man-in-the-Moon Marigolds*, by Paul Zindel. Beatrice, the mother, has been intimidated into staying home from a science fair assembly in which her younger daughter is a finalist. After arranging by phone the removal of an elderly boarder, she notices the children's pet rabbit and decides to destroy it.

The Beginning: "Dawn of a New Life"
1. Slam phone down.
2. Burst into laughter.
3. Pour another drink.
4. Take drink to chair and sit comfortably.
5. Accidentally hit rabbit cage with foot.

The Middle: "Afternoon of Leftover Strings"
6. Examine cage and rabbit.
7. Rise and find a towel.
8. Pick up towel and throw over shoulder.
9. Get bottle of chloroform.
10. Cross to cage.

The End: "Evening of Final Resolution"
11. Pick up cage.
12. Take cage upstairs.

EXERCISES   Make and perform scores for several of the problems given below. Use pencil and paper; *write them out*. Remember a score must be a sequence of physical actions constituting logical and appropriate behavior in particular circumstances. Make the circumstances specific; find definite answers to the questions of *who, what, where,* and *when*. Choose actions that will communicate your meaning to an audience. Don't develop a habit of acting only for your own benefit. Your score should designate the beginning, the middle, and the end. Each of these units should have a suitable name.

After you have made the score, plan a simple arrangement of exits, windows, furniture, whatever you need for the action. Provide yourself with actual or substitute objects (magazines, coffee cups, and so forth); don't try to pantomime nonexistent props. We will attempt this kind of sensory work later. Work by yourself in this exercise, and don't imagine another character onstage. This practice conditions you to imagine responses from an actor who isn't there, and live responses to other actors is a vital part of acting.

This is basically a silent improvisation. Don't make up dialogue; use speech or sound only as necessary to call out or to release inner responses. Don't try to feel emotion. Don't try to be dramatic. Simplicity is one of the first (and one of the hardest) things to learn. All of these "don'ts" are for the purpose of starting you off in the right direction and of making you aware that actors work within a set of definite limitations. In fact, it is only after limitations have been established that freedom can be achieved.

Perform each score many times. Technique is developed through repetition. Each repetition should stimulate your imagination to greater belief. It is not necessary in these exercises to realize all of the circumstances of the play. The situations described should stimulate the actor to provide circumstances from his imagination. You are not yet ready to create a character or to give a performance.

(1) In *The Crucible*, by Arthur Miller, a Puritan farmer named John Proctor returns to his home in the evening, exhausted from having planted crops since daybreak. He puts down his shotgun, washes his face and hands, and eats his supper.

(2) On a cold winter morning Zenia in *Ethan Frome* (a dramatization by Owen and Donald Davis of Edith Wharton's novel) is suffering from a bad cold. She takes medicines, gets a cup of hot water, and, sitting by a wood-burning stove, inhales the steam.

(3) In *Hedda Gabler*, by Henrik Ibsen, Hedda is a discontented woman spitefully jealous of a young author with whom she had had a relationship before her marriage. She finds the manuscript of his latest work, tears it to pieces, and burns it.

(4) In *The Taming of the Shrew*, by William Shakespeare, Katharine is a headstrong bride who is being "tamed" by her husband. One of his tactics is to keep her from eating. Hungry and defiant, Katharine steals into the dining room, searches for food, and hides it in her dress.

(5) In *Sticks and Bones*, by David Rabe, Ozzie believes his belligerent son David, who has just returned from Vietnam, may have hand grenades concealed in his duffel bag. He searches secretly and cuts his fingers on an overseas cap which David has made into a dangerous weapon by sewing razor blades into it.

(6) In *A Streetcar Named Desire*, by Tennessee Williams, Blanche DuBois, nervous and exhausted, comes to visit her sister. Finding no one home on her arrival, she explores the small apartment, searches for liquor, and takes a drink to quiet her nerves.

(7) In *Misalliance*, by George Bernard Shaw, Gunner is an ineffectual, impoverished young man who has decided to shoot the wealthy Mr. Tarleton. He steals into Mr. Tarleton's house, investigates the scene, hides when he hears someone approaching.

(8) In *Desire Under the Elms*, by Eugene O'Neill, Eben Cabot checks to be sure that money hidden by his skinflint father is still there. He finds it under the floorboards of the farmhouse kitchen, counts it, and returns it to its hiding place.

(9) In *The Glass Menagerie*, by Tennessee Williams, Laura Wingfield, an extremely shy girl, is entertaining a "gentleman-caller" at dinner. Laura's mother is anxious for her to impress the young man favorably. Suffering acutely from her shyness, Laura becomes sick at the table. She is forced to retire into the living room where she escapes into a dream world by playing with her collection of tiny glass animals.

(10) In *Romeo and Juliet* (Act II, Scene 5), by William Shakespeare, Juliet impatiently awaits the return of the Nurse from an errand to bring news of Romeo. She keeps watching for the Nurse's arrival and attempts to control her impatience. Finally the Nurse appears offstage, and Juliet runs eagerly to meet her.

(11) In *Summer and Smoke*, by Tennessee Williams, Alma is an intelligent, tensely sensitive girl who has developed an abnormally reserved attitude toward young men. On an autumn evening she walks in the park realizing that her prudishness has been responsible for her losing a brilliant young doctor with whom she has been deeply in love for a long time. She drinks from the fountain, and quiets her nerves by taking a relaxing pill. When an unknown young man appears, she decides to make up for her past mistakes by attempting to attract his attention.

(12) In *The Shadow of a Gunman*, by Sean O'Casey, Donal Davoren is an Irish Nationalist who hears noises outside and realizes that his room is going to be raided by the police. He searches for an incriminating letter, finally finds it, and destroys it.

(13) In *Purlie Victorious*, by Ossie Davis, Purlie has involved Lutiebelle, a backwoods serving girl, in a scheme in which she will try to pass herself off as Purlie's educated and sophisticated Cousin Bee. After Lutiebelle has examined the beautiful clothes Purlie has bought for her to wear—slips, hats, shoes, nylon stockings—she picks up her own humble belongings and tries to escape.

(14) In *The Prisoner of Second Avenue*, by Neil Simon, Mel Edison is a Manhattan apartment-dweller who has recently lost his job, has had his apartment robbed, and is being kept awake by noise from a neighbor's apartment. Unable to sleep, Mel emerges from his bedroom wearing a baseball glove on his left hand and carrying a baseball in his right hand. He keeps throwing the ball into the glove as he paces—grim, unshaven, and hostile —into the living room. He cannot escape the noise. He walks though all the available walking space like a prisoner taking his daily exercise. He keeps throwing the ball into the glove with increasing intensity. Finally he throws the ball against the wall from which the noise appears to be coming; then he crosses to the kitchen to look for something to eat.

(15) In *The Price*, by Arthur Miller, Victor Franz is a policeman who returns to the building where he grew up. The room, stacked with furniture and personal effects, has the appearance of a dusty attic. Once inside the room, Victor halts, glances up, then walks at random a few feet. He looks at his watch and removes his gun belt and jacket. As he surveys his family's belongings, he is affected both by a nostalgia for his youth and by painful memories of the Depression.

(16) In *Waiting for Godot*, by Samuel Beckett, Estragon is an "everyman": simple, bored, hungry, and fatigued by waiting. As the play opens, he is sitting on a low mound, trying to remove his boot. He pulls at it with both hands, panting. He gives up, exhausted, then tries again.

Finding a Purpose

3

Chapter 2 stressed the importance of an actor's beginning his task by making a score of appropriate physical actions, and by carrying them out without attention to his own feelings or the feelings of the character he is creating. Recognizing again that emotion is a vital element of the actor's art, we repeat that it cannot be sought directly. Even in scenes of tragedy, the actor does not think about his feelings, but about what he has to *do*. Emotion means literally "outward movement." By definition the word implies an "impulse toward open action." The preceding chapter has emphasized the importance of remembering the true meaning of this word, of being concerned with *action* rather than *feeling*. The question never is, "How would I feel if I were this character in these circumstances?" The question always is, "What would I do?"

The purpose of this chapter is to extend the uses of action as the basis of inner technique. We have already learned that one action must follow another in a logical sequence. We know too that actions must be truthful, that the actor must believe they are what he really would do if he were the character in the given situation. In addition to being logical and truthful, actions must also be *purposeful*. To have any meaning, whatever happens onstage must have a purpose. It must serve some end beyond accomplishment of the action itself. The meaning, both for the actor and the audience, rarely lies in the action but in the purpose for which it is done. Even loading a gun or mixing poison is not in itself dramatic. We must know *why*, toward whom the lethal effort is directed. Clearly played for the right reasons, any number of homely, everyday actions—packing a suitcase, moving the furniture, lying down on the floor—may be tensely dramatic.

So to the four "w's" discussed in Chapter 2 we now add an all-important fifth. *Why?* The answer to this question gives the actor the reason for carrying out the physical action. The answer is all-important because actions without a reason that is compelling to the actor and clear to the audience have no dramatic interest for either. Again, the answer to this question is often given or implied by the dramatist. Often it must be contributed by the actor from his insight and his imagination.

The ways of making action purposeful are among the most valuable of all acting techniques and will bring you greater belief in what you are doing as the character. They will give you a reason for being on the stage, and thus relieve your tension. They will provide a principal means of conveying the import of the play to the audience.

In this book we are going to call the purpose for which you carry out your physical actions your *intention.* Others call it different names. The problem in terminology is described by Robert Lewis:

> It has been called many things in many books and some people don't call it anything; but it is a process that is going on, if they are really acting. I myself don't care if you call it spinach, if you know what it is, and do it, because it is one of the most important elements in acting.[1]

Intention is the term that many actors and directors use. By definition it is: "A determination to act in a certain way or to do a certain thing." So let's agree that *action* will mean the sequence of physical actions. The *What. Intention* will mean the reason for doing them. The *Why.*

The technique of executing simple physical actions motivated by a compelling psychological purpose ultimately became the basis of Stanislavski's approach. He called it the technique of psychophysical actions. It is both simple and profound. It enables the actor to do consciously onstage what he does spontaneously in life. Fully utilized, it enables him to involve his entire physical and mental being in the performance of his stage tasks. It is an approach that good actors have always used more or less consciously, but no one before had ever articulated it so that it could be specifically helpful in actor training. It has had a vast effect on modern acting. Jerzy Grotowski, the renowned Polish director and innovator, called Stanislavski's work on physical actions one of the most stimulating influences coming from his exhaustive study of major actor-training methods.

Stating the Intention

At this point we would do well to return to the exercises in Chapter 2, and to extend them by carrying out the actions to satisfy a clearly *stated* intention. Finding the right statement is important because the search forces us to dig again into the circumstances and into our own resources. As with the actions,

[1] Robert Lewis, *Method—or Madness?* (New York: Samuel French, 1958), p. 29.

we find the intention by examining both what the playwright gives us and our own experience. It is also important to state the intention in a form that compels us to execute the action. The stating and playing of intentions in the problems with which we are now concerned will be relatively easy. Later this process will bring us to "beats" and the super-objective.

To the problem from *The Wild Duck* (we have already made a score of physical actions and separated them into structural units) we will add this circumstance: Hjalmar's concern over Hedvig's being gone comes from the fact that recently he has unjustly hurt the child by declaring he can't live in the same house with her and making her aware that he suspects she is not his child. In addition to accomplishing the physical action of finding Hedvig, we now have a psychological intention. Hjalmar is frightened that she may have run away because she feels she is not wanted at home. He must find her to let her know he loves her. State your intention as: "I must make Hedvig know I love her."

EXERCISE   (1) Play the score of actions from *The Wild Duck* with this intention fast in your heart. And let your imagination work!

(2) Again carry out the same actions but change your intention to: "I want to punish Hedvig for disobeying me." Keep firmly to this intention even during the action of bringing in the dead child. Use your imagination to justify this intention.

Note carefully the way an intention is stated:

1. It begins with "I want to . . . ." or "I must . . . ." to make the desire to carry out the physical actions personal and compelling to the actor.
2. "I want to . . . ." or "I must . . . ." is followed by an *active* verb because any statement of intention must germinate action. It must always be: "I want to walk straight and steady." It must never be: "I want to be drunk." It must be: "I want to kick you downstairs." It must not be: "I want to be angry."

Think always in terms of what you must *do*, not in terms of what you want to *be*.

Doing, Not Being

One of the most common mistakes made by young actors is to attempt to act by *being*, rather than *doing*. The actor who concentrates upon *being drunk*, *being angry*, *being happy*, *being sad*, *being afraid* is certain to fail. He must concern himself, just as he does in actual life, with what he would do in each situation, not with what he would be.

When you are angry, your mind is not taken up with being angry. You are concerned with the cause—the person or thing that has made you angry; and you may deal with the cause in any one of a number of ways. You may overlook it. You may seek release from your anger in some act of physical violence. You may forgive. You may plan some dreadful revenge. Certainly you are not saying to yourself, "I must be angry." Your attention is given to doing something about the tricycle you have fallen over or about the person who has placed you in an embarrassing situation.

When you are frightened, you do not *want to be afraid*. Your want lies in quite the opposite direction. You want to dispel your fear in some way. You may want to escape or to seek comfort from someone. You may want to calm your fears by turning your attention to something else. You may want to investigate the source of danger.

A state of being is not actable because it provides nothing specific to do. It leaves the actor stuck with a general emotion. It leads him into stereotyped movements and gestures—clenching his fists to show he is angry, putting his hand to his forehead to show he is thoughtful, or contorting the muscles of his face to show he is in pain.

Burning your hand may *be* painful. But you *want* to relieve the pain by applying salve, butter, cold water, or some other remedy. When a celebrity is pointed out in a crowd, you may *be* curious. But you *want* to get in a position from which you can see him to advantage. You may even want to get his autograph. To be in pain or to be curious is not actable. To relieve pain or to satisfy curiosity *is*. You can easily carry out the actions of applying a remedy to your burned hand or of working your way into a favorable position.

In *When You Comin Back, Red Ryder?*, by Mark Medoff, the scene is a diner in the desert of New Mexico in the late sixties or early seventies. Stephen/Red is a nineteen-year-old who wishes to escape the mundane world and become famous as his movie hero. Angel, the waitress, is a few years older and accepts her life. She has a "crush" on Stephen and wants him to stay. In the opening scene, the conversation is about coffee, their names, and coupons, but Stephen/Red's intentions are "I want to steer Angel's attention away from me," and Angel's, "I must force Stephen to pay some attention to me." In this scene there are many actions to be played, including reading a newspaper, drinking coffee, and eating a donut.

The Crucible, by Arthur Miller, deals with the famous witchcraft trials in Salem, Massachusetts, in 1692. The theme is the frightening effect of injustice and the misapplication of authority. John Proctor is a hard-working farmer of independent spirit about thirty years of age. His wife Elizabeth, also about thirty, has discovered that John had an adulterous affair with Abigail, a girl who worked for them and has since been dismissed. Abigail is one of the children bringing charges of witchcraft against innocent people, including Elizabeth. Earlier, she has admitted to John that their allegations are not true.

Elizabeth's Puritan ethic has made her husband's single infidelity into a situation of major proportions. At the opening of Act II her intention is "I must make John go to Salem to expose and denounce Abigail." John's is "I must please Elizabeth and restore normalcy to my home."

EXERCISES   To realize more fully the importance of *doing* rather than *being*, and of how to help yourself by stating your intention with an active verb, work carefully on the following problems:

(1) Choose a word from the list below and make it the basis for a series of actions. Do not let this instruction lead you into a trap. As you study the list you should now realize that you can't act any of these words. They describe effects. You must give yourself a circumstance providing a reason for *action that will produce the effect.* Then forget the effect and give your attention to carrying out the action. For example, this circumstance would provide an action for the word "cautious": *You have just escaped from a war prison. In darkness, starved and exhausted, you are making your way across an area filled with booby traps. You find a knapsack which might contain rations.* State your intention as: "I must work my way through the area without exploding a trap."

This circumstance would provide an action for the word "spiteful": *You have not been getting along with your roommate. You resent his constantly asking you to loan him money so that he can satisfy his extravagant taste for clothes. You return home to find he has "borrowed" from your coin bank money you were saving to buy a present for your sister. You take several articles of his new clothing, cut off all the buttons, and put them in the box where he keeps his coins when he has any.* State your intention as: "I must get even with my roommate for his selfishness."

Choose another word from the list. Give yourself similarly appropriate circumstances. State your intention. Make a score of your actions. Structure your score and name each of the three units. Carry it out with imagination. Observe the instructions given for the exercises in the preceding chapter.

embarrassed	distracted
bashful	excited
frantic	exhausted
nervous	irritable
terrified	scornful
breathless	nonchalant
ruthless	tantalizing
spiteful	languorous
awkward	bewildered

coarse	drunken
affected	maudlin
cautious	violent
jealous	dazed
jovial	sickly
quarrelsome	apprehensive

All of these words come from playwrights' directions to actors in a single volume of modern American plays. They illustrate how dramatists (and often directors) ask for effects and, consequently, how actors must be able to think of effects as actions and intentions. A frequent comment to actors from directors is: "Don't play the effect (even though he may have just asked for it), play the action!"

(2) Choose one of the following "everyday" actions. Give yourself circumstances providing an intention you can attempt to realize with genuine interest and excitement. Take, for example, polishing silver: *You are in an antique shop in a foreign country. You discover among many dusty articles a blackened silver bowl which you think is the work of Benvenuto Cellini. Beneath the tarnish may be revealing marks. If you are right, the proprietor obviously does not suspect its origin.* State your intention as: "I want to get the tarnish off this bowl without attracting the notice of the proprietor."

Take, for another example, walking five steps: *You are in the hospital with a serious illness. You are very weak and short of breath. You are under strict doctor's orders to stay in bed. You decide to test your strength by walking a short distance to a chair. You reach the chair exhausted but convinced you are beginning to recover.* State your intention as: "I must start to use my muscles if I am ever going to regain my strength."

Choose one of these "everyday" actions. To solve the problem you need specific circumstances, a properly stated intention, a score of definite things to do, and imagination. Execute all physical actions precisely, clearly, and with complete commitment. Don't hurry them. Give them form. Observe all previous instructions.

looking through a window
opening a door
stroking an animal
hunting for a lost ring
lying down on the floor
arranging furniture in a room
building a fire
feeding fish in an aquarium
drinking tea
wrapping or unwrapping a package

crawling on your hands and knees
packing a suitcase
washing your hands
picking flowers
walking five steps
digging a hole in the ground
acquainting yourself with a room you've never been in before
examining a bundle of clothes
waiting for someone to come home
hanging a picture
sitting perfectly still (Here your intention must justify the *absence* of physical action.)

Plays are filled with simple actions for which the actor must find intentions that stimulate his imagination and make the actions significant to the playwright's meaning.

Working Against an Obstacle

By now it must have become apparent that stated or implied in each intention there has been an *obstacle*. An area full of explosives is an obstacle to the successful escape from a prison camp. A shrewd antique dealer is an obstacle to picking up a Cellini masterpiece for a few liras. The interest in a play or scene (or in an acting exercise) lies in the possibilities it provides the actor to realize an objective against odds—odds sometimes so great that the struggle ends in defeat, either glorious or ignoble. Plays in which there is no struggle have little interest for either actor or audience.

A question that must be answered as you crystalize each intention is: What is the *obstacle?* What is going to make it difficult to accomplish the intention? If there is no difficulty, there is no problem—no scene—no play! The obstacle, like the intention, may be either physical or psychological. Frequently there is a combination of both. The physical and psychological are often so interrelated that it is not possible, or desirable, to separate them.

The problem from *The Wild Duck*, as we can discover from digging more thoroughly into the play, is an example of this interrelation. The physical obstacle to Hjalmar's accomplishing his intention is that Hedvig is not in the places he looks, nor does she answer his calls. The psychological obstacle is that Hjalmar does not have a real father-love. He is a selfish shallow person, given to self-dramatization. It is because of these shortcomings that he has hurt Hedvig so deeply, and he is more than a little responsible for her suicide. The love that he would like now to profess, like the grief after her death, is not quite

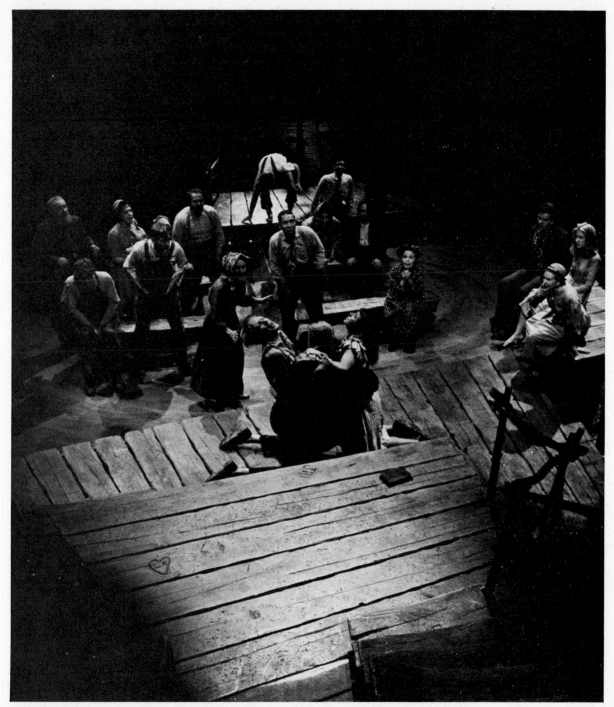

A scene from the Arena Stage, Washington, D.C., production of *Dark of the Moon* by Howard Richardson and William Berney. Staged by Edwin Sherin with settings by Robin Wagner, costumes by Marianna Elliott, and lighting by Leo Gallenstein. (Photo — George de Vincent.) Study the actors for concentration of attention and physical involvement.

real. In the problem from *Summer and Smoke,* among the exercises at the end of Chapter 2, the obstacle is entirely psychological. The eager Young Man presents Alma with no difficulty. The obstacle is her own shyness, her lack of confidence, her pride, her fear of rejection, her moral scruples.

In playing either of the scenes, the actor—especially the beginning actor—does well to concentrate upon the physical. Psychology must be translated into action. Alma should concentrate upon quieting her frayed nerves by physical means and attracting the Young Man's attention. Hjalmar will play the scene best by continuing to conduct a specific search, protecting Hedvig from pain when he carries the body, searching for the extent of the wound. He can't directly play against the psychological obstacle. His fondness for self-dramatization—here he sees himself in the role of the loving grieving father—should help the actor by increasing his desire to realize his intention. Gina, Hedvig's mother, is an interesting and moving contrast to Hjalmar. Her love is real and selfless. She has no need to parade it.

On the stage, as in life, psychological intentions and obstacles can stimulate great desire to accomplishment. The motivation for nearly every winner is psychological. The runner does not want only to cover the distance faster than anyone else; he is motivated by desire to bring honor and prestige to himself and to the team, to win admiration and fame, perhaps by a determination to set someone right who said he could not do it. A man is motivated to build a home not just by desire to complete the physical structure, but to provide protection, security, beauty for himself and his family. A proud collector would have a very special desire to get possession of a Cellini bowl. From these illustrations come three important points for the actor:

1. Psychological intentions and obstacles can stimulate the actor's imagination more strongly than physical intentions and obstacles.
2. The actor must make a personal commitment to overcome the obstacle and accomplish his intention. This commitment generates real feeling. It is the actor's most dependable source of emotion.
3. We must feel the challenge physically as well as intellectually. We don't win races by wishing to, thinking about it, or feeling victorious. Stage tasks, similarly, are accomplished only by purposeful action.

It is necessary for the beginning actor to realize much more fully than he usually does the importance of the *obstacle.* His psychophysical actions, if they are to have any dramatic interest, must be performed to overcome a counter-action that exerts a positive force against the accomplishment of his intention. Neither as character nor as actor can he afford to be indifferent to this opposition. One of the commonest ways in which student actors render their performances ineffective is their tendency to assume an attitude of nonchalance towards the challenge of overcoming the obstacle. Even more basic is a failure to understand clearly what the obstacle is. Consequently, they fail to discover what means the dramatist has provided, either directly or by implication, for overcoming it; and they fail likewise to provide additional definite strategy from their imaginations. Notice here the words *clearly*, *specifically*, *directly*, and *definitely*. They are all vital to the acting process and apply to circumstances, intentions, obstacles, and actions. Generality in any of these matters will always yield inferior results.

Strategy means "the art and science of employing armed strength to meet the enemy in combat." While conflict between the character and the obstacle is not always open warfare, the actor would do well to conceive his whole performance as a strategic plan to overcome the forces that are working against him. Far too often in answer to the question, "What are you doing in this scene," the young actor says casually "Oh, I'm just talking to this banker about loaning me some money." Or, "Why, I'm just asking my husband what he did while I was away this afternoon." There should be no "just's" in such answers. The actor must have, supplied by the dramatist or by his own imagination, an urgent need to get the money or to find out what was happening during the afternoon. A hardheaded banker or a secretive husband provides a genuine obstacle that must be overcome. When the circumstances demand a subtle strategy of which the opponent will be unaware, the inner urgency must be all the greater. Satisfactory answers in the above instances might be "I must get this money to pay the debts I have incurred before my father finds out about them" and "I must find out whether the gossip about my husband and the girl next door is true." If these answers sound melodramatic, remember such material is the stuff of which drama is made. The material of Shakespeare's plays in the hands of a hack writer becomes soap opera, and the Greek tragedies become horror stories. Attempt always to simplify the conflict by finding the character's elemental need; don't try to complicate it.

British critic Kenneth Tynan has aptly written:

> . . . good drama, of whatever kind, has but one mainspring—the human being reduced by ineluctable process to a state of desperation. Desperate are the cornered giants of Sophocles; desperate, too, as they huddle in their summerhouses, the becalmed gentry of Chekhov; and the husband of French farce, with a wife in one bedroom and a mistress in another, is he not, though we smile at his agony, definably desperate? . . . How, in this extremity, will they comport themselves? It is to find out that we go to theatres. . . .[2]

The actor must conceive the carrying out of his <u>intention</u> as a "desperate quest" to overcome an <u>obstacle</u>.

---

[2] Kenneth Tynan, *Curtains* (New York: Atheneum, 1961), p. 77.

EXERCISE   You were asked to use the problems at the end of Chapter 2 as exercises in making and carrying out a score of physical actions. Without being aware of it as a technique, you certainly performed the actions for some purpose. It would not be natural to do otherwise. Now, after this introduction to intentions, choose again a problem from Chapter 2 and extend it consciously to include finding the intention—both physical and psychological—and playing the action to accomplish your objective. To make the technique most helpful be sure to:

1. Find the intention in the given circumstances. It must allow you to satisfy the needs of your character and the demands of the play.
2. Make it attractive to *you*. You personally must feel compelled to carry it out.
3. Make it truthful. You must without reservation believe it is what you would do if you were the character in the circumstances.
4. Provide an *obstacle* either derived from the circumstances or appropriate to them.
5. Be sure it provides you with physical action.
6. Begin your statement with "I must. . . ." or "I want to. . . ." followed by an active verb.

Adapting to Other Characters

So far the problems have involved only one person. But dramatic art is a collective art. An individual actor's creation must always be conceived in relation to other characters who either help or hinder him in accomplishing his objectives. He must consider other characters in planning his actions. He must also be able to adapt, and sometimes to abandon his plans as he is confronted with the unexpected. He must *watch* and *listen*. He must be alert and ready to adjust what he does and says to the needs of the moment.

In life the person who can't adapt to changing circumstances will never get across the street alive. And he needs to make adjustments not only to passing trucks, but also of a subtler kind. He must deal with people not only logically, but psychologically. The kind of adaptation he makes—whether it is bold, delicate, daring, cautious—is important to its success. There are an infinite number of situations requiring a wide range of adjustments.

On the stage this vital activity far too often becomes a matter of merely remembering lines and movements as the actor repeats his role in rehearsal and performance. A remembered performance is necessarily a lifeless performance. The actor needs constantly to make real adjustments to other characters. Learning to keep his performance alive by constantly adapting to the needs of the moment is a necessity in the actor's training.

(1) For work in the technique of *adaptation* try this "coach and actor" exercise. Work in pairs. One actor serves as "coach," telling his partner firmly and quietly (the class should be able to hear too) what actions to perform. His instructions should constitute a logical sequence of physical actions having a beginning, a middle, and an end. The coach should prepare carefully in advance. He should be certain the sequence can be psychologically motivated, but he should not tell his partner what the motivation is. As he proceeds, the actor must discover a motivation and adapt accordingly. The coach should vary the tempo-rhythm of his instructions as the actions develop toward a climax, and as he senses his partner's responses. Later discussions should compare the motivation the coach had in mind with what the actor discovered. The actor's job is to find *a* motivation, not to guess what the coach intended. There is no absolute right and wrong. Although some motivations might be illogical under the circumstances, two quite different motivations could be well justified.

(2) In the following problem the "coach" becomes an actor within the imaginary circumstances. The two characters are a window dresser and an assistant. The window dresser is on the sidewalk directing the assistant where and how to place the objects for display. They are separated by a plate glass window so all communication must be visual rather than oral. The physical intention clearly is to get the window dressed, and the physical separation provides a definite obstacle. From your imagination supply additional specific circumstances. Know exactly what objects are being arranged for display. Some other members of the group might be used as mannequins. The dresser should know exactly what effect he wants to achieve. Supply psychological intentions and obstacles as well as the obvious physical ones. Remember the necessary element of urgency. Structure the exercise giving it a beginning, a development leading to a climax, and a conclusion. All exercises accomplish their purpose more fully when they are followed by a discussion regarding the clarity and urgency of the intention, the precision of the physical actions, the strategy for overcoming the obstacles, the adaptations, the effectiveness of the structure.

Improvising Group Scenes

The actor may obtain further practice in adaptation through exercises in group improvisation. Like everything related to acting, improvisation provides him with specific objectives which he must accomplish in a specific way. Improvisation is *not*, as it is sometimes loosely thought to be, a game of "making up dialogue." Although you may need to speak, making conversation is in no sense your objective. Your objective is the same as it has been in the previous problems: *to realize a clearly defined intention through a logical sequence of actions.* Remember that speaking is an action. In life there may be aimless talk, but onstage, the actor speaks only to help him achieve his purpose. Lines, dialogue, speech (whatever term you prefer) must be conceived as actions employed to accomplish your intention.

Improvisation, then, is a further extension of the exercises you have already been doing. It involves more complicated and interesting problems, bringing you closer to your ultimate aim. We must begin with given circumstances in which you will find your intention. Again, it must be active, attractive, and truthful. The added complication comes from the fact that you can't know what you will need to do because you don't know what the others are going to do, nor what obstacles they may make for you. You need to be ready to adjust moment by moment. And again, the actions with which you adjust must be truthful and logical; you must believe they are what you would really do if you were the character in the circumstances.

EXERCISE   For a first effort in group improvisation we will set circumstances that permit communication through psychologically motivated physical actions and expressive sounds—*without the use of dialogue.* The situation is suggested by the first scene of *Romeo and Juliet,* in which the servants of the rival houses of Capulet and Montague confront each other in the Public Square. Because the two families are ancient enemies, the servants feel compelled to challenge each other whenever they meet although they may have forgotten (or perhaps never knew) the cause of the age-old hatred. The servants are an uneducated lot, not dangerously armed, and not overly courageous. Their object is to insult and perpetrate minor physical assaults. In this exercise the objective is to be accomplished through physical actions (including gesture and facial expression) and vocalized sounds—no articulated words. The servants of one house should create obstacles for the others. Each actor should strive to play his intention as fully as possible. Remember, though, that actions must always be logical and appropriate within the given circumstances. The scene should not become chaotic. Each action must be purposefully performed. The circumstances prescribe a number of obstacles to a realization of the intention: the natural timidity of the characters, the need for self-protection, the need for a degree of furtiveness because these encounters in the public streets have been forbidden by law.

Let the *beginning* consist of the meeting in the street and some cautious advances by one or two of the servants followed by hasty retreats. Let the *middle* develop the confrontation, as some of the servants, egged on by others, become bolder in their actions and ultimately involve the whole group. Let the *end* consist of the arrival of someone in authority who breaks up the quarrel.

The group could decide to set the scene in circumstances other than those of Verona in the Italian Renaissance. In *West Side Story*, a modern musical based on *Romeo and Juliet*, the enemies were not "two houses both alike in dignity," but rival street gangs in New York. It would be valuable to work on the same situation in different sets of circumstances.

EXERCISE

George Washington Slept Here provides a situation for work in improvisation. The Fuller family—Newton, Annabelle, and daughter Madge—having restored an old Colonial house in Pennsylvania, is entertaining weekend guests. Rain has kept them constantly indoors. On Sunday afternoon they sit around the living room in bathing suits hoping the weather will clear and permit a little pleasure in a dreary weekend.

Before starting actually to improvise, each member of the group needs to provide from his imagination a few additional circumstances. An actor can't work to any purpose, either in an improvisation or in a play, until he knows who, where, what, and why. *Who* he is. *Where* he is. *What* he wants. *Why* he wants it. For an improvisation the answers do not need to be detailed, but they must be specific. For this problem from *George Washington Slept Here*, the group needs first to decide who will be Newton, Annabelle and Madge. Other actors must know who they are in relation to the Fullers—Madge's boy friend, her college roommate, her cousin to whom all the boys are attracted, an athlete who doesn't mind the rain, a business associate of Newton's (decide specifically what business he and Newton are in), a hired girl, and so forth. Don't seek to be melodramatic or bizarre. Supply yourself with a character who would readily be found at such a party, and whose behavior you can easily understand. Many young actors seek to be interesting through being exotic. A domestic Annabelle really trying to make her guests comfortable and happy is more engaging than a phony maharajah. Who knows what a maharajah does at a house party on a rainy afternoon?

Now, set up the living room with the necessary chairs, tables, sofas, doors, windows—probably a fireplace and a bar. Technically, this is the process of making a *ground plan*. For the present, however, though there is no point in consciously ignoring stage requirements that provide actors with positions in which they can be readily seen, concern yourself primarily with an appropriate arrangement of the room. Each member of the group must clearly understand the essentials of the plan. Then his imagination allows him to accept a placement of miscellaneous chairs and tables as a finely restored Colonial house, and he can relate to them exactly as he would if they were real. An imaginative actor can be genuinely upset when some dolt treats a folding chair like the thing it is instead of like the rare antique it has been designated as being.

Having established the who and where, decide upon the what and why. This means finding your intention and the reason for it. Everyone will want to pass the afternoon either as pleasantly or as profitably as possible, but to realize this general objective you need specific action. Madge's roommate may want to sit by herself and read a book in preparation for an examination she has to pass the next day. The business associate may want to discuss business, while Newton wants to see that his guests are properly supplied with drinks and food; restoring the house was his idea and it is essential to his ego that everyone have a good time. Madge's boy friend may want to get the cousin into a corner. Madge may want to keep him from doing it. Annabelle may want to organize a card game, keep Newton from drinking too much, see that Madge doesn't neglect the guests, and keep the harassed and inexperienced hired girl functioning as a proper maid.

The value of improvisation lies in your learning to make real contact with other actors, to heed what they do and say, to adapt the playing of your intention to the need of the moment, to work freely and logically within the imaginary circumstances. What you learn should carry over into everything you do because all good acting is to some degree improvisational. Even a scene that has been "set," demands constant adjustment—a living connection with fellow players. The choices you make in the adjustments must be credible and appropriate. The social situation of a house party places restrictions upon both hosts and guests. Behaving logically within the circumstances is the beginning of truthful acting. Avoid choices that are sensational, that are calculated for dramatic effect, that repeat what you have seen other actors do, or even what you have done in the past. Improvisation is best when your imagination leads you truthfully into *spontaneous* adjustments.

Don't talk more than necessary! Don't try to make what you say clever, dramatic, or literary. In fact, don't think about it. You are an actor, not a playwright. An actor's job is to use his lines to accomplish his intention.

A time limit should be set—at the beginning ten to fifteen minutes for a group exercise. After it is over, the work should be carefully analyzed (preferably by a competent observer) so that each actor is aware of the points where he has or has not behaved logically and truthfully, and where his adjustments have fallen short of what could have been expected. Each actor can help himself and sometimes help others by recalling where he was making real contact, where his actions seemed true and spontaneous, and where they did not. The analysis should not be concerned with whether the scene would be entertaining or exciting to an audience. Improvisation is a means, not an end. You will defeat its purpose if you think about results other than truthful behavior.

Doubtless your first attempts will not be fruitful. Improvisation is a technique which takes time to learn. It is time well spent, and it is essential to your training.

The following situations provide opportunities for group improvisations. In each case additional circumstances must be supplied from either the play or the imaginations of the actors. Each character must clearly understand his intention and attempt to realize it through actions appropriate to the circumstances.

(1) *Street Scene*, by Elmer Rice, takes place on the sidewalk in front of a crowded tenement house in New York City. The summer night is stiflingly hot. The tenants are hanging out of the windows or sitting in the street. Attention centers on Mrs. Maurrant's windows because it is known another man is with her while Mr. Maurrant is away.

(2) In *Gammer Gurton's Needle*, an early English farce—the authorship of which has never been determined—Gammer has lost her needle while sewing a patch on Hodges's breeches. In those days a needle was a rare and greatly prized possession, and the entire village becomes involved in a search. Plan an improvisation in which the group are sixteenth-century villagers hunting for the needle. Add actuality by having someone who is not taking part hide a needle somewhere on the stage. Read the play to find out where the needle was found.

(3) In *Pygmalion*, by George Bernard Shaw, a group of people leaving a concert are stranded in the rain in front of St. Paul's Cathedral in London. They are trying to protect themselves from the weather, keep their tempers in check, and hail taxicabs, which prove to be very scarce late on a rainy night.

(4) In *Desire Under the Elms*, by Eugene O'Neill, neighbors gather to celebrate the birth of a son to old Ephraim Cabot and his young wife. There is drinking and dancing and many a sly remark casting doubt upon the child's paternity.

(5) In *The Weavers*, by Gerhart Hauptmann, a group of mill workers, who for a long time have not been able to afford decent food, sit down to a dinner of roast meat. Most of them enjoy it, but old Baumert's pleasure is brief because the rich meat soon makes him ill.

(6) In *J. B.*, by Archibald MacLeish, a prosperous family celebrates Thanksgiving with a traditional turkey dinner. As head of the family, J. B. realizes that they have much to be thankful for.

(7) In a later scene from the same play, J. B. has suffered tragic losses culminating in the destruction of his property in war. He and his wife, Sarah, along with several others who have had less to lose, survey the destruction. The others feel varying degrees of sympathy for Sarah and J. B.

(8) In *The Visit*, by Friedrich Duerrenmatt, enormously wealthy Claire Zachanassian returns to the small town she left years ago as a disgraced and penniless girl. The townspeople give her a gala welcome at the railway station hoping she will become their generous benefactor.

(9) In *An Enemy of the People*, by Henrik Ibsen, Dr. Stockman, a leading citizen, has proposed idealistic actions which are contrary to the practical interests of the majority of the townspeople. A group gathers outside his house to make a protest. In attempting to defend his views, Dr. Stockman meets with physical violence.

(10) In *The Queen and the Rebels*, by Ugo Betti, a group of travelers is detained at the border of a foreign country by government officials. Each traveler has a reason for wanting to proceed as quickly as possible, and they blame each other for their unhappy situation.

(11) In *The Birthday Party*, by Harold Pinter, the presence of two unidentified strangers at a birthday celebration mystifies the guests. The actors playing the strangers must find reasons to justify their presence and behavior.

(12) In *R. U. R.*, by Karel Capek, a group of mechanical men manufactured by Rossum's Universal Robots gain control of the human beings who made them.

(13) Improvise the first scene of *Julius Caesar* in which Flavius and Marcellus disperse the commoners who have gathered in holiday mood to pay homage to Caesar. Find the basic circumstances in Act I, Scene 1.

(14) In *Fiddler on the Roof*, by Joseph Stein, the Jews of Anatevka, a poor Russian village, are told they must leave their homes. They are sad at leaving their birthplace but hopeful that their new lives will be easier. The villagers slowly load their wagons with their meager possessions—trunks, pots, clothing—across the stage before exiting at different times in opposite directions, saying goodbye.

(15) In *The Odd Couple*, by Neil Simon, a group of poker players nervously and absentmindedly attempt to play their hands while trying to disguise their awareness of their friend Felix's depression. Felix has just split up with his wife, and his friends wonder, as they play their cards, whether Felix may attempt to do something desperate.

(16) In *The Royal Hunt of The Sun*, by Peter Shaffer, Spanish soldiers led by Pizarro climb the Andes in search of gold. Although they are motivated by greed and by loyalty to the Spanish crown, the soldiers face exhaustion as they make "a stumbling, tortuous climb into the clouds, over ledges and chasms."

Taking It Easy

In working on the exercises in Chapters 2 and 3, you must already have become aware of one of the actor's greatest problems—freeing himself from muscular tension and achieving a state of relaxation that will permit freedom of action. This is a difficulty from which he is never entirely liberated because the problem is not a simple matter of outgrowing self-consciousness as he gains experience. All actors develop more or less conscious techniques of eliminating harmful muscular tension. And harmful tension may be described as more tension than is needed to execute a movement or to maintain a position. Good movement is characterized by economy of effort.

Relaxation is necessary to both the internal and external aspects of acting. It is much more fundamental than the facility it provides for gesturing gracefully and moving easily about the stage. Without it the actor can't give his attention to the subtle process by which a character is brought to life. He can't freely carry out his actions when he is suffering from excessive tension. Stanislavski made this point vividly clear by demonstrating that it is impossible to multiply thirty-seven times nine while holding up the corner of a piano. The actor's tension is often just as great as the tension required to lift a heavy weight; and the problems that demand solution are no less complicated than a problem in multiplication.

Relaxation is equally important in differentiating one character from another as the actor goes from role to role. When he is suffering from tensions, no matter what actions he performs, the audience sees his own nervous mannerisms. Then, instead of the character he wishes to create, the audience sees an externalization of the actor's need to relieve his tension; and his nervous mannerisms will be the same regardless of the character or the situation. This sameness is one of the reasons that some actors always seem to play themselves even though they attempt a variety of characters.

It is generally recognized that physical exercise to develop coordination and muscular control is an essential part of the actor's training. Fencing and some form of dancing are required in many schools of drama. They are valuable in developing poise and alertness, and there is always the possibility of an actor's having to dance or fence onstage. Athletic training—swimming, tennis, gymnastics—is highly desirable. Anyone seriously interested in acting will engage in a program to provide a coordinated and responsive body.

Training the Body

There is, at the present time, no universal agreement as to just what program of body training the actor should engage in. If all the possibilities were readily available, he would have considerable range of choice. They include acrobatics; circus skills of juggling, tumbling, and trapeze; Oriental disciplines such as yoga and T'ai Chi Ch'uan; various techniques in mime; and a number of programmed exercises.[1] Each approach has its exponents and its detractors. There *is* agreement that each program will yield some benefits if the actor commits himself to consistent practice of it, and further agreement that some program adapted to the actor's needs is necessary. Relaxation and physical readiness are only in part a matter of general conditioning. An athlete whose movement on the tennis court is a model of economy and coordination may be awkward and ill at ease when he attempts a simple assignment in acting. In recent years intensive efforts have been made to discover a genuinely effective program in body training for the actor. It is in this area that there have been most significant changes both in concept and practice; and there has been increasing emphasis on carefully directed work in stage movement. Several of the influential approaches to actor training—those developed and being developed by Jerzy Grotowski, Peter Brook, Joseph Chaikin, and Arthur Lessac—are oriented to physical training as a means of developing the actor's total instrument. In this regard Grotowski says that "the most elementary fault, and that in most urgent need of correction, is the overstraining of the voice because one forgets to speak with the body." [2]

Practically, body training is designed to accomplish two basic objectives that are closely related: (1) proper body alignment, and (2) freedom from excess muscle tension. Accomplishment of these objectives enables the actor from a standing, sitting, or lying position to move off in any direction with a mini-

---

[1] For a description of some of the possible choices in physical training see *The Drama Review*, Volume XVI, Number 1 (March 1972), "The Acting Issue."

[2] Jerzy Grotowski, *Towards a Poor Theatre* (New York: Simon and Schuster, 1968), p. 185.

mum of effort and without a preparatory shifting of weight. Together they produce strong efficient movement without any forcing. Proper alignment, sometimes called *centering*, is the correct relationship between the principal weights of the body—head, chest, and pelvis. It is actually a normal posture, but it is seldom achieved without conscious effort because most of us suffer from bad physical habits and from adverse psychological and environmental influences. It can be clearly seen in the movement of certain primitives who have not been similarly victimized. Natural alignment is best achieved under the guidance of a competent teacher. However, a description of it should be helpful.

We unconsciously achieve proper body alignment when we are lying on our backs on a reasonably hard surface. It is then easy to eliminate all tension, and when we do so the weights of the body come naturally into a correct relationship. We have to learn to transfer this relationship and this feeling of relaxation from a prone to an upright position. In this alignment we are *standing tall*, and the "tip at the back of the top of the head" is the tallest point. In this head position the bottom line of the chin is parallel with the floor, and the front neck muscles are relaxed—an essential in ridding ourselves of vocal tension. The shoulders are rounded forward to obtain the widest possible space between the shoulder blades. We may think of the shoulder blades as a double gate that is always kept open. Square-shouldered, closed-gate military posture produces tensions and inhibits the natural expressiveness of the body. The abdominal muscles are held in firmly and the buttocks are "tucked under" so that the spine is straight from top to bottom. Standing in this position against a wall, there should be little or no space between the wall and the small of the back. The arms swing freely from the shoulders, and the knees are relaxed.[3]

Practice until you can achieve a proper alignment. Remember it is not something to be used only onstage. It is an easy natural posture that should be maintained both onstage and off. It should become your normal life posture. It will improve your appearance, eliminate any eccentricities in your movement, decrease fatigue, and increase your efficiency in physical and mental activities.

The second objective of body training—muscular relaxation—is a quality that characterizes all fine acting. It is not a dormant state. It is rather a condition in which, with tension removed, we have attained our utmost capacity for accomplishing any activity. Our courage and self-confidence are at their greatest. It has been variously called "blissful relaxation" (Morris Carnovsky), the "potent state" (Moshe Feldenkrais), the "creative state" (Stanislavski). Tension cannot be eliminated, however, and this state achieved in a few easy lessons. It demands time and effort. It is, in fact, a lifelong process. The advice most frequently given to an actor who has not attained it is "Just relax. Take it easy."

[3] For a more detailed description of correct posture see Arthur Lessac, *The Use and Training of the Human Voice* (New York: Drama Book Specialists, 1967).

A class in American Mime taught by Paul J. Curtis, Director of the American Mime Theatre. (Photo—Jim Moore.) Mime is a highly valuable discipline in actor training.

The advice is sound, but more often than not it produces the opposite of the desired effect. It is likely to make the actor more aware of his tension and, consequently, to increase it.

Along with the kind of training and practice discussed above, the actor needs to induce a state of relaxation through justifying his actions and concentrating upon performing them. We will give our attention to *justification* and *concentration* here and in the following chapter.

Relaxing Through Justification

We have already mentioned that athletes are often unable to transfer their muscular coordination from the playing field to the stage. The gallery of spectators watching a proficient tennis player as he serves and returns does not unnerve him in the least. In fact, he is hardly aware of being watched. But the few observers at a rehearsal may make him painfully self-conscious, unable to function with any degree of ease.

The difference between his performance on the tennis court and on the stage is that as an athlete his actions are justified. He knows *why* he is doing them, and he has developed a technique for doing them efficiently. All his attention is directed toward accomplishing a purpose that seems right and clear. He is relaxed mentally as well as physically. He forgets himself and concentrates on winning the game. As an actor, he is unable to forget himself because he can't justify his actions to the extent that they compel his attention. Furthermore he does not have a technique capable of providing him with confidence in his ability to do what the situation requires.

"Forgetting himself on the stage" and "losing himself in the part" are phrases frequently heard in describing a state of being that an actor can achieve. To gain freedom from tension the actor must "forget himself," but there must be no misunderstanding as to what happens when he does. There is a popular notion that he goes into a trancelike state, becomes unaware of his surroundings, surrenders himself to his emotions, and loses control of the situation. Such a state would be undesirable, and fortunately it never occurs. "Forgetting himself" means the same thing to the actor as to the athlete. It does not involve loss of control or anything resembling self-hypnosis. It is rather a condition in which control is at its fullest. It would be more accurate to say it is a state in which the actor *finds* himself. It occurs when he is free from—that is, when he forgets—any anxiety over his shortcomings and concerns himself entirely with carrying out his stage tasks.

Worry over what audiences may think or over the responsibility of keeping them "entertained" is the greatest enemy of relaxation. The athlete is just as dependent as the actor on the approval of the spectators. But during the game he forgets them and concentrates on winning. This is his purpose. He knows if he accomplishes it by fair means the spectators will be satisfied and overlook any minor errors or shortcomings of form. The actor's purpose is to create a believable character by carrying out specific actions. To accomplish this he must be able to concentrate on the actions by freeing himself from worry over nonessentials. He must be able to relax so that his energies will serve his purpose freely and fully. He must overcome his consciousness of himself. He eliminates tension by becoming absorbed in carrying out his action.

About Inhibitions

Occasionally actors are encumbered by social inhibitions that prevent them from expressing themselves fully and naturally. In such cases, it may prove helpful to realize that social inhibitions take many forms, and that they vary substantially from society to society, from era to era, and from individual to individual. In our society, for instance, men rarely touch each other except to shake hands. In other societies, such as Mexico or Italy, it is perfectly acceptable for men to embrace and to walk arm in arm in public. Even succeeding generations within the same culture have different sets of social inhibitions. Our great-grandparents would almost certainly have been inhibited had they been asked to wear bikinis or shorts. An important key to freeing inhibitions, then, is understanding the customs and mores of your character's society.

The relationship between social inhibitions and the individual person is more complex. Why is it that some actors are less encumbered by social inhibitions on stage than others? Can an actor from a conservative background learn not to wince (either internally or externally) at using suggestive behavior or foul language on stage? What are the actor's rights and responsibilities in these delicate areas?

There are no easy answers; however, actors should turn down roles in which they feel themselves exploited. In many plays produced recently, nude scenes have been included for no apparent reason except as an inducement to backers and a "come on" to audiences. On the other hand, once you have accepted a role, then it is your responsibility to carry out the actions appropriate for the characterization, even when those actions are not what you would do personally. If you believe in a play and in your role and concentrate on the reasons why characters behave the way they do, you soon will lose your inhibitions. As you involve yourself in the role, the inhibitions slip away, replaced by the internal logic of the role and an increased empathy with the character.

In an age of total nudity onstage, the actor is often forced to be a critic, to decide whether or not the playing of a character will justify itself artistically. In David Storey's The Changing Room, which takes place in the locker room of a rugby team in England, all the players appear nude while changing from street clothing into their uniforms. The nudity is not central to the action of the play, but it is necessary because it is a realistic part of the play's locale. Obviously, an actor would have to solve the difficulty of self-consciousness in order to make believable the easygoing, uninhibited locker room banter. If an actor feels too self-conscious about his body to rehearse the play and create the role, he will not serve the play and should turn down the role.

The late Judith Lowry, who played roles well into her nineties, was often required to use foul and abusive language onstage because it created such a vivid comic effect. When questioned by her granddaughter, Lowry explained that it was not Judith Lowry saying those things, but a character whom she was creating, someone make-believe.

Now we will concern ourselves with exercises that will help to remove tensions and self-consciousness—exercises that will help the actor to follow the direction, "Just relax. Take it easy." Throughout the exercises, remember that relaxation is a mental, as well as a physical state.

EXERCISES

These may be done either individually or by a group. You must have enough room so that your movements are not restricted. You should not wear clothes that will hamper your freedom. These exercises involve consciously tensing and relaxing your muscles.

(1) Fill as much space as you can vertically. Make yourself as tall as possible. Stretch upward as far as you can. *Justify* this action by imagining you are removing a burned out light bulb that you can barely reach.

(2) Fill as little space as you can vertically without bending or stooping. Make yourself as short as possible. Imagine you are walking through a low cave.

(3) Fill as much space as you can horizontally. Make yourself as wide as possible. Stretch as far as you can from side to side. Imagine you are holding back two boulders that may roll together and crush you.

(4) Fill as little space as you can horizontally. Make yourself as narrow as possible without decreasing your height. *Justify* this exercise by imagining you are walking through a narrow tunnel.

Practice these exercises alternately feeling the alternation of tension and relaxation. Check carefully to see that you are making full use of every muscle that will help you accomplish your purpose. When you are stretching upward, be sure your feet, legs, abdomen, chest, shoulders, arms, hands, fingers are fully extended. When you are as tall as you can be, stretch a little more. Then relax as much as possible without losing any height. Check especially the facial muscles. Relax them completely because they can't make you any taller.

(5) Again stretch upward as far as possible. Again check carefully against excess tension; use no more tension than necessary to maintain the position. Now, beginning with your fingers, slowly relax. Continue downward with your arms, neck, shoulders, chest, abdomen, letting yourself fall forward until the upper part of your body is hanging like a rag doll. Maintain tension only in your legs and thighs to keep you from collapsing into a heap on the floor. Alternate the upward stretch and the "rag doll" positions, getting the feeling of purposefully tensing and relaxing your muscles.

(6) Sit well back on a straight chair, feet flat on the floor about six inches apart, hands resting on your knees. Take a comfortably erect position, and eliminate any tension not necessary to maintain it. Now fall forward at the waist, letting your face rest upon your knees. Eliminate all tension not necessary to keep you in the chair. Alternate the two positions.

(7) Return to the sitting position checking again for excess tension. Now concentrate on relaxing the facial muscles. Beginning with the forehead and the temples, let the energy drain out of your face until the lower jaw hangs loose and you feel like an idiot child. Maintain good sitting posture. If you "salivate," don't worry. Use your handkerchief.

(8) Make your body feel like an inflated balloon. Resist the temptation to puff out your cheeks. Deflate yourself. Alternate these two muscular states.

Throughout these exercises you have been asked to check yourself against excess tension. Most of us have tensions of which we are not aware. Relieving them is an ever-present problem, in life as well as on the stage. We go about our daily activities—walking, sitting, driving, even lying down—using more than the required energy. We should develop a habit in whatever we are doing of frequently checking ourselves to discover what muscles are unnecessarily tense and then proceed to relax them. We often find we are holding onto a pencil as if it would jump out of our fingers or we are walking with tense shoulders or standing with our knees locked, talking with a tight jaw, reading with a frown.

A habit of finding tensions and relieving them yields several benefits. Although it may be impossible, onstage or off, to keep tensions from occurring, the habit will induce a state of more general relaxation. It enables us to eliminate tensions at will—a facility of great value to the actor who is always subject to nervous strain. Perhaps most important, it helps the actor to discover his own nervous mannerisms. Different people reveal tensions in different ways. Some by contracted muscles, some by random movements. Among the commonest are shaking the head, pursing the lips, frowning, snapping the fingers, raising the shoulders. Take stock to find your personal signs of tension and get rid of them. You will discover that elimination of tension is not easy; it demands concentration. As you relax one muscle, another tenses in its place; it becomes a process of "chasing your tensions." Considerable practice may be necessary to achieve success.

Through systematic work, an actor will develop a "controller" inside himself that will instantly find the spot of unnecessary tension and as instantly eliminate it. This process of spotting and removing tension must be developed into an automatic habit in life as well as on the stage. It is necessary not only in quiet scenes that obviously should be played with relaxation, but in climactic scenes of physical excitement. At such moments there is a natural tendency to increase the tension, and the need for relaxed control is even greater.[4]

Justifying Your Exercises

The next group of exercises is to provide further practice in *justified* physical training by which the actor can transfer the gained benefits to the stage. All exercises can be made more valuable by supplying circumstances to justify the action. Only exercises that involve the actor's imagination and his internal resources are entirely profitable. Mere repetition of physical activity produces only part of the desired results. In performing any action make your gestures and movements free and unrestrained. Arm movements should come freely from the shoulders. Many young actors tend to gesture with the forearms only, holding the elbows close to the body. Be sure the wrists are free from excess tension, but they should not be limp. Your "controller" should constantly check the shoulders where tension is very likely to occur. Delsarte, whose theories of expressive movement were too systematized but not entirely unsound, believed that the shoulders were the most expressive part of the body and that all emotions were first registered there. Tense shoulders will not respond to inner impulses. In walking, swing the legs freely from the pelvis with the knees relaxed.

---

(1) *Believe* you are picking apples from branches that can be reached only by standing on your toes and extending your arms to their utmost. To avoid bruising it, place each apple carefully in a basket on the ground. Let your imagination bring this situation to life. Your objective is not to *pretend* you are picking apples. Let your imagination make the tree and the apples true, **EXERCISES**

[4] See Magarshack, Introduction to *Stanislavsky on the Art of the Stage*, pp. 44–45.

and let it compel you to purposeful action. Check frequently to discover and eliminate excess tension.

(2) Supply additional circumstances that will justify the action to an even greater extent. Pick the apples for a number of different purposes:

As if you were a horticultural student hoping to win a prize at the state fair.
As if you were stealing apples from a neighbor's backyard.
As if you were preparing a basket of fruit to take to a sick friend.
As if your father had forced you to pick a bushel of apples before he would let you take the car.
As if you were Eve picking apples in the Garden.

(3) Household tasks offer opportunities for exercises in relaxation through justification. Believe you are:

Hanging wallpaper.
Painting the ceiling.
Putting up window draperies.
Scrubbing the floor.
Waxing the floor.
Shaking throw rugs.
Pumping water.
Chopping wood.
Spading the garden.

In every case supply circumstances to provide justification for the physical task. Wax the floors and make them shine because your mother-in-law is coming to visit. Chop wood because the temperature is falling below zero and your wife has pneumonia. In every case commit yourself completely to the action, using fully all the muscles needed to perform it. Continue frequently to check and eliminate excess tension.

In performing these exercises, and in all other physical activities, strive to make the movements precise and clear *stripping away whatever is unessential.* Jacques Lecoq, whose work in mime provides actors with excellent body training, says "movement begins first with economy, that minimum of effort for a maximum of result. . . ." One of his general principles is to break movement down to its essentials, which

involves the ability to separate action into its components. In order to shovel, one: *stands* with the instrument poised, *thrusts* it into the earth, *presses* the blade deeper with one foot, *turns* in preparation to one side in order to *throw* the contents of the shovel to the other side. Such is one series of functional gestures. They are executed with precise economy, eliminating any unnecessary movements like shifting of weight, grimacing, wiping hands, hitching trousers, or whatever. Of course, these movements are often a part of real-life shoveling, but they are not needed in order to shovel; there are no slippery shafts or extra hard earth or loose trousers in the simple act.[5]

As a means of making your movements precise and economical, practice analyzing them and breaking them into their components. Then do only what is absolutely necessary. You may be surprised at the strength and clarity you can achieve. Much acting is cluttered with realistic but unessential details.

(4) Athletics offer additional opportunities. Believe you are:

Throwing a baseball.
Serving a tennis ball.
Kicking a football.
Driving a golf ball.
Hurling a javelin.
Thrusting a foil.
Putting a shot.
Lifting weights.
Punching a bag.
Shadow boxing.

Supply imaginary circumstances in each case. Put your whole body into the action. Check yourself constantly to see that all muscles except those needed to perform the action are relaxed. Concentrate on keeping your face free of tension.

(5) The following are exercises for walking (or moving) in various circumstances. Each will require some modification of your natural walk. Again commit yourself fully, but don't permit any excess tension. Supply additional circumstances as needed. Move as if you are:

A hunter stalking a deer.
A soldier marching in a parade.
A goose-stepping soldier marching in parade.
A high-fashion model at a showing.
A candidate for the title of Miss America parading on the runway.
A burglar hugging the sides of the buildings in a dark alley.
A trapper on snowshoes.
A boy crawling through a low tunnel.
A soldier crawling on his stomach under gunfire.
A drum major or majorette.
A thief forcing a victim to march by holding a revolver against his back.
The victim being forced to march.

[5] Bari Rolfe, "The Mime of Jacques Lecoq," *The Drama Review* (Volume XVI, Number 1, March 1972), p. 37.

A native balancing a can of water on his head (no fair using your hands).
A guerrilla fighter creeping up on an enemy.

Make a regular practice of doing relaxation exercises before each rehearsal and performance. Condition yourself to begin any kind of work session with your muscles relaxed.

(6) In this group of exercises you will make fuller use of your body by combining movement with inarticulate sounds. Use the widest pitch range and the most varied intonations of which you are capable. Your "controller" should continually check for tension in your throat. Do not constrict the larynx. It is not the purpose here to imitate the sounds and movements of animals, but rather to realize their quality. These problems may be worked on individually or in groups of two or three. In each case have clear intentions and obstacles.

A dog barking.
A lion attacking his prey.
A crowing rooster. Be sure to play an intention.
A hissing snake.
A meowing cat.
A howling wolf.
A soldier at bayonet drill. In training for a bayonet charge, recruits are required to make frightening sounds and use fearful facial expressions to intimidate the enemy. This follows a primitive practice in which warriors going into battle painted their faces in grotesque patterns and uttered terrifying noises.

Directing Your Attention

Concentration was mentioned in Chapter 4 as an important aid to relaxation. It also serves to channel the actor's energies toward the accomplishment of a purpose; and it is the principal means of controlling the attention of the audience, which is one of the actor's primary responsibilities. If the audience hears what the actor wants it to hear and sees what he wants it to see during every moment of a performance, he has gone a long way toward fulfilling his function. On the other hand, if attention constantly strays to other points on the stage or in the auditorium, he has little chance of success no matter what the other virtues of his performance may be. His chances are even less if the spectators withdraw altogether to think about personal matters which have no connection with the production.

The audience is likely to be interested in whatever interests the actor. If this statement can't be accepted without reservation, certainly the reverse is true: the audience is not likely to be interested in what does not interest the actor. *Attention demands attention.* When you are walking down the street and see a number of people looking up at a high building, you are either very preoccupied or very self-satisfied if you are not curious to find out what is attracting their attention.

But concentrating, like "just relaxing," is easier to say than to do. Too many young actors are like the fellow described by Stephen Leacock who jumped on his horse and rode off in all directions. Their attention is scattered to all points of the compass. Their minds wander from what they think the audience is thinking about them, to what is going on offstage, to what their next lines are, to what they will be doing next, to whether they will be able to get through a difficult scene in the next act, to whether someone else is going to break up, and so on. It is safe to say that many a student actor never focuses more than 10 percent of his attention on anything related to the character he is trying to create. Thus 90 percent of his energy is dissipated.

An actor can make full use of his talent only by learning to concentrate his energies. *Creativeness onstage, whether during the preparation of a part or during its performance, demands complete concentration of all of his physical and inner nature, the participation of his physical and inner faculties.*[1] Maximum concentration is another characteristic of a fine actor. He must be able to control his attention in spite of the pressure of the audience, the distraction of backstage activities, the mechanical demands of the role. Concentration requires conscious effort. It is one of the specific skills that an actor must possess, and like any other skill it can be attained only through hard work and a developed technique. And he must at all times know *where* to direct his attention.

EXERCISES

Any activity that requires concentration, especially in the presence of distracting influences, is excellent discipline for the actor. A person training for the stage needs to develop his power of attention through general exercises in concentration. Their value is derived only when they are practiced regularly over a period of time. No exercise has served its purpose until it can be done satisfactorily with a minimum of effort. Students of Stanislavski suggest the following kinds of activity for developing an ability to concentrate:

(1) Read expository material in the presence of a group that constantly tries to interrupt and distract. Hold yourself responsible for remembering each detail you have read.

(2) Solve mathematical problems under the same conditions.

(3) Memorize a passage of prose or poetry under the same conditions.

(4) With a group sitting in a circle, one person says any word that comes into his head. The second repeats the word and adds another which has no logical relation. The next person repeats the two words and adds a third. The process continues around and around the circle until no one is able to repeat the entire series. Anyone who fails is eliminated. The exercise provides training in both concentration and memory.

(5) Under similar circumstances, play a game of numbers. The numbers may be unrelated, or you may progress by each person's adding 4 or 7, 11 or 19! The game can become quite challenging.

[1] Constantin Stanislavski, *Stanislavski's Legacy*, ed. by Elizabeth Reynolds Hapgood (New York: Theatre Arts Books, 1958), p. 174.

(6) Do Rapoport's "Mirror Exercise" in which "two people . . . stand opposite each other; one makes a movement, the other copies him exactly as in a mirror. The director of the group looks on and points out any errors." [2] Do the exercise first with abstract, nonrepresentational movements. Then do it performing realistic physical tasks such as sewing on a button, manicuring the nails, applying makeup. By using a prearranged signal, the "director" indicates that the initiator and the mirror image change roles. There should be no break in the movement when the change occurs. After some practice the two actors will develop a rapport in which neither seems to initiate the movement. They will feel they are moving simultaneously under the direction of some inner impulse.

(7) Extend the above exercise into a Sound Mirror. Along with the movements the first person utters gibberish, which the other repeats accurately.

(8) Concentrate on coordination of arm movements. With the left arm fully extended continue making a large circle in the air; with the right arm continue making a square by extending it straight out from the shoulder, then up, then to the side. Once coordination is established, reverse the arms making the circle with the right arm and the square with the left. You may find this exercise surprisingly difficult.

(9) Do a "Copy Exercise" in which one of the group performs a sequence of simple actions such as entering a room, removing a coat, getting something to eat from the refrigerator, and sitting down to read. Others concentrate on watching and then repeat the movements in exact detail and with the same tempo-rhythms. If available, video equipment can be used to advantage permitting each actor to see for himself how accurately he has observed and repeated the movements.

Concentrating on Action

We have been much concerned with the importance of action. In earlier exercises you have been asked to write down—make a score of—the physical actions you would undertake if you were in the situation of an imaginary character. Actions are tangible and specific for both the actor and the audience. They bring a character to life and reveal the dramatic events of the play. Since they are never divorced from some desire, their advantage lies not just in the actions themselves, but in the meaning and feelings they have the power to evoke. An actor has the greatest advantage when he can focus his attention

---

[2] I. Rapoport, "The Work of the Actor," in *Acting: A Handbook of the Stanislavski Method*, ed. by Toby Cole (New York: Lear Publishers, 1947), p. 38.

on carrying out a simple stage task. A proper object of concentration is the carrying out of psychophysical actions.

When Ethan Frome waits outside the meeting house for Mattie Silver, he warms himself against the winter cold by stamping his feet and slapping his arms. Here is a situation in which the actor may concentrate on a physical action. The desire to keep warm in winter is common enough and the action to satisfy it simple enough, that through *concentration of attention* no actor will have difficulty in inducing belief. And the extent of his belief will depend upon the degree to which he is able to commit "all of his physical and inner faculties."

In the opening scene of *Romeo and Juliet*, the Capulet servants make faces and "bite their thumbs" at the servants of the Montagues for the purpose of insulting them and inciting them to a quarrel. In *Ceremonies in Dark Old Men*, by Lonne Elder III, Mr. Parker spends his time loafing in his barber shop (he never has a customer) and playing checkers with a neighbor while his daughter Adele supports him and her grown-up brothers. Late in the afternoon he gets out the checkers for another quick game before Adele comes home from work. He concentrates on setting up the game, beating Mr. Jenkins, and watching the door for his daughter's return. In *A Doll's House*, by Henrik Ibsen, Nora wants to keep her husband from going to the mailbox, knowing he will find a letter which may ruin their marriage. She concentrates on dancing a tarantella to keep his mind from the mail as long as possible. In the great Sleepwalking Scene, Lady Macbeth concentrates on rubbing the bloody signs of guilt from her hands. It is said the French actress Rachel attempted to lick off the blood with her tongue instead of rubbing it away.

Good plays are filled with opportunities for concentrating attention on physical action. Good dramatists are very skillful in providing such opportunities. Sometimes the action is to satisfy a simple desire like Ethan's wish to keep warm—sometimes to satisfy a wish such as Nora's, complicated by emotional frustration and deep psychological need. When the dramatist has not provided it, the actor makes his problem easier by finding action to satisfy the needs of his character. Good actors and directors display great imagination in inventing physical action which is organic to the character and the situation.

EXERCISES   Learning to act is an accumulative process. Return to any of the earlier problems on actions and intentions. Work until you can repeat the exercise without any feeling of distraction from outside influences, until you are satisfied that every bit of your energy—all of your physical and inner faculties —are concentrated toward carrying out the action. Here are more problems providing opportunity to work on concentrating attention on physical action. Plan and rehearse a sequence of actions for the following situations.

Supply additional circumstances giving yourself specific details that will lead you to believe what you are doing.

Write out a score. Be sure each series of actions is structured with a beginning, a middle, and an end. State an intention that you *must* accomplish. Perform with the greatest possible economy discarding any details that do not help in achieving your purpose.

(1) You are visiting a museum, and you accidentally break a valuable antique vase.

(2) You are sitting on a park bench in a strange city feeding crumbs to the pigeons.

(3) You are searching for a lost article that is very important to you.

(4) You are mixing a dry Martini for a connoisseur.

(5) Late on a cold winter night you are standing on a street corner waiting for a bus.

(6) You are packing your suitcase in preparation for running away from home.

(7) You are soaking and bandaging a painfully swollen ankle.

(8) You are bailing water from a leaking boat.

(9) You are administering first aid to someone who has been injured in an accident. Seek the help of another actor to serve as the victim.

(10) You are taking your first steps after a serious illness.

(11) You are searching for interesting pebbles along the seashore.

(12) You are stranded alone on a deserted island. You are trying to attract the attention of a plane flying overhead.

Concentrating on Other Actors

Another way in which the actor directs his attention is toward other actors. He attempts to influence the people with whom he is playing. He yields to or resists their influence in turn. The "connection" established by this process is one of the actor's surest sources of stimulation and one of the most rewarding theatre experiences for the audience. Drama consists fundamentally of one character's attempt to force his will upon another. This attempt provides the essential element of conflict. The ups and downs of the struggle provide interest and suspense which is resolved when finally he either succeeds or fails. *King Lear* begins with Lear's attempt to force his will upon his daughters by requiring extravagant declarations of love from them. Othello's tragedy comes from Iago's determination to ruin his contentment. *The Taming of the Shrew* is a straightforward clash between Katharine and Petruchio.

Nora dances to keep Helmer from going to the mailbox. She concentrates upon the action of the dance and, at the same time, she is concerned with how

Douglas Turner Ward (center) and members of the Negro Ensemble Company in a scene from *The River Niger* by Joseph A. Walker. (Photo—Bert Andrews.) Study the picture as an example of concentration of attention.

she is influencing her husband. As she perceives he may be thinking of his mail, the tarantella becomes more animated. A director might do well to tell the actor playing Helmer to go to the box as soon as Nora's dance fails to hold his attention. In *The Winter's Tale*, Hermione pleads with her husband to convince him he is wrong in suspecting her of being unfaithful. She knows her honor and her life depend upon her ability to exert her influence.

This "character connection" is accomplished through concentration. The actor concentrates on using his actions and his lines to get what his *character* wants from the other *actors* in the play. Through lines and actions he attempts to arouse real feeling and stimulate genuine responses in the other actors. In this exciting way the imaginary world of the play merges with the real life of the actor. His real effort to exert his influence and the real responses he is able to induce are the vitality of any performance. Its life is the communion between the actors. In the opening of *Romeo and Juliet*, the Capulet servants concentrate on making the Montagues mad. They actually make every effort appropriate to the characters and the situation (we must always accept the given circumstances!) to provoke the actors playing opposite them to anger. Hermione strives to win real sympathy from the actor playing Leontes. The circumstances require him to refuse her; his own feelings will make Leontes' decision more difficult. They will provoke an inner conflict and heighten the impact of the scene.

To excite an audience actors must excite each other. Stanislavski wrote: "Infect your partner! Infect the person you are concentrating on! Insinuate yourself into his very soul, and you will find yourself the more infected for doing so. And if you are infected everyone else will be even more infected." [3]

Making an Action of Speech

Speaking is of great importance in this vital "inter-influence." Both in life and onstage we use words as a means of getting what we want, as a way of realizing our intentions. We use words to ask, beg, demand, plead, explain, persuade, woo, threaten—and for many other purposes. We are not yet ready to consider the problems of line interpretation (an important part of the actor's job), but it is necessary to come to an understanding of *why* the actor speaks, and to begin to use speech to serve its proper function. A mere reading of the lines, no matter how intelligent or how beautiful, is only a part of the actor's responsibility. The common tendency to read lines as smoothly and easily—and consequently as glibly—as possible must be avoided from the start. It is not essential to speak smoothly and easily, to utter what Charles Marowitz calls "a mellifluous cascade of sound." It is essential to speak for a purpose.

The basic function of stage speech is to help the actor accomplish his purpose. His first task is to discover how each line serves this aim. This is a thinking process—not highly intellectual, to be sure—but it does demand understanding of what his purpose is and how the line relates to it. It demands, too, that he think clearly of this relation at every rehearsal and performance. What is in the actor's mind at each moment of the play determines the extent of his influence. Acting is thinking! Two factors tending to defeat the thinking process are a desire to speak smoothly, and a tendency to stop thinking during the many necessary repetitions. The actor must train himself to keep his thoughts alive. He must discover a genuine need to use the playwright's words.

He must also whole-heartedly accept the concept that *speech is an action.* Speaking is doing. In some primitive languages the word to act and to speak is the same. The actor needs constantly to concentrate on influencing other actors through his words. Just a simple "good-morning" has no justification on the stage until the speaker concentrates on influencing the listener in some way or other. The greeting may "infect" the listener with casual indifference, deep

[3] Constantin Stanislavski, *Building a Character* (New York: Theatre Arts Books, 1949), p. 118.

love, intense hate. It may say any one of a dozen things, each intended to evoke a different response. It may say for example:

I am in a friendly, leisurely mood. Let's have a chat.
I am perfectly friendly but in a hurry. Please be brief in what you have to say.
I got up on the wrong side of the bed. Don't say a word.
The occasion demands a civil greeting. Don't presume it means anything more.

In each case the actor concentrates his attention on influencing the behavior of the listener.

Inter-influence is, of course, two-way influence. The actor concentrates not only on *affecting* others. He also *listens* to what is said to him, and he resists or yields to the desires of the speaker. The "art of listening" is often mentioned as one of the specific skills required of the actor. The art consists of concentrating on what is said by hearing and responding to it at each rehearsal and performance as if it had never been heard before. He creates what William Gillette aptly called "the illusion of the first time." It is the illusion, necessary both to him and to the audience, that no matter how long he has worked upon a part—no matter how often he has rehearsed or performed it, each time is a new and fresh experience. Close *connection* between actors is necessary in creating this illusion. In this way live feelings are aroused each time and in a sense the experience *is* new.

EXERCISE   Do a "Greeting Exercise" the object of which is to *infect* another actor so he will respond as you would like him to. You are limited to one phrase of greeting and one physical action. You should carefully choose your intention to evoke the desired response, and your partner should not know what your intention is nor the imagined circumstances in which you are playing it. Possible situations might be:

Intimate friends who have not seen each other for a long time.
A former husband and wife meeting socially for the first time after an unpleasant divorce.
A peasant meeting a king.
Two prima donnas who habitually try to avoid speaking to each other.

When your partner has *adapted* to your greeting, you should adapt to his response and continue to improvise a short scene. Discuss later whether your partner responded as you desired.

A short dialogue near the beginning of Ibsens's *The Wild Duck* gives both actors an excellent opportunity to speak for a purpose. The scene is the study in the house of Mr. Werle, a wealthy manufacturer. Sounds of a large dinner party are heard from stage left. At right a small door leads to an office where Werle's clerks do copy work. A servant enters and speaks to the butler.

SERVANT. I say, Pettersen, here's an old fellow who . . .

PETTERSEN. Who the devil's here now?

> OLD EKDAL *enters from center. He wears a threadbare cloak with a stand-up collar, woolen mittens; in his hands a stick and a fur cap, under his arm a parcel done up in brown paper. He has a reddish-brown, dirty wig, and a small mustache.*

PETTERSEN. (*Going toward him*) Good lord! What are you doing here?

EKDAL. (*In the doorway*) Must absolutely go to the office, Pettersen.

PETTERSEN. The office was closed an hour ago and . . .

EKDAL. Heard so at the door, my lad. But Graberg's in there still. Be a good fellow, Pettersen, and let me slip in this way. I've been this way before.

PETTERSEN. All right, you can go. (*Opens door*) But mind you leave the proper way, for we've company.

EKDAL. Know that—h'm! Thanks, Pettersen, my lad. Thanks. (*In a low tone*) Idiot!

The intention of each of the characters is clear. Ekdal must persuade Pettersen to let him into the office. Pettersen must keep the disreputable old man from embarrassing the company. Each actor must know how his lines serve to help him accomplish his purpose. He must find in the play, or he must supply from his imagination if the playwright has not provided them, circumstances that make the accomplishment of the purpose necessary. It is the actor's responsibility to find reasons for his actions and words which are both logical for the character and stimulating to the actor—reasons which he personally can understand and accept.

Old Ekdal through a miscarriage of justice has fallen from better days. He now does copy work for Werle, earning small amounts that he promptly spends on drink. He is cleverly persuasive when the need for liquor is upon him. Pettersen has long been a servant in Werle's house. He has pride in his position. Nothing must mar the dinner party. The intentions in each of the lines may be stated as:

SERVANT. I must get Pettersen's help in handling this old reprobate before he makes a scene.

PETTERSEN. I must protest about any interruption just as I'm getting ready to serve coffee.

EKDAL. (*Entrance*) I want to let Pettersen know I can cause him a lot of embarrassment if he doesn't let me through.

PETTERSEN. I must take care of this situation quickly.

EKDAL. I must let him know I'm not going to be got rid of, that I'm going to take full advantage of the situation.

PETTERSEN. I must get rid of him.

EKDAL. I want to take advantage of a position which could cause him embarrassment. I call him "lad," even though he's almost as old as I am. I tell him I know there's someone still working in the office. I remind him it won't be the first time I've slipped through the study.

PETTERSEN. I must get him out of the way before anyone sees him. I must warn him he's going to suffer for it if he tries to come through here again.

EKDAL. I want to let him know I am well aware of what goes on here. I want him to think I'm grateful and humble. I want to give myself the satisfaction of saying what I really feel.

Just before Old Ekdal's appearance, a dialogue between Pettersen and another servant does not clearly provide a reason for the lines.

PETTERSEN. (*Lighting a lamp on the mantelpiece, and placing a shade upon it*) Just listen, Jensen; there's the old gentleman standing up by the table and proposing to Mrs. Sorby's health in a long speech.

JENSEN. (*Bringing down an arm chair*) Is there any truth in what people say that there's something between them?

PETTERSEN. Lord knows!

JENSEN. For he's been quite a rake in his time.

PETTERSEN. Maybe.

JENSEN. It's in honor of his son that he's giving this dinner, they say.

PETTERSEN. Yes, his son came home yesterday.

JENSEN. I never knew before that Mr. Werle had a son.

PETTERSEN. Oh yes, he has a son. But he's always stopped up there at the Hojdal works. He's not been in town all the years I've been in service here.

How does Pettersen want this information to affect Jensen? What is Jensen's purpose? This is a dialogue for which the actors must supply circumstances from their imaginations. They might imagine that Pettersen is a talkative old fellow, delightfully scandalized by what goes on in Werle's household, always eager to impress others with his knowledge and his importance as butler to such a wealthy man, but always discreet enough never to disclose any family secret. Jensen, a waiter hired only for special occasions, wants to keep Pettersen talking. He is eager to hear the gossip because he enjoys repeating it when he is working in other houses.

In developing a role an actor may be certain of the action of each line only after he understands the desires that motivate the character's total behavior. Understanding this motivating desire is a problem to be bypassed at the moment. We will come to it in Part II, which considers the actor in relation to the play. At this time it will best serve our purpose to work on small scenes without assuming the responsibility of finding their total meaning.

Work improvisationally in the following situations. Your intention here is to influence your partner—to elicit specific responses from him. And his intention is to influence you. This means a mutual influence, a give and take that is the essence of a lively stage performance. It means you are sensitive to every detail of your partner's presence, you hear and understand what he is saying; and he, in turn, is equally aware of you.

Remember improvisation is free only within certain limitations. It requires a definite preparation. Your intention—the response you want to provoke—should be stated in advance. You should provide additional circumstances to supplement those briefly given here, and your behavior should be appropriate within those circumstances. The exercise should be structured into its three parts, and the "key lines" used in the beginning unit. You might do well to determine in advance other key lines to be made part of the other units.

This kind of preparation gives you direction and purpose. It does not eliminate spontaniety and immediate adaptations. It is like playing any game. You know the rules and the objectives. You do not know what offensive actions your partner will attempt, nor what defenses he will use against your attacks.

(1) In *Who's Afraid of Virginia Woolf?*, by Edward Albee, a married couple have just returned home after a party. Martha wants to continue drinking and having a good time. George is tired and wants to go to bed. Key lines are:

MARTHA. Come on, make me another drink.

GEORGE. It's two o'clock in the morning.

(2) In *In the Wine Time*, by Ed Bullins, Lou and Cliff are a young married couple sitting on the street in front of their house on a hot summer night. They are drinking wine, and their conversation alternates between bantering and wrangling. Key lines are:

LOU. What should I do when I find lipstick on your shirt . . . shades I don't use. (*Silence.*) What should I say when I see you flirtin' with the young girls on the street and with my friends? (*Silence.*)

CLIFF. (*Tired.*) Light me a cigarette, will ya?

(3) In A *Hatful of Rain*, by Michael V. Gazzo, Polo lives in a small apartment with Johnny and Celia, his brother and sister-in-law. Johnny's neglect of Celia leaves her alone with Polo a great deal of the time. She recognizes their growing attachment for each other and asks Polo to leave. Key lines are:

CELIA. . . . . I don't want to take any chances.

POLO. What chances?

(4) In *The Time of Your Life*, by William Saroyan, Blick, a plainclothesman, questions Kitty Duval in a waterfront bar in San Francisco. He is intent on charging her with prostitution. Key lines are:

KITTY. . . . I sang and danced in burlesque all over the country.
BLICK. You're a liar.

(5) In *The Tiger*, by Murray Schisgal, Ben grabs an unknown girl named Gloria in the street and carries her to his basement room. Key lines are:

BEN. Je m'appelle Benjamin.
GLORIA. No, not quite; hold your lips like this and let the words run into each other. Like this. Je m'appelle Benjamin. Try it.

Provide circumstances in which a seduction logically becomes a French lesson.

(6) In *Thieves' Carnival*, by Jean Anouilh, Gustave is caught by Juliette in the act of robbing her aunt's drawing room. He binds her to a chair and gags her with a handkerchief, but the precaution is unnecessary. She ends up helping him with the theft. Key lines are:

GUSTAVE. Are you comfortable? You're not choking, are you? Look, Juliette, if you swear not to call out, I'll take the gag off. Do you swear?
(*She nods.*)
All right then, I trust you.

(7) Extend the problem from *Summer and Smoke* described at the end of Chapter 2 by improvising the scene in which Alma "picks up" the Young Man (see pages 24 and 34). The Young Man is a traveling salesman— eager, but inexperienced. Key lines are:

ALMA. The life of a traveling salesman is interesting . . . but lonely.
THE YOUNG MAN. You're right about that. Hotel bedrooms are lonely.

(8) In *All the Way Home*, by Tad Mosel (based on James Agee's novel *A Death in the Family*), Jay Follet receives a call from his brother Ralph to tell him their father is ill. Although it is late at night, Jay prepares to drive some distance to his father's farm leaving his wife and young son at home. His wife Mary helps him get ready for the trip. Key lines are:

MARY. Is it very grave?
JAY. Lord knows.

(9) In *Career*, by James Lee, Sam and Barbara are college students, much in love. Barbara is proud of Sam for saving two hundred dollars which she assumes he is going to use to go on to law school. One night, in front of Barbara's house, Sam has to break the news that he has other plans. Key lines are:

SAM. . . . Barbara, I'm going to be an actor. . . . I'm going to New York.
. . . That's where I have to go if I'm going to be an actor . . .

BARBARA. Well, I hope you have a very successful career. I'm going in. Good
night.

(10) In *The Caretaker,* by Harold Pinter, Aston has befriended a tramp
named Davies by taking him into his house and providing for him. Unable, after some time, to put up with the tramp's peevish and ungrateful
ways, Aston has to make clear to Davies that he wants him to leave. Key
lines are:

ASTON. You make too much noise.

DAVIES. But . . . but . . . look . . . listen . . . listen here . . . I mean.
. . . What am I going to do? (*Pause*) What shall I do? (*Pause*) Where am
I going to go?

(11) In *The Zoo Story,* by Edward Albee, two men quarrel violently over
which one has the right to occupy a particular park bench. Key lines are:

PETER. This is my bench, and you have no right to take it away from me.

JERRY. Fight for it, then. Defend yourself; defend your bench.

(12) In *The Effect of Gamma Rays on Man-in-the-Moon Marigolds,* by Paul
Zindel, Ruth, a high-school student who thinks more about her appearance
than her studies, is getting ready to leave for school. Her divorced mother,
Beatrice, is a nervous high-strung woman who doesn't know how to support,
nor how to handle her two teen-age daughters. Key lines are:

BEATRICE. . . . If you don't hurry up you'll be late for school.

RUTH. Well, I couldn't very well go in without Devil's Kiss, now could I?

BEATRICE. Doesn't anyone go to school these days without that all over their lips?

(13) In *Yerma,* by Garcia Lorca, Maria is bursting with happiness when she
comes to tell Yerma she is going to have a child. Yerma shares her joy, but
she is also filled with longing because after two years of marriage she is still
childless. Key lines are:

YERMA. Tell me about it. . . . You . . . tell me . . .

MARIA. . . . Have you ever held a live bird pressed in your hand?

(14) In *Dutchman,* by LeRoi Jones, the scene is a subway car. A white
woman, a stranger sitting beside a young black man, tries to tempt him ero-
tically. Key lines are:

LULA. (*Grabbing for his hands, which he draws away.*) Come on, Clay. Let's
rub bellies on the train. . . . Get up, Clay. Dance with me. Clay.

CLAY. Lula! Sit down, now. Be cool.

EXERCISE

(1) In *Kataki*, by Shimon Wincelberg, an American soldier during World War II parachutes to a lonely island inhabited by a single Japanese soldier. They are enemies, their only weapon a knife, and no common language for communication. Gradually they learn that they must become friends or die. Improvise scenes from this situation with both actors speaking *only gibberish* so that neither will understand the words of the other.

(2) Act II of *The Kingdom of God*, by G. Martinez Sierra, takes place in a "maternity home (for women who have 'come to grief') which has been established in some old noble mansion in the north of Castile." Among the inmates is The Dumb Girl, strongly possessive of her baby, who utters only strange unintelligible sounds. The Mother Superior attempts in several languages and through gestures to find out who the girl is and where she came from. Improvise the scene with the Mother Superior using *gibberish* so The Dumb Girl actually will not understand what is said to her.

(3) Return to any of the situations in the previous group of exercises and improvise them in gibberish. This kind of improvisation can be made a valuable part of your work—creating an increased awareness of the function of lines in accomplishing intentions. Too often actors speak lines concentrating too much upon the words and not enough upon their purpose. Overcome immediately any feeling of ridiculousness that may occur in speaking gibberish. Remember when an actor is working with a purpose, he is ridiculous only when he is afraid of being ridiculous.

Seeing Things

An actor must make the study of human nature one of his major concerns. The great actors of France have long been famous for their ability to dazzle an audience by means of their technical perfection and the incisiveness of their character portrayal. One of the greatest was Constant Coquelin, creator of the role of Cyrano de Bergerac. Coquelin wrote, ". . . it is one of the necessary qualities of an actor to be able to seize and note at once anything that is capable of reproduction on the stage." [1]

The process of "seizing and noting" is a technique called *observation*. It is another of the necessary skills. We are already aware that an actor does not have within his experience the knowledge to play the variety of characters he must undertake. He must constantly make use of what he can observe in the world around him. He must endlessly enlarge his impressions of life. These are the materials from which he creates. He must go further than Coquelin suggests by making it a practice to seize and note not only anything that is capable of reproduction onstage, but also anything that reveals truth or provides understanding about what may be produced there.

The technique of observation involves a conscious effort to develop a fuller awareness of what is going on around us, a fine sensitivity to what we see, hear, taste, feel, and smell. Jean-Louis Barrault is fond of telling a story about Charles Dullin, the noted French director whose productions were always vital and vibrant. Dullin himself was marvelously childlike in his appreciation of everything in his environment.

[1] Benoit Constant Coquelin, "Acting and Actors," *Harper's New Monthly Magazine* (May 1887), pp. 891–909.

Once Dullin was asked, "How can you stare at the same scenery every day? You stare out of the train window as if seeing the scenery for the first time, even though you travel on this same train practically every day."

"Because," he responded, "every night, before I go to sleep, I 'kill' the old Charles Dullin. Each morning, I am reborn." This was Dullin's method for maintaining his powers of observation: each day he saw the world anew through the eyes of a child.

The world—especially this modern world—is so full of a number of things that we tend to take most of them for granted. We don't really look at people's faces, hear their voices, nor listen to sounds, or even taste the food we have paid dearly for in an expensive restaurant. This indifference is movingly expressed by Emily in *Our Town*, by Thornton Wilder. Returning from the dead to relive a childhood experience, she sees people going insensitively about their everyday tasks. She says of her family at breakfast, "They don't even take time to look at one another." The actor must learn to observe familiar things as if he had never seen them before, and he must remember the experience. Through remembered observation he will build a reserve of materials which he can put to creative use. And he will enrich his life, which, to be practical, will also enrich his acting.

Observation is both intellectual and sensory. The mind tells us the uses of things, classifies them, analyzes them in any one of a number of ways, permits us to retain them in memory. Recognizing that a flower is a carnation and not a buttercup, red and not yellow, a variety of the clove, pink, spicy scented, double blossomed, used for bouquets and buttonholes is an intellectual response. We perceive the flower, however, through the senses. Experiencing a carnation is not just knowing about it. It is seeing the color, smelling the fragrance, holding it, touching it. The basis of observation is sensory perception. And fortunately we have a memory for sensory as well as intellectual experience. It allows us to retain and recall not only our knowledge of the carnation, but also the sensory experience of it.

EXERCISE

(1) A first step in developing a technique of observation is to train yourself to experience the regular events of everyday life. To get into the habit, take time to perceive fully these common activities. Remember observation involves all the senses—sight, hearing, taste, touch, and smell.

Peeling and eating an orange, apple, peach, pear.
Shaving.
Brushing your teeth.
Manicuring your nails.
Putting on your shoes.
Putting on and taking off a coat.

Hearing a bird call, a siren, a clock ticking.
Arranging a bouquet of flowers.
Tasting a strong cheese.
Eating celery, artichokes, corn on the cob.
Eating marshmallows, caramels.
Cleaning fish.
Scouring a pan with a metal pot cleaner.
Shelling peas.
Sandpapering a piece of furniture.
Walking barefoot on wet grass, hot sand, cold tile.
Pouring and drinking a cup of hot coffee.
Drinking cold lemonade.
Smelling and tasting vinegar, lemon juice.
Warming yourself by an open fire.
Cracking and eating pecans, walnuts, peanuts.

(2) Concentrate on these observations until you can repeat them without the object. Don't think of this as an exercise in pantomime that may lead you to concentrate on only the visual aspect. Your objective is to re-create the entire sensory experience. You not only see the orange and handle it accurately, you feel it (texture, weight, form), smell it, taste it, feel it in your mouth. See if you can get genuine sensory responses to imaginary objects. This part of the exercise has two important purposes: it trains you to observe more closely, and it develops your *sensory memory*.

(3) Spend a period of time each day making a careful observation. Don't neglect any of the senses. Concentrate for one week on taste experiences, another week on touch. After five weeks begin again.

(4) Occasionally set a time limit. Observe an object for 60 seconds. Put it away and see how much you can recall. Check for accuracy. Do it again.

(5) After observing students in various classes, re-create the entire sensory experience of
    Walking into class late.
    Sitting down.
    Taking off a hat and coat.
    Leaving class when the period is over.

(6) Write a 500-word "biography" of a perfect stranger, beginning your narrative by observing the person's hands, and drawing inferences about his or her character from the type of shoes, watch, or glasses he or she wears.

(7) Close your eyes. Can you remember the following details about the room you are in?

What color are the walls?
How many windows are in the room?
What color is the rug?
How high is the ceiling?

(8) Sharpen your sensitivity to different times of day and night, different weather conditions. With all your senses observe:

A rainy day.
Summer noon.
Autumn evening.
Midnight.
Winter morning before daylight.
Late summer afternoon.
Winter sunlight.
Spring morning.

Combine these conditions with different locales:

Home.
A city park.
A small town.
A busy street corner in a big city.
The country.
A lake.
The seashore.
A strange town.

Use your sensory memory to recreate the feelings these various combinations arouse in you under conditions different from those that evoked them. Find a short scene, or invent a sequence of actions appropriate to these feelings. Perform the actions using your sensory memory to create the atmosphere. Move and speak in harmony with the atmosphere you create; imagine the air is filled with it and you are moving and speaking through it.

(9) The following problems consist of picking up an object, carrying it, and disposing of it. Your work should be based on direct observation and sensory memory. Be sure your whole body is involved in performing the action; don't act with just your hands and your arms. Remember the standing instruction to plan your action in three parts. Each exercise should have a definite beginning that makes the situation clear, a development into a conflict with an obstacle, an ending with some form of resolution. Find correct tempo-rhythms for each part.

A piece of ice.
A very hot dish.
A piece of sticky candy.

A scene from *Sweeney Todd*, book by Hugh Wheeler with music and lyrics by Stephen Sondheim. Staged by Harold Prince; costumes designed by Franne Lee; production designed by Eugene Lee; and lighting by Ken Billington. (Photo—Martha Swope.) In this scene, Sweeney has just claimed another victim in his search for revenge against society. Notice the adoration with which he holds his razor—both the tool of his trade and the instrument of his revenge.

A prickly pear.
A live snake.
A dog that has been struck by a car.
A live fish.
A worm.
A crown on a cushion.
A bloody knife.
A lighted candle.
A bucket full of water.
A cross.
Three heavy suitcases.
Two overfilled bags of groceries.
A person who has fainted.

In addition to increasing his awareness of what goes on around him and to developing his sensory memory, the actor may use the technique of observation in these three specific ways:

1. By observing characteristics of human behavior (manners of walking, talking, gesturing, and so forth) which he may reproduce quite literally on the stage.
2. By observing characteristics, incidents, situations which through his imagination he may adapt for use on the stage.
3. By observing animals, plants, inanimate objects for the purpose of abstracting qualities which may help him in creating a character.

In a description of her working methods, Helen Hayes gives examples of these uses of observation. After defining acting talent as "a peculiarly alert awareness of other people," she continues:

When I was preparing for my role of the duchess in Anouilh's *Time Remembered*, I had some difficulty capturing the spirit of the role, until . . . I heard some music written by Giles Farnaby for the virginal—you know, one of those sixteenth-century instruments. . . . That old duchess, I told myself, is like the music, light, dainty, period, pompous, tinkling. And, poor me, I'd been playing her like a bass drum. I had one scene in *Victoria Regina* that I played like one of my poodles. . . . I had a poodle that used to just sit, and he'd look almost intoxicated when I'd say, "Oh, Turvey, you are the most beautiful dog," . . . and believe me every night for a thousand and some performances of that play, I saw that poodle. There was a famous moment in *Coquette*—I didn't know what really true way to accept the news that my lover had been shot and was dead. . . . I remembered a picture on the front of one of the tabloids—the *News* or the *Mirror*—of a mother standing over her son's grave. He was a gangster, in Chicago, and this coffin was being lowered, and this woman was standing there and she was holding herself as if she'd had a terrible, terrible pain in her insides. And I knew this was the complete, complete reaction to something like this.[2]

These ways of observing will be explored through illustrations, explanations, and exercises.

Observing People

Let's return to the hypothetical, but entirely possible, production of *Romeo and Juliet* for which we were rehearsing a few chapters ago. Let's suppose you are now cast, not as Juliet or as Romeo, but as Juliet's old nurse. Let's see how *observation* can help in understanding, and ultimately in believing this character.

What manner of person is Juliet's nurse?

She is old.
She is large
She is short of breath.
She is good-natured.
She likes to tease.
She loves Juliet.
She is talkative.
She likes to put on airs.
She is bawdy.
She is an opportunist.
She is without real moral fiber.

Obviously this role is not a "natural" for the young actor. Although the process of self-exploration will doubtless reveal at least the germ of these characteristics within your own experience (indeed, you will never come to believe the character otherwise), here is an acting problem in which your own resources will need re-enforcement. How can you provide yourself with a picture of this vulgar, jovial old soul?

A simple answer would be, find some person like this nurse. Observe her carefully. Seize and note the way she rolls from side to side when she walks, the way she pants after any physical exertion, the way she rolls her head and holds in her stomach when she laughs. Copy these mannerisms and practice them until you can reproduce them accurately. Keep practicing until with each reproduction you obtain an inner grasp of the character because you know the external manifestations are true.

[2] Lewis Funke and John E. Booth, *Actors Talk About Acting: Fourteen Interviews with Stars of the Theatre* (New York: Random House, 1961), pp. 93–94.

Unfortunately, you probably do not have among your friends even a reasonable facsimile of Juliet's nurse. You will rarely play a character for whom you can find a counterpart living in the next block. The process of observation usually consists of piecing together details supplied by a number of different persons and, very possibly, noted at widely different times. The actor needs continually to observe those with whom he comes in contact. The way in which a fellow train passenger smacks his lips to express his approval may be a mannerism exactly suited to the next role you will play. The way in which a casual acquaintance smokes a cigarette may reveal a great deal of his character and provide the observant actor with an understanding of a person that he may have to portray onstage.

The material an actor can use in bringing to life such a character as Juliet's nurse is supplied by observation not only during the period in which he is working on the role; the actor trains himself to be observant constantly and to retain the details. Mannerisms of a talkative landlady at whose house you roomed three years ago might be vastly helpful in bringing you to a belief of this same quality in the Nurse. Memory of the way a neighbor used to put on airs when she dressed up to go downtown might help you to understand the behavior of the Nurse when Juliet sends her forth to find Romeo. Memory of the way an uncle used to tease you when you were a child might help you to appreciate the pleasure the Nurse derives from exasperating Juliet when she returns with Romeo's message.

EXERCISE   (1) Each day during the next week make a special effort to use your powers of observation. Note carefully mannerisms, gestures, ways of talking, walking, eating that reveal character traits. Visit a busy railway station, hotel lobby, or some other place where you will have opportunity to observe different people. Practice reproducing the observed details until you can do them accurately and until you feel you have captured some of the inner quality of the person. Prepare a short scene for which you supply circumstances leading to action that you believe would be true of the character you create.

(2) Observe someone doing a specific job expertly. Study him and practice until you can perform the job with skill and authority. Observe:

A short-order cook.
A barber.
A manicurist.
A shoeshine boy.
A mother bathing a baby.
A mother changing a baby's diapers.

A golfer driving a golf ball.
A tennis player serving a tennis ball.
Someone knitting.
Someone rolling and lighting a cigarette.
Someone shuffling and dealing cards.
A juggler.

(3) Observe a painting—an original if you have access to a museum—which reveals character. Recreate with your own body the posture, the facial expression. Make the character move; imagine how he would walk, sit, use his hands. If it is a period picture, read about the manners and customs of the period. Make him speak. Invent a scene in which you can bring him to life in a sequence of actions. Observing paintings of people in earlier times is an especially helpful source for playing characters in period plays.

(4) Observe a room belonging to an acquaintance or, better yet, to someone you are meeting for the first time. Study the furniture. Speculate on the reasons for its choice and its arrangement. Observe the manner of the decoration. Are the colors carefully planned or haphazard? Is the room neat or disorderly? What feelings does the room evoke in *you*? What does it tell you about the person who occupies it?

Adapting Observations Through the Imagination

The preceding exercises prescribed that you supply circumstances which would stimulate believable action true of some person you had observed. Supplying such circumstances involves imagination, and it leads to the second way in which an actor puts his powers of observation to work—the adaptation of observed facts to meet the needs of an acting problem. For the literal fact often serves only as a suggester of imaginary circumstances, a spur which promotes the action.

Stanislavski provides a striking illustration. Walking down the street one day, he observed a forlorn-looking woman wheeling a caged bird in a baby carriage. He knew, of course, nothing of the circumstances. Very probably the woman was moving into a new apartment. The carriage was a practical means of transporting her pet bird, and her forlornness probably derived from the fact that moving is an exhausting job. Stanislavski's imagination, however, supplied circumstances which provided him with a richer understanding of human experience, as well as a memory which may at some time have been useful in developing a character.

He adapted the observed fact in this way: The woman was a widowed mother who a short time before had lost her two children. To dispel her grief, she had

Young Girl at Open Half-Door by Rembrandt van Rijn, 1606–1669. Courtesy The Art Institute of Chicago (Mr. and Mrs. Martin A. Ryerson Collection).

The Scullion by Théodule Ribot, 1823–1891. Courtesy The Art Institute of Chicago (Mr. and Mrs. Lewis L. Coburn Memorial Collection).

Observe these paintings carefully, noting all external details and what they tell you about characterization. Improvise a scene in which you place one of these characters in imagined circumstances.

directed her affection to the bird, caring for it as if it were a child. Each afternoon she took it for an airing in the carriage exactly as she used to take the children.

Such a combination of observed fact and imaginary circumstances is one of the actor's sources of stimulation. It is a means of providing physical objectives in which he can believe. There are many possibilities for a short scene based upon the incident of the woman and the bird cage. Can you see her bathing the bird, feeding the bird, caressing it, talking to it, getting it ready to go for the ride?

Many questions immediately arise for which your imagination has to supply the answers.

How old is the woman?
What does she look like?
What kind of place does she live in?
Is she rich or poor?
What kind of bird does she have?
How long have the children been dead?
How did they die?
What is the bird's name?
Is the substitution of the bird only a temporary outlet or does it indicate some permanent mental derangement?
What attitude does the woman have toward friends who see her behavior with the bird?

Having answered these and other questions, you can visualize a series of actions which would bring this character and this situation to life. You can concentrate upon realizing these physical objectives so that the *action* will lead you to *belief* in the situation and the character, and the belief in turn will produce the desired *emotional state*. Feeling comes not directly but through association.

OBSERVATION + IMAGINARY CIRCUMSTANCES

ACTION

BELIEF

FEELING

EXERCISE

Make careful observations of human behavior. When you see a situation that stimulates your imagination, supply circumstances that you can use as the basis for an improvisation. Why, for example, might a sailor in a night club be dancing with a child's doll? Why might an old woman selling pencils on the street be reading a report of the New York Stock Exchange? Remember the purpose of these imaginary circumstances is to provide a reason for action. Action means definite physical objectives showing behavior you can believe is true of the person observed. Work out the details carefully.

Rehearse the scene until there is no part of it that does not seem right and logical. *Warning:* Do not attempt to substitute a "made-up" situation for the original observation. Without the observed fact you have no way of knowing whether your imaginary circumstances are true. *Imagination must have a basis in reality.*

Observing Animals and Objects

The study of plants, animals, and inanimate objects as a means of understanding a character is a third way in which an actor may use the technique of observation. The process involves the principle of *abstraction*—a principle in art quite generally misunderstood by the layman, but one which for our purpose may be simply explained and illustrated. *To abstract* means literally *to separate, to take away*. The principle is applied here by observing an object for the purpose of taking away from it (seizing and noting) such of its qualities as may be useful in developing a character.

The qualities of elegance, glitter, and aloofness abstracted from a crystal chandelier might be an important element in coming to understand some of the characters in Restoration drama. The comfortableness, the homeliness, the unpretentiousness of an old leather chair might provide an insight into another character of quite a different kind. The qualities to be abstracted from a gnarled and weather-beaten tree could be an *observed fact* for developing another type of person.

Close observation of an eggplant might help in preparing to play Juliet's nurse. On examining its appearance, one is impressed by its bulky form, its grossness, its unvaried purple surface—a growth that has matured in size without acquiring character. On feeling it, one becomes aware of its bland smoothness. On cutting it open, one finds the inside to be a yellow-white mass—pliant and spongy—with no core at all.

If an eggplant could walk, it would waddle from side to side; it would have difficulty carrying its bulk; it would perspire, and fan itself, and gasp for breath. Its bright purple color, symbolic of royalty and dignity, seems pretentious when everything else belies those qualities (the Nurse putting on airs before Romeo and his friends). Its smoothness suggests a good nature stemming from a lack of principles. Its "corelessness" parallels the Nurse's lack of moral fiber indicated by her inability to understand that one man is not as good a husband as any other. Her consequent advice to Juliet is that she might as well marry Paris now that Romeo is banished and she may have "no use of him."

People are often compared to animals, and in such comparison the actor may find another use for observation. We say that a certain young girl is kittenish, that a certain person is clumsy as a bear, that one man is foxy, another wolfish, and that still another is a snake in the grass. These comparisons are examples of observing animals, abstracting their essential qualities, and applying them to some aspects of human behavior. In the motion picture of *The*

Women, adapted from the popular play by Clare Boothe, each character was introduced as a different kind of animal. The gossiping, sharp-tongued Sylvia Fowler was a cat. The spreading, complacent Edith Potter was a cow. The vicious, husband-snatching Crystal Allen was presented as a panther.

A more famous example of observing the qualities of animals and applying them to dramatic characters is found in Ben Jonson's *Volpone*. The play is a vicious satire on greed. Each of the characters is appropriately named after some beast of prey. Volpone, or the Fox, is a rich merchant whose ruling passion is greed. But he is also sly, and he has hit upon a scheme of pretending that he is dying so that his equally rapacious friends will court his favor with extravagant gifts in the hope of being made his heirs. His friends include Corvino, or Little Crow, who offers his young wife; Corbaccio, or Old Crow, who sniffs at Volpone's body to make sure he is dead; Voltore, or the Vulture, who is exactly what his name implies. Slyest of all is Mosca, or the Fly, who turns the tables on Volpone by trying to prove him legally dead.

Returning once again to *Romeo and Juliet*, let's suppose you are cast as Juliet's cousin Tybalt. Shakespeare gives a clue which helps to discover both the internal and external characteristics. Three times Tybalt is compared to an animal! Mercutio first refers to him as "More than prince of cats." Later, in challenging him to a duel, Mercutio addresses him as "Good king of cats," declaring that he means to take one of Tybalt's nine lives. And after Tybalt has mortally wounded him, Mercutio says he is a "dog, a rat, a mouse, a *cat*, to scratch a man to death." With this suggestion in the lines, it would be a poor actor who did not exploit these catlike qualities that have motivated Mercutio's comparison.

First of all, what is a cat like? Whereas the word *kitten* may connote playfulness and cuteness, the word *cat* is generally associated with spitefulness, slyness, and malice. A reference to a dictionary will confirm this distinction: "the cat family (Felidae) includes besides the domestic cat the lion, tiger, leopard, puma, etc." When Mercutio calls Tybalt "king of cats," he is not thinking of a household pet. More likely he is seeing a sleek black panther.

In this species of cat, it is possible to find several characteristics that might stimulate an imaginative actor:

1. From his first entrance when he *creeps up behind* Benvolio with the line, "Turn thee, Benvolio, look upon thy death," Tybalt is a *threatening, menacing figure*. Later at the Capulet ball, he is *lurking* among the other guests threatening harm to Romeo. Still later, it is his determination to inflict harm that causes his own death and Romeo's consequent banishment.

2. Mercutio's description of Tybalt's manner of dueling indicates that he is an *expert*, but *unsportsmanlike fighter*. He fights *viciously and inhumanly* by the "book of arithmetic," unwilling to give his opponent any advan-

tage. He is willing to kill Mercutio "under Romeo's arm" as Romeo attempts to come between them.

3. His expertness in dueling would require *grace of movement* and *unusual muscular coordination*.
4. Mercutio's description indicates that Tybalt is an *extremely elegant creature* possessing a kind of haughtiness which does not sit comfortably among the old customs and manners.

An actor assigned to play Tybalt might well spend some of his time studying pictures or visiting a zoo to observe the characteristics and behavior of a panther. He could watch the panther's lurking stealth, its leanness, its elegant sleekness, its easy graceful movement, its latent strength and energy, its inhuman green-yellow eyes. Through his imagination he could visualize a person possessing these same qualities. And that person, with these definite internal and external characteristics, might be the starting point of belief in Tybalt.

Equus, by Peter Shaffer, deals with the psychiatric case history of Alan Strang, a seventeen-year-old who has blinded six horses with a metal spike. In the course of the play, the trauma peels away as he relives the experience. Because Alan has a love-hate relationship with horses, the actor should explore and incorporate many of their characteristics into the role: the nervous behavior of a young colt; the skittish, restless running back and forth; the gracefulness of motion; the head held high, moving from side to side to observe the world; the lack of trust, which needs to be allayed; and the playfulness of a young colt stretching its limbs. The actor should experiment with all of these qualities for Alan Strang, drawing upon direct observation of horses in action.

An actress preparing for the role of Maggie in *Cat on a Hot Tin Roof*, by Tennessee Williams, might do well to study the alley cat. She struggles to wrench life out of an alcoholic husband with the cunning, persistence, and sensuality of the feline. Maggie, who is the "cat" of the title, has scratched and clawed her way out of poverty. She is determined to hang on to her marriage, with the tenacity of an alley cat struggling to stay alive in the streets. Maggie can purr also when it becomes necessary. Her attempts to seduce her husband Brick and flatter Big Daddy are catlike. When Maggie walks, her whole body is in motion with feline grace. When she is spiteful, the claws emerge from their sheath. The actress working on the part must observe the human qualities in cats as well as the feline qualities in humans.

EXERCISE

(1) Choose for observation an animal or inanimate object. Study it carefully. Remember you can observe through all of your senses, not only through sight. In addition to how the object or animal looks, consider how it feels, how it smells, how heavy it is, possibly how it tastes. List all of its characteristic qualities.

Plan a short individual scene, either with or without lines, in which you impersonate a character with these qualities. Remember you will not be trying to make yourself believe you are a radish, or an old shoe, or a Shetland pony. You will have *abstracted* the essential qualities, and through your imagination you will visualize a person with the same characteristics. You will use your imagination to "supply circumstances" that would require the person to *act* in a true and revealing manner. Carrying out this action will help you to believe you are a *person with the same characteristics as your chosen animal or inanimate object*.

Suppose, for instance, you have chosen for observation a Scotch terrier puppy. Your list of its essential qualities might include the following:

He is shaggy.
He is cute.
He is playful.
He is friendly.
He is lively.
He is clumsy.
He likes attention.
He likes sympathy.

You might decide a child of ten or twelve years would have these qualities. Plan a series of actions that will lead you to believe you are a playful, friendly, clumsy child. Place your character in various imaginary circumstances, such as

receiving a present unexpectedly,
being left alone and told not to go out of the house,
falling from a tree and hurting his leg.

Determine your behavior in each of these circumstances by observation of the Scotch terrier.

(2) Create characters based on observations through each of the senses:

On hearing music of different periods, music played on different instruments, music of different types; on hearing whistles, clocks, bells, nature sounds, city sounds, and so forth.
On tasting lemon juice, whipped cream, vanilla, different spices, herbs, and so forth.
On touching furs, fabrics, surfaces, shapes of objects.
On smelling flowers, perfumes, soaps, foods, and so forth.

(3) Find a character in a play in whose development you could make use of observations of an object or an animal. Improvise a scene of action true to the character in which the details are based upon qualities of the observed object.

Relating to Things

The foundation of acting is carrying out a sequence of actions (remember, speaking is an action) that is logical within the given circumstances and that accomplishes a specific objective. The ultimate purpose, however, is not the action itself, nor even the achievement of the objective, but a revelation of its significance. The final interest of the audience is not in the events of the play—important as they are—but in what they mean to the characters involved. The action in which King Lear gives away his realm and the reasons why he does it must be clearly played, but the real import lies in how what he does affects him and the people around him. Marguerite's discovery of the jewels which Faust has placed in her way as a means of seduction is meaningful for the effect they have upon her and her neighbor, Martha. The basis for realizing this meaning is the technique of *relating to objects and to other actors*.

Stanislavski wrote, "You must have something that will interest you in the object of your attention, and serve to set in motion your whole creative apparatus. . . . Imagined circumstances can transform the object itself and heighten the reaction of your emotions to it. . . . You must learn to transfigure an object from something that is coldly reasoned or intellectual in quality into something that is warmly *felt*." [1]

In *Faust*, Goethe's most famous drama, Faust, an old scholar, has sold his soul to the devil in return for a year of restored youth. One of the youthful pleasures he seeks is the seduction of the innocent Marguerite. Martha is Marguerite's older and more experienced neighbor. The task confronting the actresses playing Marguerite and Martha is first of all a perceptive observa-

---

[1] Constantin Stanislavski, *An Actor's Handbook*, ed. by Elizabeth Reynolds Hapgood (New York: Theatre Arts Books, 1963), p. 25.

tion—both intellectual and sensory—of the casket of ᴊwels Faust has left in Marguerite's way. They must experience the color, sha e, brilliance, the feel of them dripping through the hands, the way they look hung about their throats and from their ears. Since the "prop" jewels will not be real, the actresses will need remembered observation or sensory recall. They will have to use their sensory memory to realize the beauty and fire of precious stones. If this memory is not among their resources, it may be necessary for them to visit a jewel collection in a museum or at a jewellers.

The actresses must now go further. They must "transfigure" the jewels "into something that is warmly felt." They (especially Martha) are overcome with the beauty of the stones. They desire them, they covet them. The jewels become a burning temptation, a successful lure in Faust's seduction. This *relationship* to the jewels constitutes their dramatic function and importance. It is also an effective means of stimulating the imagination and inducing the actors to believe and to feel. The value of the technique lies in making the relationship specific and personal. It is made specific by finding the exact response the character would have to the object of his attention. The same object can evoke a variety of responses depending upon the character and the circumstances. Consider the varying relationships to a casket of jewels by a hungry beggar, a wealthy dowager contemplating a purchase, a customs inspector, a jewel thief. The relationship is made personal by finding a response which the actor understands through his own experience, which through his imagination stimulates feeling.

The task confronting the actor playing King Lear in his first scene involves establishing relationships both to objects and to other characters. In his headstrong action of dividing his kingdom among his three daughters, he responds differently to each of them and his response changes—most dramatically in the case of Cordelia—as the scene progresses. His relation to Albany differs from his relation to Cornwall; his treatment of Burgundy differs from his treatment of the King of France. Each of these characters (and several others since it is a large and complex scene) is at some time the object of his attention, and with each he must make a specific and personal connection. He uses his experience and imagination to discover how Lear would feel about each of these people. He *observes* the actors he is playing with and uses them to induce live responses.

In addition to relating to the other characters, Lear has the task of relating to various objects. Good playwrights and directors are skillful and imaginative in supplying objects to help the actor find the truth of a scene. Such objects achieve their fullest meaning when they are both logical realistically and symbolic dramatically. Lear's throne, his crown, the sword of state carried before him all symbolize the kingdom which is his source of power, and which he is now about to give away. The map, indicating the division of the kingdom, is Lear's plan for seeking freedom in his old age from the cares of state; it is also the bait to lure his daughters to flatter his vanity by making extravagant declara-

Production of *A Streetcar Named Desire* by Tennessee Williams at the School of Theatre, University of Bahia, Salvador, Brazil. Staged by Charles McGaw. Study the picture as an illustration of relating to objects and to other characters.

tions of love before the assembled court. Thwarted by Cordelia's refusal, he rashly changes his plan and violently tears the map. Realizing Lear's relation to these objects—"transfiguring them into something that is warmly felt"—will help the actor to concentrate his energies, to believe what he is doing, help to arouse his feelings, help him to communicate the meaning of the play to the audience.

Relating to objects is such an effective technique that many of the great moments in drama supply the actor with this opportunity. Othello extinguishing the candle just before he murders Desdemona, "Put out the light, and then put out the light." Hamlet relating to the skull as he talks about the transitoriness of life, "Alas! poor Yorick. I knew him, Horatio. . . ." Lady Macbeth relating to her hands, which, in her deranged mind, she believes are covered with the blood of the murdered Duncan, "Out, damned spot! out, I say!" Shylock relating to the knife he is sharpening on the sole of his shoe to cut out a pound of Antonio's flesh. His action motivates Bassanio's "Why dost thou whet thy knife so earnestly?" This line indicates Shylock's concentration on his physical action.

EXERCISES

For the beginning exercises in relating to objects you need a solid nondescript article about 18 inches long, about 9 inches in breadth and thickness. A rolled-up coat secured with a string, a small pillow, or a block of wood will do nicely.

(1) Handle the article as if it were a baby. Your task is not only to use sensory memory so you handle it accurately, but to establish a specific relationship. Handle it as if you were:

a strict mother
a doting grandfather
an annoyed father
an inexperienced baby-sitter
a bachelor uncle

Supply various circumstances for the baby's condition. Handle it as if the baby were:

sick
asleep
soiled
crying
dead

(2) Handle the article as if it were:

a cat
a puppy
a skunk
a pumpkin
a watermelon
a time bomb
a valuable antique vase
a bouquet of roses
a fish you have just caught
a tureen of hot soup

In every instance supply circumstances which will provide you with a specific relationship.

(3) Working in pairs or in groups, you may make further use of the above problems as exercises in relation, recall, observation, and concentration. Without saying what it is, one actor determines an identity for the nondescript article and establishes a relation to it. Another actor observes carefully so that when the object is passed to him he can establish the same identity and relation. He then *changes* the identity and relation and passes the object on.

(4) Return to the exercise in the previous chapter that involved picking up, carrying, and disposing of a number of objects. Extend the problem by establishing definite and different relationships toward each object. For example,

Pick up the dog *as if*:
It were your favorite pet.
You were a passing motorist who loves and cares for animals.
You were a road worker getting the animal off the pavement.
You were a child "investigating" the mangled dog out of curiosity.

Pick up the snake *as if*:
You were afraid but had to remove it because it had crawled onto your
    porch.
It were a pet snake.
You were a caretaker in a zoo or a circus.
You were a snake charmer.

Pick up the unconscious person *as if*:
She were a dearly loved friend.
You were a hospital orderly handling a patient.
You had drugged him in order to carry out some "dark" purpose as in a
    mystery drama.

At this point in your exercise work, it is not too early to discuss briefly the actor's responsibility to the audience—a matter that we will take up in more detail later. We have already mentioned that *what* the actor does and *why* he does it must be clear to the spectators. It must also be interesting! Before it can be made clear to the audience, it must be clear to the actor; and far too many student actors attempt an assignment with only a vague general answer to the important questions: What? And Why? Furthermore, to be clear it must be *seen* and *heard*. Again, many young actors are not adequately concerned with sharing what they are doing. They speak and act without an awareness that they must communicate with the audience both orally and visually. Inaudible speech and actions that are too small or too covered to be visible do not fulfill their purpose. The notion that the actor should begin by making his actions small and believable and later enlarging them for the benefit of the audience conditions him to a habit that is difficult to change. Early in his training he should become aware of the necessity for clarity and for sufficient energy to communicate with the spectators.

Attempts to be interesting can lead the actor into a trap. They can easily become attempts at comedy, novelty, or sensationalism that are not logical within the circumstances. The actor must recognize that human behavior is interesting. An audience likes to see real people dealing with real problems. The way to generate interest in these exercises is to make the circumstances specific, to provide conflict by having a definite intention that can be realized only by overcoming a definite obstacle, and to let the audience follow the development of the conflict to a climax and a resolution. If you plan carefully and concentrate on carrying out your plans, you have a solid foundation for an interesting improvisation.

Plan a sequence of actions providing opportunity for working on the problem of relating to objects in these situations: **EXERCISES**

(1) You are an archeologist entering the tomb of an Egyptian king. You are the first person to enter there in over 3,000 years.

(2) You are setting the table for a special dinner. You are using heirloom silver, china, and crystal.

(3) You are a child holding a funeral and burying a pet of whom you have been very fond.

(4) You are unwrapping a present which you have long anticipated receiving. Its beauty even surpasses your expectation; *or*, you can't restrain your disappointment.

(5) You are a young ruler involved in a ceremony which Catherine of Russia was required to perform. Before the court she had to open the coffin of her predecessor, the Empress Elizabeth, who had been dead for six months. She had to remove the imperial crown from the dead woman's head and place it upon her own.

(6) You are hungry and penniless in a strange town (provide your own circumstances as to *why* this is so). You are in the street looking into the window of a bakery which is filled with delicious foods.

(7) You are putting together a home-made bomb (supply circumstances as to *why*). The handling of the materials is dangerous, and your relation to them will be further colored by your purpose in making the bomb.

(8) You are a professional wine taster (tea taster, coffee taster, what you will). You are deciding to which of five wines you will award the Grand Prize.

(9) You are counting a large sum of money.

(10) You are eating a meal.

(11) You are looking at an album of family photographs.

(12) You are on a long expedition in which "water discipline" is essential. You have one canteen that must be your entire water supply for another twenty-four hours. Relate to the canteen during a rest break.

EXERCISES   In almost all plays the actor is confronted with the task of relating to objects, and thus provided with a means of "setting in motion his creative apparatus." The following are situations requiring this technique. Using the given circumstances as a basis, plan and carry out a sequence of actions involving you in a specific relationship with the object.

(1) In *Arms and the Man*, by George Bernard Shaw, the romantic Raina is in love with a soldier who is reported to have performed great deeds of heroism for his country. Alone at night and thinking of "her hero," she takes up his portrait, caresses it, and returns it reverently to its place.

(2) In *Oh Dad, Poor Dad, Mama's Hung You in the Closet and I'm Feeling So Sad*, by Arthur Kopit, Jonathan is a young man dominated by his mother and kept from contact with the world. When a box of books is opened after he and his mother have moved into a new hotel, he ecstatically greets his old friends—Trollope, Daudet, Turgenev, Gautier.

(3) In *No Place to Be Somebody*, by Charles Gordone, Johnny Williams has been given a copy of Sweets Crane's will. Sweets is an old man who be-

friended Johnny when he was a boy, but with whom he no longer wants to have an association. Johnny does not read well and has difficulty figuring out that Sweets intends to leave him a good deal of property. In defiance he throws the will on the floor.

(4) In *And Miss Reardon Drinks a Little*, by Paul Zindel, Anna is a school-teacher who befriends animals. She is a strict vegetarian and refuses to have about her anything made of fur. When she receives a present of a pair of fur-lined gloves, she rejects them violently.

(5) In *The Ballad of the Sad Cafe*, a dramatization by Edward Albee of a novella by Carson McCullers, a group of men in a small Southern town come at night to the general store to buy corn liquor. They value the liquor highly because it has a special quality which brightens their drab lives as mill workers.

(6) In *Miss Julie*, by August Strindberg, the valet Jean is about to elope with the aristocratic Countess Julie. When she wants to take her pet canary, he grabs the bird and kills it with a meat cleaver. This situation provides a good exercise for two people. The sight of the dead bird fills Julie with hatred and contempt for Jean.

(7) In *Peer Gynt*, by Henrik Ibsen, Peer's mother, Ase, lying on her death bed asks Peer for her Bible and seeks comfort from it.

(8) In *My Heart's in the Highlands*, by William Saroyan, young Johnny Alexander lives a happy life with his improvident father. Often there is little to eat, and he swipes grapes from a nearby vineyard. He eats slowly and appreciatively.

(9) In *Riders to the Sea*, by John Millington Synge, Cathleen is an Irish peasant girl. Her brother Michael has been reported drowned. She is opening a bundle of clothes recovered from a body that has been washed ashore to determine whether the clothes are Michael's.

(10) In *The Rivals*, by Richard Brinsley Sheridan, Bob Acres is a young country bumpkin. Having come to town to woo the fashionable and romantic Lydia Languish, he is making every effort to improve his appearance and polish his manners. He grooms himself and practices postures and dance steps in front of a mirror. Here the object of attention is the actor himself.

(11) In *Hedda Gabler*, by Henrik Ibsen, Hedda is a selfish and destructive woman who cherishes the pistols that belonged to her father, General Gabler. She enjoys using them for target practice, firing into the garden from the window of her drawing room.

(12) In *Sticks and Bones*, by David Rabe, David has been blinded during military service in Viet Nam. When he returns home, he explores the living room by relating to the once familiar objects with his white cane.

(13) In *That Championship Season*, by Jason Miller, the Coach cherishes a huge silver trophy that was won by his basketball team some years before. It is a symbol of a glorious achievement. Improvise a situation dramatizing his relationship to the trophy.

(14) In *Mother Courage*, by Bertolt Brecht, Katrin is a young mute. Although she follows the army with her mother, she has been kept from any knowledge of men. Having observed the ways of the prostitute Yvette, she steals Yvette's plumed hat and red boots and practices walking about seductively. When an alarm sounds for an approaching enemy attack, she hides the articles of finery, contemplating further use of them.

(15) Mother Courage is a tough, practical old woman who makes a living following the army as a peddler. Her simple honest son, Swiss Cheese, has been killed in an attempt to guard the regimental cashbox. When shown his body (the cover is pulled back from a stretcher), Mother Courage refuses to recognize her son for fear action will be taken against her by the soldiers. Play the scene with the relation to the body that the circumstances require of Mother Courage. Change the circumstances and play it with a different relation.

(16) In *Day of Absence*, by Douglas Turner Ward, Mary is an incompetent mother who is wakened in the morning by the crying of her baby. The baby needs attention because the Negro servant on whom the family is completely dependent has not appeared for work. Mary is sickened in her attempt to change the baby's "didee," a task for which she is absolutely inept.

(17) In *Androcles and the Lion*, by George Bernard Shaw, Androcles is a meek little man who befriends all stray animals. Walking near the jungle, he is confronted by a lion that is limping and roaring because it has a thorn in its paw. After an initial fright, he extracts the thorn and earns the great beast's gratitude. Enlist the aid of a partner and improvise this scene, realizing Androcles' changing relationship toward the lion.

(18) In *Rosencrantz and Guildenstern Are Dead*, by Tom Stoppard, Rosencrantz and Guildenstern are betting on the flip of a coin. Each toss comes up heads—an impossibility. Rosencrantz pockets each coin as he wins it, betraying no surprise at all. He feels, however, a bit embarrassed in taking so much money from his friend.

(19) In *Butterflies Are Free*, by Leonard Gershe, Don Baker is a good-looking young man who has just moved into an apartment in Greenwich

Village. Although Don has been blind from birth, he accepts his blindness as more of an inconvenience than a handicap, and he is fiercely protective of his ability to care for himself. He tells Jill, his next-door neighbor, that part of the reason he does not bump into things around the apartment is because he has "memorized" his room. To prove it, he walks around the room with grace and confidence, calling off each item as he touches or points to it: bed, bookcase, guitar, cane, books, front door, and tape recorder.

In these exercises remember your primary task is to discover a definite relationship to the object involved and to communicate that relationship by carrying out a score of psychophysical actions. Objects—properties or "props," as they are called in stage lingo—are excellent actors when they are given a chance to be so.

Relating to Other Actors

When an actor concentrates attention on another actor by trying to influence his behavior, he can hardly fail to establish a relationship. Both consciously and unconsciously he will make logical and psychological adjustments to the other person, and such adjustments depend upon an awareness of the other's presence and personality. It is often helpful, however, to use, in conjunction with concentrating upon another actor for the purpose of accomplishing an objective, the techniques we have been working with in relating to objects—that is to "transfigure" the other *actor* into "something that is warmly felt"; the nature of the transfiguration depends, of course, upon the given circumstances.

It is frequently true, both in life and on the stage, that we attempt to evoke the same responses from two or more people toward whom we feel quite differently, or with whom we have different relationships. Returning to the opening scene of *King Lear*, we discover that, while Lear wants to influence each of his daughters to make a declaration of love, his relation to each of them is not the same. He knows that Goneril is shrewd, cold, ambitious, willing to do whatever is necessary to gain a share of the kingdom. He knows that Regan is a follower, that she wants what Goneril has and will do what Goneril does. He loves Cordelia "most" because of her straightforward honesty; from her he expects a genuine protestation. While Lear may be vain enough to enjoy a public declaration of love from each of the three, toward Goneril his attitude is reasoned—a kind of bargaining relationship: tell me you love me and I'll give you a share of my kingdom. Being able to predict Regan's response, his attitude is almost one of indifference—mingled with contempt, perhaps, because she does not act independently. Cordelia is truly an object of affection, and he reaches out to her for love and comfort in the loneliness of his old age.

The actor playing Lear establishes these relationships by (1) imagining himself as the old king in this situation, by answering the question: "What would I do in relation to Goneril, Regan, and Cordelia if I were King Lear in these circumstances?" and (2) using his real responses to the actresses playing the daughters. We have pointed out earlier that real responses between the actors are one of the principal sources of vitality in any performance.

Stimulating these responses is a technique sometimes called "playing off of another actor," and it is one that should be thoroughly explored and practiced. It means that, although you behave toward them as if the other actors were characters in the play, you see them as themselves and you make full use of your sensory and intellectual responses to them. It means that if you were King Lear you would not, all by yourself, conjure up an image of what the three daughters should be and pretend that your three partners were a realization of that image. This approach traps an actor into "playing by himself" and deprives him of the stimulation that comes from a genuine relationship. He should rather respond as fully as he can to the qualities of the three actresses with whom he is playing. Thus the same actor playing Lear with different actresses as the daughters might give performances with quite different nuances, but each performance would have equal truth and vitality.

EXERCISES   The following are for the purpose of developing real connections and responses between the actors. They do not involve imaginary circumstances. They may be done in pairs or in small groups.

(1) Play catch with a real ball. As the game progresses try to surprise your partner.

(2) Continue the game with an imaginary ball. Use sensory memory so that you can handle the ball as if it were real. Watch carefully when, how, where it is thrown and catch it accordingly.

(3) Working in pairs, or with a group divided into two teams, engage in various games or contests using imaginary athletic equipment. Develop team spirit and establish a relationship with the other players. Engage in

volleyball
badminton
pingpong
a tug of war
shadow boxing

(4) Peter Brook describes an exercise that is a variation of shadow boxing. The actors fight in pairs taking and giving back every blow, but never touching, and never moving heads, arms, nor feet. The movement is from

the torso only. Within these limitations, the fight must be carried on with full physical action and with complete commitment to winning.

(5) Engage in a conversation. If you are not well-acquainted with your partner, find out about his background, his family, his interests, his hobbies. Encourage him to talk about himself. During the conversation seek attractive features in the other actor which will promote a pleasant and favorable relationship.

(6) Engage in a conversation on a controversial subject. Seek to get an actual exchange of ideas and opinions. Stimulate the other actor to express himself.

(7) Extend these exercises in relationships into your everyday life. Along with *observing* other people, analyze your responses to them. Notice carefully how you are responding and what it is about them that produces your response. This is one way of following Coquelin's practice of "seizing and noting" anything in life that might be useful to you on the stage.

Return to any of the earlier problems based upon scenes involving two or more actors. Establish a specific and real relationship with your partner. Remember you make the relationship specific by discovering the attitude of your character to the other characters. You make it real by (1) letting yourself respond to the imaginary relationship, and (2) actually using the qualities and features (personality, appearance, voice, feelings) of the other actors as belonging to the characters they are playing.   **EXERCISE**

Relating to Images

It has been emphasized throughout that while evoking feeling is one of the actor's principal jobs, feelings can't be sought directly. They come not by squeezing and forcing, but only as a result of forgetting about them and concentrating attention on accomplishing a specific task. Learning to act consists to a great degree in learning techniques that will produce the desired emotional responses, which will enable the actor to respond *on cue* according to the requirements of the play. So far we have studied how to use physical actions, intentions, relations to objects and other characters. Another technique is relating to things in the mind, using *images*.

The image technique is familiar because we use it—both voluntarily and involuntarily—in everyday life. Alone in a strange town, we see specific pictures of home. We see the porch with its comfortable chairs, the living room with its soft lights, the table set for dinner. We hear voices in the kitchen. We smell rolls baking in the oven. Immediately we are filled with feelings of homesickness. Tired and bored at home, we see pictures of strange far-away places. We see towering hills, quaint villages. We hear the tinkle of cowbells on a Swiss mountain side. Immediately we are filled with a desire to get away. Waiting for someone who is late in arriving, we can't keep pictures of accidents out of our minds. We see the person we are waiting for struck by a passing car, lying in the hospital, perhaps the victim of street robbers. We cannot dispel the feelings of worry and fear. Planning to surprise a friend with a present, we see him unwrapping the package. We see him taking the gift out of the tissue paper, holding it up to examine it. We see his smile, and we are filled with feelings of happiness and affection.

The process by which imagination determines the actor's responses and behavior onstage is very much like the way they are determined in life. Sergei Eisenstein, the renowned Russian film maker and an advocate of the "inner technique," discusses the process in some detail. He is describing how an actor would prepare to play the part of a respected government employee on the point of committing suicide because he has lost a large amount of government money at cards.

> I believe it would be almost impossible to find an actor of any training today who in this scene would start by trying to "act the feeling" of a man on the point of suicide. . . . We should compel the appropriate consciousness and the appropriate feeling to *take possession* of us. . . .
>
> . . . How is this achieved? We have already said that it cannot be done with the "sweating and straining" method. Instead we pursue a path that should be used for all such situations.
>
> What we actually do is to compel our imagination to depict for us a number of concrete pictures or situations appropriate to our theme. The aggregation of the pictures so imagined evokes in us the required emotion, the feeling, understanding and actual experience that we are seeking. . . .
>
> Suppose that a characteristic feature of our embezzler be fear of public opinion. What will terrify him will not be so much the pangs of conscience, a consciousness of his guilt or the burden of his future imprisonment, as it will be "what will people say?"
>
> Our man finding himself in this position, will imagine first of all the terrible consequences of his act in these particular terms.
>
> It will be these imagined consequences and their combinations which will reduce the man to such a degree of despair that he will seek a desperate end.
>
> This is exactly how it takes place in life. Terror resulting from awareness of responsibility initiates his feverish pictures of the consequences. And this host of imagined pictures, reacting on the feelings, increases his terror, reducing the embezzler to the utmost limit of horror and despair.[2]

[2] Sergei Eisenstein, *The Film Sense*, ed. by Jay Leyda (New York: Harcourt Brace Jovanovich, 1942), p. 42.

As Eisenstein points out, the life process that would drive this character to suicide and the creative process that would stimulate him to the same action on the stage are very similar. In life a picture of the circumstances that led him to such foolhardiness would be constantly in his mind. At the same time, the embezzler would be driven to despair by an image of how he would be cast off by his associates when the crime was discovered.

The technique of using images, then, begins with pictures of definite circumstances supplied voluntarily by the imagination. These pictures lead in turn to action, to belief, and to feeling. Again we must recognize that feeling is the end and not the means, that the actor is concerned with *causes*, not with *effects*. He is like the interior decorator who wants to create a beautiful room. The decorator concerns himself with color and fabric, with line and form. He knows they are the means to beauty and that properly controlled they will produce a beautiful effect. He knows he would get nowhere if he tried merely to create beauty without a specific knowledge of how to use his materials.

The material that the actor uses is a series of pictures that stimulate him to action and that his imagination enables him to keep vividly before him. Resorting to a technique of advertising, we may formulate a slogan to state this important principle: *When an actor acts he sees a picture*. He keeps the images before him as if they were on a television or a motion picture screen. He sees them in color, synchronized with sound. He can locate the screen in various positions depending upon the requirements of the moment. If the scene is introspective, he may keep the screen in his mind. If he is trying to influence another character, especially if he wants the other actor to see vividly what he is talking about, he may place the screen on the actor's face. He may place it in a position in which he directs the attention of another actor to it. He may want to locate the images in the auditorium, sometimes creating a giant screen across the rear wall. This technique is well described in the following passage.

> The actor needs . . . an uninterrupted series of visual images which have some connection with the given circumstances. He needs, in short, an uninterrupted line not of plain but of illustrated given circumstances. Indeed, at every moment of his presence on the stage, . . . the actor must be aware of what is taking place outside him on the stage (i.e., the external given circumstances created by the producer, stage-designer, and the other artists) or of what is taking place inside him, in his own imagination, that is, those visual images which illustrate the given circumstances of the life of his part. Out of all these things there is formed, sometimes outside and sometimes inside him, an uninterrupted and endless series of inner and outer visual images, or a kind of film. While his work goes on, the film is unwinding itself endlessly, reflecting on the screen of his inner vision the illustrated given circumstances of his part, among which he lives on the stage.[3]

[3] Magarshack, Introduction to *Stanislavsky on the Art of the Stage*, p. 38.

EXERCISES   (1) These problems are for developing the habit of seeing definite images from word stimuli. For each of the following concrete words visualize a detailed and specific picture. See yourself in the picture; think what you would do if you were there. Let yourself respond. Remember you can't *make* yourself feel, but you can *let* yourself feel. You can make this exercise more valuable by writing down what you see; or, if you can draw, make a sketch of it. Describe your picture and your actions to the members of the group. Make them see the images as vividly as you do.

fountain	ship
tree	beach
shoe	mansion
chair	fish
sister	trumpet
wedding	courtyard
funeral	shack
palace	automobile
candy	fire
flower	vase
queen	teapot
bench	pie

(2) Repeat the same process for the following abstract words. It is important that the actor learn to realize abstract concepts in concrete images which are meaningful to him and which can stimulate responses. *Happiness* might be a picture of a child laughingly chasing his shadow. *Injustice* might be a picture of an injured woman denied admission to a hospital because of her color.

power	bliss
speed	misery
love	fame
happiness	grief
poverty	calmness
wealth	indifference
mercy	beauty
elegance	disgrace
cruelty	jealousy
kindness	glamor
injustice	bigotry

In these exercises you have been creating a "film" of visual images and describing them vividly to the group. In the process you have been obliquely using another helpful technique called the *inner monologue*. What the actor is thinking—what is in his mind—each moment he is onstage is vastly important to his performance. The inner monologue is a technique for controlling his thinking and making it serve his overall purpose. It is used when he is not speaking the playwright's words, that is, during pauses in his own speeches and during the lines of the other characters. It is one of the actor's truly creative contributions because, except in some special instances, it is not given by the dramatist. It should be carefully planned, *written out*, memorized, and *thought* at each rehearsal and performance, just as the actor memorizes and speaks the playwright's lines.

The special instances where the dramatist provides the inner monologues are soliloquies and asides in which he supplies thoughts to be spoken to the audience. Hamlet's "To be, or not to be," and Macbeth's "Tomorrow, and tomorrow, and tomorrow" are examples of superb inner monologues. Eugene O'Neill experimented with the inner monologue in *Strange Interlude* in which he wrote "thoughts" for the actors to speak between the lines of regular dialogue.

In telling the group the images you had in your mind in the above exercises, you were, in a sense, speaking an inner monologue. You were making the inner monologue an *outer* monologue and thus receiving an initiation into this useful technique. The next series of exercises will allow you to make further application of it.

EXERCISE

Perform an action that you do not want anyone to know about, for example: opening someone's mail, searching someone's desk, breaking your diet, drinking secretly. Your inner monologue, which for purposes of practice you will speak as you are carrying out the action, should make use of images and should be an attempt to justify to yourself what you are doing. Be sure you have an intention, an obstacle, and a dramatic structure.

EXERCISES

Plays abound in opportunities to use images. The situation need not by any means be so desperate as one in which the embezzler is driven to suicide. Eisenstein mentioned that he was pointing a path that should be followed in all situations. Work on several of the problems described below. The pictures should be definite and detailed, not vague and general. They should be from life experience, not from the theatre (that is, don't use an image of another actor in a similar circumstance). *Write* them out, memorize them; and, along with appropriate psychophysical actions, make them part of an improvisation in which you accept as one of the circumstances that the character speaks his thoughts. A reading of the play from which the situation is taken will stimulate your imagination. But don't memorize the playwright's lines. Use your own words, and commit yourself to sharing your images with the group.

(1) In *Ethan Frome*, by Owen and Donald Davis, Zenia enjoys being ill. She is constantly complaining of her ailments and nagging her husband to provide medicines that will make her comfortable in what she insists is her "last illness." She pictures herself as desperately sick. She even sees herself dead. From such images she gains a good deal of pleasure. She especially likes to make Ethan feel guilty for not treating her as well as she thinks he should.

(2) In *Richard II* (Act V, Scene 5), by William Shakespeare, the deposed king, alone in the dungeon, talks to himself. He pictures his past glories and also his past follies, and attempts to rationalize his present situation.

(3) In *She Stoops to Conquer*, by Oliver Goldsmith, Mrs. Hardcastle is the victim of a deception planned by her mischievous son, Tony Lumpkin. At night on a country road she believes she is being confronted by highwaymen. Her imagination calls forth pictures of all manner of dreadful things that might happen to her.

(4) In *Raisin in the Sun*, by Lorraine Hansberry, Ruth, a young Negro wife, is preparing with her husband's family to move from crowded quarters into a large house in a white neighborhood. She anticipates the greater comfort their new home will provide as she packs bric-a-brac, accumulated over the years, into a carton. The objects provoke images from the past, and her anticipation evokes images of the future.

(5) In *The Three Sisters*, by Anton Chekhov, Masha is desperately unhappy because her soldier lover is being transferred to another post. She sees a bird flying overhead that symbolizes to her a life free of sadness and frustration. She pictures the freedom of a bird in flight in contrast to her life in which she is committed to living with a dull husband in a small provincial town.

(6) In *The Ballad of the Sad Cafe*, a dramatization by Edward Albee of Carson McCullers' novella, Cousin Lymon yearns for a close human relationship such as he imagines is shared by men on a chain gang working and singing together. He conjures in his mind glamorous images of the "togetherness" of life in the penitentiary.

(7) In *Mooney's Kid Don't Cry*, by Tennessee Williams, Mooney is trapped in a small city apartment with a baby and a nagging wife. He dreams of escaping to the life of freedom and fresh air he used to have when he was a lumberman in the Northern woods.

(8) In *The Doctor in Spite of Himself*, a farce by Molière, Martine has been soundly beaten by her drunken husband. She says, "These cudgel blows set

heavy on my stomach," and pictures to herself how she is going to get revenge for the beating she has received.

(9) In *The Taming of the Shrew* (Act IV, Scene 1), Petruchio in a speech beginning, "Thus have I politicly begun my reign," tells how he is going to continue taming Katharine. The images of the discomfort he expects to cause her give him considerable pleasure.

(10) In *Blood Wedding*, by Garcia Lorca, the Mother has lost her husband and her son in a long-standing feud with the men of the Felix family. Her mind is filled with pictures of past violence and bloodshed, and with hatred of her enemies.

(11) In *Desire Under the Elms*, by Eugene O'Neill, the brothers Peter and Simon are planning to run away from the hard life on a New England farm and seek easy wealth in the California gold rush. They picture acres of nuggets and streets paved with gold. This exercise could serve for either one or two actors.

(12) In *The Gentleman Caller*, by Ed Bullins, the Maid has been a model of servitude for many years. She pictures the time black people will come together and overcome the forces that have oppressed them.

(13) In *The Basic Training of Pavlo Hummel*, by David Rabe, Pavlo is a wide-eyed, totally inept soldier, born and raised in a middle-class environment. He wants to be thought of as a tough street kid. He conjures up romantic pictures of stealing automobiles and being chased by the police.

(14) In *The House of Blue Leaves*, by John Guare, Bunny is an ever-hopeful, failure-plagued dreamer. She tells her friend Artie a dream she had about a Buick nicknamed the Green Latrine, in which she attempts to give rides to Jackie Kennedy, Bob Hope, President Johnson, and Cardinal Spellman. They refuse her offer of a ride. A melee breaks out, the Green Latrine blows four tires, and the people rush to separate cabs. Later, on "The Johnny Carson Show," Cardinal Spellman and Bob Hope tell the story, and Bunny, in her dreams, once again feels the object of the world's ridicule.

(15) In *Ashes*, by David Rudkin, Colin and Anne are an Ulster couple living in England, whose single-minded desire is to produce a child. When Colin returns from the funeral of a relative killed in a Belfast bombing, his discussion of violence sums up an entire society reaping a whirlwind of ashes.

(16) In *The Zoo Story*, by Edward Albee, Jerry is an "outsider" in life, a man unable to fit into contemporary society. When he meets Peter, the epitome of the society he both abhors and desires, he tries to lure Peter into conversation. Peter is fascinated and a bit frightened of Jerry but listens while Jerry re-

lates the story of a dog who inhabits Jerry's apartment house. Jerry has tried to befriend the dog and, failing, has resolved to kill him. The dog emerges as an image of all Jerry's frustrated attempts at communication with other people.

Relating to Past Experiences

In working to develop the technique of using images, your pictures have certainly come partly out of your imagination, partly out of your past experience. In Chapter 1 we discovered that an actor's inner resources consist of his memory of what he has done, and seen, and read, and felt. How he uses these resources—how he puts his past experience to work—is a matter of considerable importance to him.

Fortunately, most of the time the actor does not need to concern himself with this matter. Onstage, as in life, most of the time our memory serves us without our making any conscious effort. Facts, figures, and faces, stories, images we have known in the past—even sensory and emotional experiences—come back automatically as we need them. If the actor is concentrating on performing actions, logical within the given circumstances, for the purpose of accomplishing an intention, and if he is establishing specific relationships, it is likely that his past experience will be serving him without his giving any thought to it. The actions and the relations, coming directly from the imaginary circumstances of the play and from connection with the other actors, will tap his resources and evoke the proper feeling. If, on occasion, the techniques of physical action, intentions, and relationships do not bring the desired responses, the actor may make conscious use of his past experience. Although actors to some degree have always made conscious use of their experiences (theatre history provides many such instances), as a specific technique, this practice was first explored by Stanislavski. He called it *emotion memory*, or sometimes *affective memory*. These terms, however, are not altogether suitable because he ultimately came to realize that we can bring back emotions only indirectly. We must recall the sensory experiences of the situation and, most of all, we must remember *what we did*. So *physical action memory* is a more appropriate designation. It is a technique involving five steps:

1. the original experience
2. retaining the experience
3. selecting an experience that will be useful in solving the problem
4. recalling the sensory and physical details
5. using the experience within the given circumstances.

Jessica Tandy as Olga, Hume Cronyn as Dr. Tchebutykin, Michael Levin as the Orderly, and Ellen Geer as Irina in Chekhov's *The Three Sisters*. **A production of the Minnesota Theatre Company, directed by Tyrone Guthrie and designed by Tanya Moiseiwitsch. Study the picture for character relationships.**

Most of the time the actor will go through these steps without thinking about them. An examination of them will help him when he needs to make conscious use of the process.

The Original Experience The original experience may have occurred months, even years, before it is recalled and put to practical use. It is better, in fact, to use events that occurred some time ago because you will be able to use them more objectively. Childhood incidents, because they frequently remain in the mind with peculiar vividness, are likely to be especially valuable. It must be an experience that you have felt deeply.

Retaining the Experience Retaining the experience is partly a matter of natural memory, partly a matter of conscious effort. Anyone who is genuinely aware of what is going on around him is likely to remember what has happened in the past. Any technique, however, which will aid the actor in retaining the details of an experience vividly in mind is worth developing.

The story is told of the great French actor François Joseph Talma (1763–1826), a favorite of Napoleon and later of Louis XVIII, that on hearing the news of his father's death, he was shocked to the point of uttering a piercing cry. He immediately noted the nature of his grief while commenting that the memory of it might be of use to him on the stage. Such behavior might seem cold-blooded; but there is no reason to doubt that Talma's sorrow was sincere. The story illustrates the working method of a great artist in accumulating "inner resources."

Selecting the Experience   In deciding what experiences to recall, the actor searches his past for happenings which most nearly parallel those of the character he is playing. They may be identical. They may be far removed. John Barrymore describes recall of past experience in playing the title role in *Peter Ibbetson*, a dramatization of George duMaurier's novel:

> . . . An actor's performance, at best, is the way he happens to feel about a certain character. . . .
>
> I'm a bit of Peter Ibbetson and a bit of Jack Barrymore. At least, I never utterly forget Jack Barrymore—or things he's thought or done—or had done to him. . . .
>
> I leave my dressing room to make Peter's first entrance. I am Jack Barrymore—Jack Barrymore smoking a cigarette. But before I make the entrance I have thrown away the cigarette and become more Ibbetson than Barrymore. By the time I am visible to the audience I am Ibbetson, quite.
>
> That is, you see—I hope to make this clear—on my way to the entrance I have passed imaginary flunkies and given up my hat and coat. Peter would have had a hat and coat—naturally; and would have given them up. And he's a timid fellow. He gives up his imaginary hat and coat to these flunkies just as I, Jack Barrymore—and very timid then—once gave up my hat and coat to flunkies at a great ball given by Mrs. Astor.
>
> Of course I don't always make Peter's entrance with the memory of a bashful boy at Mrs. Astor's ball. That would harden the memory—make it useless. You couldn't keep on conjuring up the same thing. You have to have different things to get the same emotion. . . .[4]

Barrymore's description is an example of recalling an experience close to the circumstance of the play. The entrance he mentions is Peter Ibbetson's entrance to a great ball given in honor of the Duchess of Towers. And Peter is a very timid fellow, painfully embarrassed in the presence of duchesses and liveried footmen. More often than not the actor can't find in his past so close an approximation to the experience of the character. Obviously, he can't have

[4] Ashton Stevens, *Actorviews* (Chicago: Covici-McGee Co., 1923), pp. 64, 66–67. Quoted in *Actors on Acting*, ed. by Toby Cole and Helen Krich Chinoy (New York: Crown Publishers, 1949), p. 516.

had experiences which parallel those of every character he might be called upon to play. He must often resort to situations in which his feelings were similar to those of the character, although the circumstances which prompted the feelings may have been entirely different.

In playing Macbeth, for instance, an actor must be able to feel Macbeth's vaulting ambition to be king and his willingness to commit any crime in order to realize his desires. But the actor certainly will not find in his past any experience which parallels Macbeth's evil course of action. A young actor's most vivid memory of ambition may be a desire to play the leading part in a production in which he has been cast as an extra. His most guilty thought may be a vague wish that the leading man would suffer some calamity which would remove him from the coveted role. Even so, this experience—the momentary wish to realize an ambition at the expense of someone else—may enable him to feel the terrible desire that drove Macbeth along his path of blood and crime.

Using experiences different from the given circumstances is called *substitution*. In the suicide in *Redemption*, Jacob Ben-Ami said he substituted the recall of the shock of taking a cold shower for the impact of the bullet. His acting of this scene is a memory still cherished by many playgoers. You might play some of Alma's scenes in *Summer and Smoke* using the recall of a painful sunburn which would cause tension and withdrawal when anyone started to touch you.

Another situation for which the actor is not likely to find a parallel is the Potion Scene (Act IV, Scene 3) from *Romeo and Juliet*. Secretly married to Romeo, Juliet has been promised by her parents to the Count of Paris. To get herself out of this entanglement, she is about to take a potion which will make her appear dead. She will then be placed in the family tomb, and Romeo will rescue her. Juliet's emotion is fear mounting almost to hysteria. She is about to take an action the outcome of which is uncertain and fraught with dreadful possibilities. She is distracted by imagining all the things that might happen to cause her plan to fail. What if the potion doesn't work at all? What if it is a poison? What if she should wake before Romeo comes and find herself alone in the tomb with the remains of all her buried ancestors?

What experience have you had which might enable you to realize Juliet's fear? Have you been in a situation, no matter how dissimilar in its actual circumstances, which induced a feeling akin to Juliet's? Have you been alone preparing to take some step the consequences of which were uncertain holding possibilities of danger, unhappiness, pain, discomfort? Have you ever prepared to run away from home? Have you ever contemplated an elopement? Have you ever prepared to go to the hospital for an operation? to go into the army? to go away to college or to move to a new town where you might experience homesickness and have to face problems which you might not be able to solve?

In searching for an experience which would help you in the Potion Scene, you need to find some incident in which you had to control yourself in face of fears that were largely imaginary. Perhaps the incident you can recall most vividly is the common one of childhood fright. It may have happened something like this:

When you were ten years old, you spent a weekend with an aunt who lived alone in a large house with no neighbors nearby. On the first evening, before you had become acquainted with your surroundings, your aunt was called to care for a sick friend. You boasted that you were used to staying alone, and since it was impractical to get a "sitter" on short notice, your aunt reluctantly left you to look after yourself for a couple of hours. You settled down in the living room feeling quite grown up and independent, and looked happily at a picture book. Gradually you became uneasy. At home there was always activity and noise. This place was terribly still. At home there were always lights all through the house and everything was bright and cheerful. Here there was a lamp with a green shade in the living room, a lamp with a red globe in the hallway. Both of them together did not drive away the shadows in the large rooms.

Suddenly you were overcome with fear. A noise on the porch started you thinking of thieves and kidnappers. You had no sooner quieted those fears than a noise upstairs started you thinking of ghosts and haunted houses. It seemed impossible to stay on in the house alone. But the outdoors was just as terrifying, and to reach the telephone you had to go down the hall and into the dining room which was completely dark.

If such an incident is your liveliest experience with fear, it will have to serve. If you can recall it vividly, it will serve you well.

Recalling the Details   Don't attempt directly to recall your feelings. Concentrate on remembering the details of the experience rather than on the emotion itself. Begin by making use of sensory recall. Attempt to remember as much as you can about the room—the lights with their bright spots, and, more particularly, the dark corners; the reflection of the light on the dark polished surfaces of the furniture; the windows, shiny black in the darkness, reflecting the quiet gloom. Remember the chair you sat on, the objects on the table beside the chair, and the pictures you looked at. Recall the odors of the room —lilacs and furniture polish. Recall the stillness and the sounds you heard (or thought you heard).

If you are unfamiliar with this technique, you will be surprised (after you give it an honest trial) how many details you will be able to bring back, and how much the memory of the way things felt and looked and smelled will help you to recapture the essence of the entire experience. For, as we have recognized earlier in the chapter, sensory recall plays an important part in aiding the actor to remember the quality of incidents that have happened in the past.

When you have brought the whole experience back into your consciousness, turn your attention to what you *did* in this situation. How did you deal with the cause of your fear—the frightening shadows, the sounds on the porch, the noise upstairs? Let's suppose you first pretended that you were not afraid and attempted to renew your interest in the pictures. Then you braved your way into one of the dark corners for another book. You tried to reassure yourself by singing as loudly as possible. You went timidly to the window to investigate the sounds on the porch, but could not bring yourself to take a good look.

Throughout the process of recall sit quietly relaxed, free of any tensions that might interfere with the flow of memory and feeling. This is, in a sense, an application to acting of Wordsworth's famous definition of poetry: "Emotion recollected in tranquility."

Using the Experience in the Given Circumstances of the Play Once the memory has evoked the response, it is necessary that you use it to fulfill the needs of the scene. You will take yourself out of the play and away from your intention (some actors are guilty) unless you use the feelings you have induced to help you play the actions and speak the lines of the character. You must be sure that what you have recalled fits the circumstances of the play. You must guard against reducing moments conceived by the imagination of a master dramatist to your own personal experiences that may be smaller in scope and quite prosaic. You should carry on this process during your work on the role at home, or during your preparation before rehearsal and performance. Your job is to have your responses ready when you need them in a scene.

Return to any of the earlier exercises. Make your playing of them more effective by using the technique of recalling past experience.   **EXERCISE**

PART 2
THE ACTOR
AND
THE PLAY

Getting into the Part

8

Throughout the preceding chapters, we have been discovering how the actor can use his intelligence, his life experience, his senses onstage. There have been frequent references to "circumstances given by the dramatist" which guide the actor in using his resources. All the exercises derived from plays have required behavior logical and appropriate to these circumstances. But we have not considered how the actor uses the *total* circumstances of the play, how he develops his part as a whole.

A character living onstage is a union of the creative talents of the actor and the dramatist. Any argument over which of the two is more important is futile because they are completely interdependent. The actor requires the character created by the dramatist to provide the initial and vital stimulus. The dramatist requires the embodiment of the character by the actor to bring his creation to fulfillment. The result of this collaboration is the finished performance to which both the actor and the dramatist have made a unique contribution. The result can be neither Shakespeare's Macbeth nor the actor's Macbeth. It must be the actor *as* Shakespeare's Macbeth. An audience can never see a character as the dramatist conceived him. They always see whatever significance a particular actor has been able to find. And the person who prefers reading his plays to seeing them is merely substituting his own interpretative abilities for those of the actor.

The actor's contribution consists of an "inner characterization" and its "outer form." To create the outer form—the way the character looks, moves, gestures, speaks—the actor draws "from his own experience of life or that of his friends, from pictures, engravings, drawings, books, stories, novels, or from some simple incident—it makes no difference." [1] But he chooses these externals to fit

---

[1] Stanislavski, *Building a Character*, p. 7.

Laurence Olivier as Henry V.
(Photo—Culver Pictures, Inc.)

Laurence Olivier as James Tyrone in *Long Day's Journey into Night*. (Photo—Michael Childers.) Part of Olivier's greatness is his versatility. He seems to be comfortable playing roles from all of the dramatic literature.

Laurence Olivier as Hamlet. (Photo
—The Bettmann Archive, Inc.)

Laurence Olivier as George Hurstwood in
the film *Sister Carrie* based on the novel by
Theodore Dreiser. (Photo—The Bettmann
Archive, Inc.)

the inner characterization. He chooses them to give an outer form to the character prescribed by the dramatist as his experience enables him to understand the character.

To a very considerable degree the actor must always "play himself." He can create another person only by drawing upon his own experiences, actual or vicarious. No matter how he may alter his outward appearance, no matter how he may change the sound of his voice (and this outer form is necessary to complete characterization), his ability to communicate the essential truth of his role—which is, after all, the core of any performance—is dependent on what he is able to bring to it from his inner resources. Even though study and observation in the preparation of a specific part may greatly enlarge these resources, they remain essentially the same as the actor attempts one character after another. The way to get to any character is through yourself.

So the final performance is "the actor in the part." It is a unique creation because no one else can duplicate it. No two actors have the same inner resources. No two actors can find identical significance in the same part because they have not had a lifetime of identical experience. The actor's confrontation with the role produces, through his own imagination and experience, a unique concept of the character. It is for this reason that two actors may differ considerably in the same role. The character created has the same father (the dramatist), but a different mother (the actor). David Magarshack extends this analogy in this way:

> Every artistic stage character is a unique individual creation, like everything else in nature. In the process of its creation there is a "he," that is "the husband," namely the author of the play, and a "she," that is "the wife," namely the actor or actress. . . . There is "the child"—the created part. There are in this process, besides, the moments of the first acquaintance between "him" and "her," their first friendship, their falling in love, their quarrels and differences, their reconciliations, and their union. . . . During these periods the producer, Stanislavsky points out, helps the process of the birth of the man-part by playing the role of matchmaker.[2]

In this process the actor becomes a creative artist in his own right without either minimizing or falsifying the creation of the dramatist. John Gielgud's Hamlet is different from Laurence Olivier's because each actor finds meaning in Shakespeare's Hamlet in light of his own experience. In so doing, each is true to Shakespeare and to himself.

The discussion and exercises so far have been designed primarily to help the actor be "true" to himself. It is now time to consider how he can be true to the dramatist.

---

[2] Magarshack, Introduction to *Stanislavsky on the Art of the Stage*, p. 77.

Discovering the Dramatist's Concept of the Character: The Motivating Force

The description of "the actor in the part," stressing the originality and uniqueness of the actor's creation, in no way supports a notion that the actor has little responsibility to the dramatist. On the contrary, one of his most important tasks is to discover what the dramatist intended the character to be. Jerzy Grotowski says that the actor must allow a role to "penetrate" him. By definition penetrate means to "enter by overcoming resistance," and the actor must make the greatest effort to remove any blocks that prevent him from yielding freely to the physical and psychological demands of the part. To accomplish this task the actor uses every means at his disposal. He familiarizes himself with whatever critical commentary may be available, and for the standard classics he is likely to find a considerable amount. He discusses the problem with his director and with others whose insight and judgment inspire his confidence. Most important of all, he *studies the play* to find every suggestion that can help him to understand any aspect of the character.

In beginning his study, the actor should keep in mind two basic questions for which he must find answers:

1. What primarily does the character want?
2. What is he willing to do to get it?

A certain character, for instance, may want more than anything else to be rich and may be willing to employ any means to satisfy his desire. He may be willing to forego all ordinary pleasures. He may sacrifice his health and the happiness of his family. He may break any law—legal or moral—that he finds to be an obstacle. Another character may want to be rich, but he may not be willing to employ such means. He may not want to gamble with the happiness and security of his family, nor take advantage of friends and associates. A certain character may want to find love, and she may be willing to sacrifice her pride and virtue to gain what she wants. Another with the same basic desire may be too proud to make any compromise. Still another may be too shy to let her desire be known.

In the answer to *what a person wants* and *what he is willing to do to get it* lies the key to his character. Here is to be found the *motivating force* behind what a character does and says. And that is what the actor is most eager to discover as he studies the play! Failure to understand the desire that motivates the behavior of the character means failure to understand the dramatist's intention. This, in turn, means failure to interpret the play truthfully.

The process is one of analysis and synthesis—a process of taking apart and putting together. The actor analyzes—takes apart—the character, studying his behavior in relation to the other characters and to the play as a whole. Then, guided by his sensitivity and imagination, he puts the parts together, organizing them to form an artistic creation.

Naming the Motivating Force

Once the actor has been able to form an idea of "what a character wants," he continues analyzing until he understands the character's desire definitely. Then he must state the motivating desire in specific terms. Finding a name for the motivating force is an important step in creating a character. The name must designate a desire which is true of the author's intention. It must also *stimulate the actor to action*. A motivating force that does not motivate action is worthless.

Stanislavski emphasized the importance of choosing the right name in discussing Argan, the principal character in Molière's *The Imaginary Invalid*. Argan, as the title suggests, is a hypochondriac—a person who suffers from imaginary ailments. Stanislavski wrote,

> Our first approach was elementary and we chose the theme "I wish to be sick." But the more effort I put into it and the more successful I was, the more evident it became that we were turning a jolly, satisfying comedy into a pathological tragedy. We soon saw the error of our ways and changed to: "I wish to be thought sick." Then the whole comic side came to the fore and the ground was prepared to show up the way in which the charlatans of the medical world exploited the stupid Argan, which was what Molière meant to do.[3]

In so naming Argan's motivating force, Stanislavski was true to Molière's intention. He has also stated a specific desire that could stimulate him to action in playing the role. Argan wanted people to think he was sick because the attention he thus received from his family and his physicians gratified his enormous vanity. To satisfy this desire he was willing to become the victim of a horde of unscrupulous doctors. He even proposed to sacrifice his daughter's happiness by marrying her to a simpering physician so there would be a medical man in his own household to attend him constantly.

About the hero in Goldoni's *The Mistress of the Inn*, Stanislavski wrote,

> . . . we made the mistake of using "I wish to be a misogynist," and we found that the play refused to yield either to humour or action. It was only when I discovered that the hero really loved women and wished only to be accounted a misogynist that I changed to "I wish to do my courting on the sly" and immediately the play came to life.[4]

---

[3] Constantin Stanislavski, *An Actor Prepares* (New York: Theatre Arts Books, 1936), pp. 257–258.

[4] Stanislavski, *An Actor Prepares*, p. 258.

Besides not being in accord with the dramatist's conception, "I wish to be a misogynist" is not adequately specific. Misogyny means hatred of women. But wanting to hate women is a general attitude that fails to suggest action. Such statements as "I want to avoid women" or "I want to take advantage of every opportunity to embarrass women" have the virtue of suggesting definite action. For this character, however, they are unacceptable because he didn't hate women at all. And what splendid possibilities for action are suggested by "I want to do my courting on the sly."

A good name for the motivating force must be the statement of *a specific desire which the character can attempt to satisfy through action.* Examples of unsatisfactory statements that cannot motivate specific action are:

I want to be unhappy.
I want to hate my neighbor.
I want to be popular.

Examples of better statements are:

I want to find comfort for my unhappiness at my husband's death by giving
    all my affection to our child.
I want to ruin my neighbor's reputation in the community.
I want people to think I am generous and witty.

The rules for naming the motivating force for the character's behavior throughout the play are the same as those in Chapter 3 for stating the intention for a smaller sequence of actions. Begin the statement with "I want to" or "I wish to," and follow with an *active* verb expressing the basic desire of the character. Don't follow with the verb *to be* or a verb expressing feeling because *being* and *feeling* are conditions, not actions, and consequently are not actable.

Another cardinal rule is that the statement must involve the actor with other characters. As we recognized earlier, a play is a conflict. Your motivating desire must demand something of the other characters and bring you in conflict with them. It is through conflict in motivating desires that plot unfolds and character is revealed.

Last, the character's motivating force must be personal to the actor. It must arouse in him a real desire to accomplish his aims. To *think* is not enough. The actor must truly *want.* Michael Chekhov says the actor must be "possessed" of his objective.[5]

Analyzing the Role

In analyzing a role to discover the motivating desires of a character as the dramatist has conceived him, the actor gives attention to
    what the character does,

[5] Michael Chekhov, *To the Actor* (New York: Harper & Row, 1953), p. 69.

A Goodman Theatre Center production of Shakespeare's *Henry IV*, Parts I and II, staged by William Woodman with costumes by Virgil Johnson. (Photo— David H. Fishman.) Study the faces as an example of actors thinking onstage.

what the character says,

what the other characters in the play say about him (always taking into consideration the speaker's purpose in saying it),

what actions are suggested in the character's lines,

what comments and descriptions the playwright offers in the stage directions.

By way of illustration let us analyze the roles of Lomov and Natalya in Anton Chekhov's one-act play *The Proposal*.

The plot of this short farce is simple. Lomov, a landowner, comes to visit his neighbor Chubukov for the purpose of proposing marriage to Natalya, Chubukov's daughter. Before he can acquaint the lady of his intentions, the two "lovers" get into a violent quarrel over the ownership of a practically worthless piece of property. After the would-be suitor has fled the house, Natalya discovers the purpose of his visit. In desperation she sends her father to bring him back. Immediately they engage in another pointless quarrel over the relative virtues of their hunting dogs. Lomov faints from indignation and excitement. He is revived and quickly betrothed. The quarrel continues more loudly than ever as the prospective father-in-law calls for champagne with which to toast the "happy couple"!

A study of the role of Lomov reveals a highly interesting character.

What he does:

He comes to his neighbor's house in great excitement.
He frets and worries about his health.
He talks constantly and volubly.
He becomes embarrassed and formal when he attempts to make the proposal.
He quarrels violently about trivial matters.
He abuses his neighbor by calling him names.
He faints from excitement and anger.
He resumes the quarrel with Natalya within a few seconds after he is betrothed to her.

He says that:

He is nervous and excitable.
He is thirty-five years old.
He does not love Natalya, but he needs a wife to look after him.
He is having chills.
He is having palpitations.
He is fainting.
His arm is coming off.
He is dying.

The other characters say that:

He is dressed in formal clothes with white gloves.
He is a "fool" and a "pup" and he is afraid of his housekeeper. (We must take into consideration that these things are said in the midst of the quarrel.)
He is dead when he faints into the chair.

The dialogue suggests these physical actions:

He drinks water to quiet his nerves.
He restores the circulation in his foot when it goes to sleep.
He twitches his eyebrows.
He staggers and faints into a chair.
He kisses Natalya when they are betrothed.

The comments supplied by the dramatist are:

"Ivan Vasilevitch Lomov, a neighbor of Chubukov, a large and hearty, but very suspicious landowner."
"Lomov enters, wearing a dress-jacket and white gloves."

After such an analysis the actor can proceed to "name" the *motivating desire*. In this farce where the characters do not present psychological complexities the problem is relatively simple. Even so, the actor must take pains to state the desire specifically and in terms that will stimulate him to action.

Since Lomov declares he has come to propose to his neighbor's daughter, we might suppose his motivating desire to be "I want to court Natalya." We soon see how wrong such a statement would be. Before he has exchanged half a dozen words with Natalya, they are quarreling about the land. And courtship seems to be the last thing in his mind. Since he frets about his health and delicate nerves, we might suppose that his motivating desire could be "I want to protect my nervous system from all disturbing influences." But again, even though he does worry about upsetting his nerves, he is more concerned with winning the argument.

Here, in fact, is what motivates his actions. He is willing to sacrifice both his need for a wife and his need to protect his nerves to the winning of a quarrel over a triviality. The strongest factor influencing his behavior is his egotism. We may state Lomov's motivating desire as "I want to trample down anything that challenges my ego."

An analysis of Natalya reveals that she is twenty-five years old, an efficient person who manages the workers on her father's farm. She enters wearing an apron and house dress because she has been "shelling peas for drying." That she would like to have a husband is shown in her desperation when she learns that the quarrel has kept Lomov from proposing. But she, too, is a headstrong egotist. She, too, is less concerned with romance than with standing up for her rights and in defending her dog when someone chances to belittle him. In spite of different character traits, Natalya and Lomov are motivated by the same desire. They both want to maintain their egos. Neither will give in one bit to the other. Therein lies the conflict (and the humor) of the play.

By now it must be apparent that discovering the motivating force is the key to getting into the part. Important as it is, actors frequently fail to understand the basic motivation clearly, to name it accurately, and to feel it fully. This failure stems from two causes: (1) many actors don't study the play with enough care and imagination; (2) the motivating force—especially for a long and complex role—is often difficult to find. For some characters it may be an ideal to be sought, rather than accomplished. But the search must not be abandoned because there is much value in the effort. These further suggestions may be helpful:

Often the motivating desire is discovered only after long study. Don't give up if you don't know it when you begin rehearsal. Keep searching as you continue to work on the role.

During the search be content with playing smaller objectives, realizing the character's intentions from scene to scene without knowing surely how they relate to the motivating desire.

Always consider a statement of the motivating desire as hypothetical. You should always be exploring and testing it, willing to change it as your understanding of the character and the play increases.

At an early stage in the analytical process the actor should determine the relative importance of the character in regard to the other characters and to the communication of the playwright's meaning. Coquelin said that one of his first concerns was discovering on what plane his character should be placed, that is whether he was in the foreground of the play, the background, or the middle ground. The meaning is obscured when a relatively minor character is played so that he receives more than his proper share of attention. Too much characterization is often opposed to the play's needs. A good actor is not guilty of such overemphasis.

It is also necessary to see the character objectively and not be concerned only with identifying yourself with the role. Some actors tend to lose objectivity and "whitewash" their characters. They make them more sympathetic than the playwright intended. Foolish characters must appear foolish, greedy characters greedy, and evil characters evil. The actor may search for reasons that make the character the way he is if he feels such a need to justify his behavior, but he should not remove a quality that is essential to the playwright's meaning.

Select a role from a standard one-act or full-length play. Make a detailed analysis of the character. State the motivating desire in terms which are true to the dramatist's conception and which could stimulate you to action in playing the part. Among the many plays which contain interesting characters for study and analysis are the following:

Edward Albee: *Who's Afraid of Virginia Woolf?*
James Baldwin: *Blues for Mister Charlie*

EXERCISE

Robert Bolt: *A Man for All Seasons*
Georg Büchner: *Woyzeck*
D. L. Coburn: *The Gin Game*
Michael Cristofer: *The Shadow Box*
Ossie Davis: *Purlie Victorious*
Lonne Elder III: *Ceremonies in Dark Old Men*
Jules Feiffer: *Knock Knock*
Frank Gilroy: *The Subject Was Roses*
Charles Gordone: *No Place to Be Somebody*
Trevor Griffiths: *Comedians*
Lillian Hellman: *Another Part of the Forest*
Henrik Ibsen: *The Wild Duck*
Albert Innaurato: *Gemini*
Hugh Leonard: *Da*
Arthur Miller: *All My Sons*
Jason Miller: *That Championship Season*
Sean O'Casey: *Juno and the Paycock*
Clifford Odets: *Golden Boy*
Eugene O'Neill: *A Touch of the Poet*
John Osborne: *Look Back in Anger*
Luigi Pirandello: *Enrico IV*
David Rabe: *Streamers*
Ron Ribman: *Cold Storage*
Peter Shaffer: *Equus*
Ntozake Shange: *For Colored Girls Who Have Contemplated
    Suicide When the Rainbow Is Enuf*
George Bernard Shaw: *Major Barbara*
Neil Simon: *The Odd Couple*
Bernard Slade: *Same Time, Next Year*
David Storey: *Home*
August Strindberg: *Miss Julie* and *The Father*
John Millington Synge: *The Playboy of the Western World*
Thornton Wilder: *The Skin of Our Teeth*
Tennessee Williams: *A Streetcar Named Desire*

Getting into Character

9

We have reached a crucial point in the techniques of creative acting. It is a point which some actors never go beyond. Earlier chapters have been concerned with how the actor uses his inner resources for performing physical actions, and for playing intentions and relationships within circumstances given by the dramatist. In the previous chapter we considered how he discovers the dramatist's concept of the character, and how he states the concept as a basic motivating desire. We have now reached the point at which we must apply these techniques to the creation of a complete character. In other words, we are faced with the problem of characterization.

In giving attention to characterization we are by no means in a situation in which something new is being added. We have been anticipating this important element from the beginning. In all previous exercises each time you answered the question, "What would I do *if I were* the person prescribed by the dramatist in these given circumstances" you have been involved with characterization. It is not basically a matter of externals. Although wigs, beards, mannerisms, dialects and accents, special props may all be used with telling effect upon both actor and audience, a character is created through the playing of intentions and relationships. Change the answer to the above question, change what you would do in a given situation and you have changed the character. Onstage as in life, character consists in what a person does and what he avoids doing.

Doing a Little at a Time

The most common error in characterization is the attempt to create the whole character at once, to grasp it with all its complexities at the very beginning. The actor is often like a starving man who attempts to cram whole handfuls of food into his mouth, instead of taking bite-sized morsels which he can readily chew and swallow.

Equipped with a technique for playing intentions and relations and informed of the motivating desire, the actor will find his best approach is to choose out of the entire play the scene, or the sequence of physical actions, which he can most readily believe. It may or may not be the first scene in which the character appears. It may or may not be an important scene. But to serve its purpose it must be one which the actor can believe is true to the dramatist's concept and to his own experience, one to which he responds, in which he can become "possessed" of the objective. To help the actor approach the problem in this way, some directors rehearse in "unchronological order." That is, they begin, not necessarily with the first scene, but wherever the actors can most easily believe the behavior of the characters.

Having chosen one small segment, the actor must learn to perform the actions believably and to relate them to the character's motivating desire. Let's suppose you are preparing to play Lomov in *The Proposal*. The scene chosen is Lomov's attempt to ask Natalya to marry him—an ill-fated attempt, to be sure, because it brings about the quarrel over the land. But at the moment Lomov is concerned only with making a favorable impression. Here is a scene for which an actor can recall a corresponding, if not identical situation from his own experience. If he has not actually proposed, he has imagined himself doing it. Or certainly he has attempted to present himself in a favorable light as a preliminary to making some request.

The embarrassment attending this kind of situation is readily comprehensible. There is always the possibility that the request will not be granted. And since a proposal may not be made in a casual manner lest the lady suspect some lack of seriousness, there is no alternative to risking a blow to one's ego. We must remember that the wish to assert his ego is Lomov's motivating desire. He would, therefore, be particularly cautious in exposing himself to embarrassment. And he would be particularly self-important in his effort to make a favorable impression.

From the lines we learn that Lomov's method of impressing Natalya is dwelling upon the long friendship between their families. We learn also that his nervousness leaves him shivering with a chill. These are two details supplied by Chekhov to help the actor solve his problem.

Seeing a Part as Units of Action

Finding, one by one, the numerous intentions which taken together constitute the part is one of the most important steps in preparing a role. The actor must discover that his part is made up of small intentions each carried out to satisfy a definite desire of the character, and each having a definite relation to the character's entire behavior. The "distance from the beginning to the end of an intention" is called a *beat*. [1] Harold Clurman says of the importance of finding the beats:

> The analysis of the play's beats, the characters' actions, can and should be made before the actual staging of the play is begun. The actors derive a basic direction from such analysis and from *the notation of the beats in their part-books*, a guiding line that is the foundation of their entire work in the play. Without such groundwork, we get a display of "general emotion" but not the meaning of the play. . . . The actor's talent becomes evident in the manner in which he carries out these actions. But talent or not, they must be clearly presented for the play to become an intelligible, coherent whole. [2]

Stanislavski usually referred to beats as *units of action*. He also stressed the necessity of seeing the part as a series of units. As soon as one unit serves its purpose in satisfying a particular desire, another desire arises which must be satisfied in another "unit" or "beat." In earlier chapters we have anticipated this analytical process by "structuring" the exercises. Each of the three units with which we have been concerned—the beginning, the middle, and the end—constitutes, in effect, a beat or a unit of action. Sometimes a unit is interrupted, and circumstances literally shove an actor into a new unit before the intention of the old one has been accomplished. This progressive movement from one unit to the next provides the *basic direction* (Clurman) or the *through-line* (Stanislavski) that guides the actor throughout the play.

All actions taken together must constitute a through-line leading to the *super-objective* or *super-intention*. All actions must have some purpose in disclosing to the audience what this super-intention is. If an action is not related to this purpose it should be eliminated. The audience understands the play through a series of logical and expressive actions. This means that onstage the actor thinks and acts consistently and logically in accordance with the demands of his role. The seeming illogic of some contemporary plays—especially those identified as theatre of the absurd—is deceptive. The dramatist has written the play for a specific purpose and he has given the characters some pattern of behavior. To express the absurdity he finds in contemporary life, he may require from the actors a series of illogical actions. But by using speech and actions illogically, by introducing the fantastic and the ridiculous, he is not writing without a purpose. He sees such behavior as a way of expressing the absence of truth and meaning in modern society. As in the case of any drama, it is the actor's job to discover what the pattern is and to communicate it to the audience as clearly as possible.

---

[1] Robert Lewis, *Method—or Madness?*, p. 33.

[2] Harold Clurman, "The Principles of Interpretation," in *Producing the Play*, ed. by John Gassner (New York: Holt, Rinehart and Winston, 1941, 1953), p. 287. Italics mine.

Creating a character means, more than anything else, clearly following a basic direction or establishing a through-line. This process entails a careful playing of the actions in each beat for the purpose of realizing the intention and clearly relating each beat to the one that follows it, even though in some special instances the relation may be that there is no relation. A definite "terminal point" at the end of each unit and a firm "attack" at the beginning, marking clearly that something new is starting, makes the play move constantly forward. *The Proposal*, constructed with clear cause and effect relationships between the beats, illustrates the kind of analytical problem with which the actor will be confronted in most classic and contemporary plays. Here are the beats and the causal relationships that provide a basic direction for playing Lomov from the beginning to his first exit:

1. He greets Chubukov, Natalya's father. His intention is *to get Chubukov's approval for his proposal.*

Progress to next beat: Success in realizing this intention leads him directly into the next one. Having overcome the first obstacle, he is beset with doubts about having Natalya for a wife. Left alone, he wonders about the wisdom of proposing.

2. His intention in this beat is *to rationalize what he is doing, to make himself believe he is doing the right thing.*

Progress to next beat: The playing of this intention is interrupted by Natalya's entrance. He might like to run away, but having declared himself to Chubukov there is no escape. He must go ahead with the proposal.

3. Natalya enters, and his intention is *to get her consent to marry him by pointing out the long and cordial relationship between the families.*

Progress to next beat: It is ironic and comic that the method he chooses to win her approval provokes a violent argument. Before he has accomplished his intention, Natalya disputes his ownership of Oxen Meadows. Since his ego can tolerate no challenge, Natalya drives the proposal from his mind and forces him into another beat.

4. His new intention is *to stand up for his rights.*

Progress to next beat: He continues heatedly to play this intention after Chubukov enters. When Chubukov calls him a "grabber," the quarrel progresses into a new phase. Both sides indulge in "name-calling."

5. His intention here is *to insult Natalya and her father.*

Progress to next beat: The strain is too much for his "delicate constitution." It causes pains in his side, dizziness, numbness. His incapacity to carry on leads to a new unit.

6. His intention here is *to protect his delicate health*, and his ultimate physical action is to run away.

In analyzing Natalya, we discover the following units and causal relationships in the first section:

1. She receives Lomov in a conventional manner. She has no notion that he means to propose. Her intention is *to discharge her social duties in receiving a neighborly call.*

Progress to next beat: Her role of hostess is interrupted by Lomov's reference to *"my* Oxen Meadows." She becomes indignant and defensive.

2. Her new intention is *to set Lomov straight for being so presumptuous.*

Progress to next beat: When the name-calling begins between Lomov and Chubukov, she, too, changes to this new tactic.

3. Her new intention is *to insult Lomov.*

Progress to next beat: After Lomov runs away, she discovers he had come to propose. She is distraught at losing a suitor.

4. Her intention is *to get Lomov back.*

And so on through the entire role.

   Characterization, then, begins with discovering the character's motivating desire and proceeds with breaking the role into small units—each with a clearly understood intention which will help in accomplishing the larger purpose. It is a constant challenge throughout rehearsals and performance. There are few actors, even of the highest professional caliber (and after playing a role a great number of times), who would claim that they succeed with equal thoroughness in believing every beat. That, however, is the aim of creative actors whether they are performing professionally, or nonprofessionally in an educational or community theatre. They work to accomplish it at every rehearsal and performance. But they realize that failure to achieve complete belief at every moment does not indicate a bad actor any more than failure to return every ball indicates a bad tennis player. A good actor succeeds in believing a large proportion of what he does, just as a good tennis player succeeds in returning a large proportion of balls. Both the actor and the athlete work to improve their techniques in order to increase the proportion of their successes.

EXERCISE

   The importance of learning to divide a role into beats or units, of clearly playing each intention, and of firmly attacking the beginning of each unit cannot be overemphasized. It is well to recognize again that here is the key both to building character and to developing plot. You should not try to proceed further until you can make effective application of this technique.

Return to the character you studied in the last chapter to find the motivating desire. Divide the role into beats. State the intention for each one. Make a score of physical actions. Play each beat relating it clearly to the character's basic motivation.

Supplying an Imaginary Background

The dramatist provides enough detail for the actor to understand the motivating desire and the essential traits of a character, but it is almost always necessary for the actor to supply an imaginary background to round out the essentials given by the dramatist.

In playing the parts of Lomov and Natalya, for instance, the actor needs to know what their relationship has been in the past. Lomov states that since childhood he has had the privilege of knowing Natalya's family. We also know that he is ten years older. So he has apparently known her all her life, and we may imagine that in years past he has frequently suffered from her treatment of him. Since Lomov constantly frets about his health, he has probably always pampered himself, avoided strenuous activity, and blamed his shortcomings on his "delicate constitution." Natalya, on the other hand, in the directness with which she receives Lomov and in the efficiency with which she manages her father's land, gives evidence of being a healthy, energetic person. She is probably the kind who in her youth would have taken great pleasure in dominating and ridiculing a hypochondriac like Lomov.

As a result of her attitude, it might well be that Lomov developed a fear of Natalya's ridicule which now makes him more than usually aggressive in her presence. It might also be for this reason that he has dressed formally and comes to make his proposal in evening clothes complete with white gloves. He may have felt that the elegance of his attire could not fail to impress Natalya and to compensate for the disadvantage at which he appeared before her when he was younger.

The evening clothes provide further opportunity for imagined circumstances. The remarks of both Natalya and her father make clear that formal evening dress is not the customary attire in their society for neighborly calls. That fact is further emphasized by Natalya's receiving Lomov in a house dress and apron. We may well imagine that he wears his evening clothes rarely and that he is extremely ill at ease in them. The narrow shoes pinch his feet. The starched collar chokes him. The tight coat hampers his arm movements. We may supply still more background by supposing Lomov bought the clothes quite a few years ago to wear at a reception for some visiting government officials. His are the only formal evening clothes in the neighborhood. He is very proud of them in spite of the fact that they are out of date and that he has gained weight since he bought them.

The actor can often make best use of the technique of supplying an imaginary background by *writing a biography* of the character narrating events of his life which the play does not include. To be valid it should contain only details which are a logical extension of those provided by the dramatist. To be useful it should contain only details which can help specifically in determining the behavior of the character by guiding the actor in his choice of intentions and relationships. In many of the great classic dramas vital matters of interpretation depend upon supplying an imaginary background. What relationship, before the beginning of the play, had existed among the characters that prompted Othello to prefer Cassio over Iago as his principal officer and, at the same time, to trust Iago with knowledge of his personal affairs of which he kept Cassio ignorant? What is Roderigo's background that he aspires to win Desdemona, has access to her only through Iago, and has the wealth to satisfy Iago's extravagant demands upon his purse? Finding answers to such biographical questions is necessary in determining the behavior of a character. Following is an example of a possible biography for Natalya Stepanovna:

My name is Natalya Stepanovna, and I am the only child of a well-to-do landowner. My father's property, which I will inherit, is extensive. Because our family has lived on this land for many generations, over 300 years, we take great pride both in maintaining and increasing it. Living on the land are many peasants who perform the actual labor of working it. Managing the property, overseeing the peasants, collecting the rents, etc., is a considerable job. Since my father is no longer young, I have the major share of this responsibility. It is a job I have naturally grown into. Having no brothers, I have always been close to my father and, since I was a small child, I have accompanied him about the farm. I have always been strong and healthy and able to compete with boys in all kinds of physical activity. I have learned to stand up for my own rights, and in business deals I can trade with the best of them.

This background, along with what I suppose is a natural temperament, has always set me somewhat apart from other girls. I despise their coy, flirtatious behavior, and the way they have of not coming out and saying what they mean. I don't like to wear fancy clothes. We are rich enough to mingle with the aristocracy and we are sometimes invited to their parties. I don't like the dances, but I do enjoy the hunt. The Count often compliments me by saying I ride like a man. We travel to Moscow occasionally where we go to the theatre and the opera, but I am always glad to get back home. I like talking about animals and planting and crops more than about music and such things as that.

I would like to get married because that's what a woman should do. I have no romantic notions about love, but a man does serve some purpose. If I don't produce any children, there will be no one to inherit our land. Lomov isn't much of a man, but there are not many marriageable men in our district. Besides our two properties join and together they would be the largest and richest farm in this part of the country. That would be a nice piece of property to manage!

Writing such a biography puts you on closer terms with the character you are playing. Learn to make the biography a part of your analysis.

Characterizing Through Externals

The discussion of Lomov's evening clothes brings us to a consideration of the place of "externals" in characterization. *Externals* are exactly what the term implies. They are manifestations of character which the audience *sees* and, in the case of departures from the actor's natural speech, *hears*. Externals are costumes, make-up, wigs, padding, dialects, foreign accents, and hand properties such as fans, pipes, canes, snuffboxes, cigarette holders. The term also includes physical attributes such as posture, a manner of walking or sitting, a distinctive gesture, or any such physical abnormality as being lame or hunchbacked. "Externalizing" a character is one of the actor's most important responsibilities. We have already noted that the audience believes what it sees. The actor must find outward forms which will aid the audience in believing the character he is playing.

Externals may also be of great help to the actor in believing a character. It is one of the general shortcomings of inexperienced actors that they make so little use of them. A skillful performance will always give evidence of imagination in finding outward forms to express inner character traits. And these outward forms are often a vital element in the actor's belief. An especially erect posture, with chin held high and nostrils pinched as if constantly trying to locate a slightly offensive odor, might aid an actress in characterizing the overpowering Lady Bracknell in Oscar Wilde's *The Importance of Being Earnest*. A mannerism of sucking his teeth might help an actor in believing the vulgarity of Mr. Burgess in George Bernard Shaw's *Candida*. Elia Kazan's notebook for *A Streetcar Named Desire* outlines effective externals for the character of Stanley Kowalski. Stanley is crude, simple, naïve, sensual—given to immediate satisfaction of physical needs. He sucks a cigar because he can't suck a nipple. He is absorbed in his own pleasures, indifferent to anything else. He has an annoying way of being preoccupied, of busying himself with other things while people are talking to him.

If Lomov's evening clothes give the actor a sense of self-importance and make him feel that more than ever he must stand up for his rights, he is making proper use of an external to aid him in believing the character. He might well make further use of externals in imagining that Lomov is fat. Chekhov describes him as "large," and it is likely that as a result of his "poor health" he takes little exercise. The excess weight with an accompanying shortness of breath, further aggravated by his tight starched collar, might well help an actor in believing Lomov's rage at Natalya's obstinacy.

An example of imaginative use of externals occurred in a university production of *The Wild Duck*. The student actor playing Gregers Werle sought some external means of helping him believe the warped unhealthy state of Gregers' mind and soul. Since Gregers' mind is warped, the actor decided to warp his body also and to play him as a hunchback. The parallel, of course, is obvious. A skilled professional probably would not need such a device. But it helped the student to believe in Gregers' abnormality, in his hatred of his father with his compromising attitudes, and in his fanatical desire to lift his friend Hjalmar "above" normal people who accept compromises and depend for their happiness upon lies and illusions.

The actor doing Willy Loman in Arthur Miller's *Death of a Salesman* should examine the effect of carrying heavy sample bags on the physique of an elderly man. The rounded shoulders, the body leaning forward to balance the weight of the samples, the feet hurting from too much pressure, the eyes looking at the ground to search for obstacles—all these external manifestations can help create a truthful characterization of the exhaustion of Willy Loman.

Sir Laurence Olivier often uses makeup to help find the character. He has been known to develop the right type of nose as a key to a role. From this center, he creates a whole physical presence. Once, when preparing to play Othello, Olivier's external preparation included body-stretching exercises as well as working on the character as an epileptic with seizures. However, the external approach must be used in conjunction with internal motivation in order to develop a complete characterization.

In finding as many ways as possible to use externals as a means to characterization, the actor must observe two cautions:

1. He must beware of using clichés, the stereotyped mannerisms or properties which because they have been so frequently repeated would occur immediately to even an unimaginative mind. A lorgnette to characterize a grand dame, dark glasses and a long cigarette holder for a debutante, a Brooklyn accent for a gangster are clichés which are best avoided. For the audience they no longer express individuality, but only general types. For the actor they are likely to mean an imitation of an imitation. They can be especially dangerous because they tempt him to resort to worn-out devices that he can execute mechanically. Consequently, they are powerless to aid him in believing the character.

2. He must be sure that the externalization either *results from* or *leads to* a specific need which he can relate to the character's motivating desire. Lomov's evening clothes make him feel important and result directly from his desire to maintain his ego. Gregers' deformity sets him apart from others and leads directly to his intolerance of their moral shortcomings. Lady Bracknell is a social snob. She is certain she is better than anyone else, and one of her purposes is to make everyone aware of it. In interviewing Jack Worthing as a prospective husband for her aristocratic daughter, she does nothing to ease his discomfort. Mr. Burgess, on the other hand, is as kind-hearted and common as he can be. He is more concerned with comfort than manners. His minister son-in-law treats him with good-natured tolerance. These externals can readily be *justified* in terms of the characters' motivating desires.

Relating Details to the Motivating Desire

What has been said about the necessity of making externals serve the motivating desire may be repeated with similar emphasis for all aspects of the characterization. Everything the actor does or says or wears upon the stage should help either to create the motivating desire or to satisfy it. The more clearly the actor understands how a particular detail relates to his objective, the more significant it will be both for him and the audience. Lomov's poor health, his delicate nerves, his evening clothes all help him to satisfy his basic need. They all help to make him an object of attention and, consequently, to inflate his ego. His fatness and his shortness of breath are direct *results* of his habit of pampering himself because of his poor health.

The motivating desire is the *unifying factor* in selecting details of characterization. Anything that does not relate to it is extraneous. It should not be permitted.

Not only should the actor avoid introducing what might be contrary to the character's basic want, he should always be wary of details which are merely neutral—that is details which perhaps do not hinder, but which bear no inherent relationship. Neutral items of characterization are deadwood. They are excess weight from which no benefit is received. Whether the actor wears a slouch hat or a homburg, whether his socks are plain-colored or striped, whether he gulps his coffee or sips it slowly should all be determined by the motivating force behind the character's actions. The way an actress has her hair done, the way she sits on a sofa, the way she says "Good-morning" should all be designed to help her believe in the person she is playing. Every detail should make a positive contribution to the total characterization.

Eugenie Leontovich with students of the Goodman School of Drama in the title role of Bertolt Brecht's *Mother Courage*. Staged by Joseph Slowik with settings by James Maronek and costumes by Uta Olson. (Photo—Voris Fisher.) The body on the stretcher is Mother Courage's son who has just been killed in a brutal endless war. Study the picture and write inner monologues for several of the characters.

Expanding the Characterization

Once an actor has sufficient insight into a character to accomplish a single intention with concentrated belief, he is ready to proceed to a second intention which may have appeared more difficult in the beginning. Let us assume you have arrived at this point in playing Lomov. The second intention on which you choose to concentrate might be at the opening of the play where Lomov greets Natalya's father and tells him that he has come to ask for his daughter in marriage.

All of the imaginary background we have already supplied will, of course, help in believing this unit. But we must now supplement it with details of the relationship between Lomov and his future father-in-law. We know they are neighbors of long standing. The play provides other important information that stimulates the imagination.

1. Chubukov says he is twice Lomov's age, which suggests he would expect to be treated with respect if for no other reason than his seniority.
2. Lomov says Chubukov has granted him favors on several occasions, which suggests that in some manner he may be in Chubukov's debt.
3. Chubukov mistakenly assumes that Lomov has come to borrow money, which suggests Chubukov is the wealthier of the two.
4. In an aside Chubukov says he will not lend the money, which suggests that, in spite of their long acquaintance and extravagant greetings, there is no real friendship between them.

These circumstances place Lomov in a position in which he has to make a particular effort to assert his self-importance. At the same time he is under the strain of establishing properly cordial relations. By supplying imaginary details about the favors Lomov has received from Chubukov and adding other circumstances from the past, you will be able to induce belief in this second unit of action.

You might next explore Lomov's surprised indignation when Natalya challenges him about the ownership of the land. An understanding of his response at this moment will lead you into his fourth beat. And thus you can continue this exploration of the beats throughout the role.

In summary, the beginning steps in developing a character are:

1. Analyze the role to discover the character's motivating desire.
2. State the desire in the form of a basic want that will stimulate specific action.
3. Break the role into beats or units that will help you accomplish the motivating desire.
4. State the intention of each beat.
5. Supply an imaginary background to complete the information about the character given by the dramatist.
6. Select externals that will help you believe the motivating desire.
7. Choose one unit in which you can readily justify the intention.
8. Make a score of physical actions for the unit.
9. Rehearse the actions until you can believably repeat them at will.
10. Continue with this process through each beat of the role.

EXERCISE   You are now ready to try your wings in the rehearsal of a play. Your initial responsibility is to create an imaginary character. Let's hope you will have the opportunity to work on a character subtle enough to make the problem interesting, but not complex enough to make it discouraging. Let's hope you

will have the opportunity of developing a character that is essentially true—
not one in which the dramatist has attempted literal representation of life
necessarily, but one in which he has made a truthful observation of life.
Melodramatic and falsely romantic characters are unusually demanding
upon the actor's powers of belief. Finally, let's hope you will have the privilege of working with a group that shares your ideals and is willing to work as
hard as you are.

Getting into the Play

10

The creation of character is one of the actor's important responsibilities and, as a creative artist, one of his most significant contributions to the theatre. But a single character is part of a much larger whole. The actor must relate his performance to the entire play. He must discover why the dramatist wrote it. What he wanted the play to say. What experience he wanted the audience to have while watching it. What thoughts and feelings he wanted the audience to take away with them when they leave the theatre. He must discover what the dramatist intended the total meaning of the play to be, so that he can honestly communicate to the audience the character and ideas given him by the playwright.

In Chapter 8, which discussed the technique of getting into the part, we learned that the actor must analyze a character with considerable care to determine the *motivating force* behind his actions. In this chapter we shall discover that a dramatist employs a group of characters, all motivated by different and often conflicting desires, for the purpose of expressing a single or total meaning. Further, we shall be concerned with how the actor employs his role as an aid in realizing the author's intention.

There are several sources that the actor can explore in this part of his analysis. It may be helpful to know something of the playwright's life and of the circumstances under which the play was written. It may be helpful to know that *The Tempest* was probably Shakespeare's last play and that in Prospero's farewell to his art—the practice of white magic—Shakespeare was saying farewell to his supreme artistry as a dramatist and a poet. This knowledge might help in realizing the calm, the dignity, and the finality of Prospero's behavior. It may be helpful to know that Molière had a young wife and that in his several plays in which an old man is married to a young girl, he was making some observations from his own experience. Some of O'Neill's plays are almost completely autobiographical, and it would be helpful to know about his relation with his parents and his older brother, and about his life as a young man in New London, Connecticut.

Good drama always reflects, if it does not deal directly with, the social, economic, and moral values of its time. So it is often necessary to learn about the prevailing social conditions at the time the play was written. An actor could hardly succeed in Congreve's *The Way of the World* without a familiarity with the amoral behavior of upper class society in Restoration England. He may need to know that Brecht was ideologically a Communist and most of his plays are a protest against a capitalistic society. For the several contemporary plays about the war in Vietnam, such as David Rabe's *The Basic Training of Pavlo Hummel*, he has to know about the conditions in training camps, the prevailing moral values in the combat zones, the breach that combat experience is likely to cause between a returning soldier and his family. The actor may need to learn about conditions among the coal miners in Pennsylvania, among sharecroppers in the South, and about the treatment of the American Indian. He may have to learn about proper procedure in a courtroom, in a hospital, on a battleship.

To understand period plays it is necessary to find out about the clothes worn at the time. The actor must know not only how to wear them and move in them, but *why* a certain fashion prevailed. Why were stocks and farthingales worn in the Renaissance? Paniers and powdered wigs in the eighteenth century? How did Restoration gentlemen use a walking stick or Victorian ladies use a fan?

Knowledge of such matters is necessary not only for an external characterization; it is likely to be essential to a full understanding of the playwright's meaning. Consequently, these are kinds of information that the actor cannot afford to ignore. His *primary source*, however, for discovering the dramatist's basic purpose is the play itself.

Finding the Dramatist's Basic Meaning

Knowing what a play is about, what total meaning the dramatist had in mind, is necessary if the actor is to fulfill his function in the cooperative effort of a dramatic production. Stanislavski wrote about this necessity: "The main theme must be firmly fixed in the actor's mind throughout the performance. It gave birth to the writing of the play. It should also be the fountainhead of the actor's artistic creation." He called this main theme the *super-objective of the entire play*:

> In a play the whole stream of individual, minor objectives, all the imaginative thoughts, feelings, and actions of an actor, should converge to carry out the *super-*

Tom Conti and Jean Marsh in *Whose Life Is It Anyway?* (Photo—Martha Swope.) In this provocative British play, Tom Conti plays a character who is almost completely paralyzed and insists on his right to end his own life.

Philip Anglim and Kevin Conway in *The Elephant Man* by Bernard Pomerance. (Photo—Susan Cook.) Like *The Gin Game* and *Whose Life Is It Anyway?* (as well as *Wings*, *The Shadow Box*, and others), *The Elephant Man* makes dramatic capital of characters whose physiological ailments and deformities shape their words and thoughts.

Jessica Tandy and Hume Cronyn in *The Gin Game* by D. L. Coburn. (Photo—Martha Swope.) Despite the infirmities of age, these characters are drawn into an anguished relationship during a series of gin games.

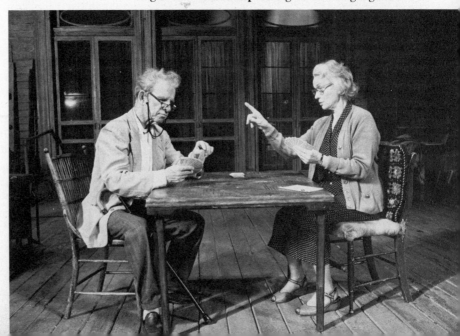

objective of the plot. The common bond must be so strong that even the most insignificant detail, if it is not related to the *super-objective*, will stand out as superfluous or wrong.[1]

Harold Clurman states emphatically that "no character of the play can be properly understood unless the play as a whole is understood." He recognizes that understanding the play resolves itself into one question:

> *What is the basic action of the play?* What is the play about from the standpoint of the characters' principal conflict? . . . What is the play's core? For Gordon Craig, *Hamlet* is the story of man's search for truth. Saroyan's *My Heart's in the Highlands,* to its New York director, was the story of people eager to give things to one another— lovers all, in a sense. For me, Odets' *Night Music* had to do with the search for a home.
>
> Whether these formulations are correct or not, the point is that the director's most important task is to find the basic line of the play. I call it *the spine* of the play because my first teacher in this field, Richard Boleslavsky, used the word.[2]

While finding the basic action is one of the director's most important tasks and sharing it with his cast is one of his most important responsibilities, the actor, if he is to be a creative artist in his own right, needs to understand the meaning of the play through his own efforts. Only then can he make it the primary source of his characterization. How does he discover this basic meaning?

In *The Proposal* we found Lomov's motivating desire to be "I want to trample down anything that challenges my ego." We decided that Natalya's actions are similarly motivated, and that the conflict results from bringing two such people together. To understand Chekhov's basic meaning, what it was that "gave birth" to the play, we must study the script with this conflict in mind.

Looking for the meaning, we must recognize that we shall not be able to find it solely from an examination of the events. Story is rarely the unique feature of a dramatic work. Essentially the same story may be used to express a variety of meanings. To find the real significance we must look below the surface to see how the dramatist has used his story to express some observation about human behavior. People who are interested only in "the story" of a play are missing a good deal of its value. And a play which offers nothing more is realizing only a part of its possibilities.

The story of *The Proposal* may be told in three short sentences. Two people quarrel. They become engaged. They continue quarreling.

Immediately we recognize the importance of a second dramatic element— character. These are not any two people. They are Lomov with his ego and his nerves and his ridiculous evening clothes, and Natalya with her ego and her efficiency and her apron. So in addition to telling the story, the action reveals these two interesting persons.

[1] Stanislavski, *An Actor Prepares,* pp. 256–258.
[2] Clurman, "The Principles of Interpretation," in *Producing the Play,* ed. by John Gassner, p. 277.

Story and character combine to form plot, and through them the dramatist makes an *observation on life* that is his basic purpose in writing the play. Revealing this observation is the actor's basic purpose when the play is produced on the stage.

What observation has Chekhov made in *The Proposal?* The play can't be merely a story of two people quarreling. A noisy wrangle has little point unless it is directed toward some further end. If the play is only the story of two people's becoming engaged, it is like half of all the dramas ever written. What purpose do the quarrel and the engagement serve? The fact that there is humor in interrupting a wrangle only long enough for the characters to become engaged does not make it unnecessary to determine Chekhov's purpose. The writer of comedy makes an observation that is as true, and often as serious, as the writer of other types of drama. And the production of comedy has significance to the extent that actors are able to make the observation clear.

In answering the question as to what observation Chekhov was making in this story of the quarrel and the engagement, we must give attention to two points:

1. Both quarrels are over *trivial* matters.
2. To both Lomov and Natalya, becoming engaged is a *serious* matter. They both seriously want to become engaged.

The play, then, must be about people who make trivial matters more important than serious matters.

In trying to understand more clearly, we logically ask *why* these people argue so violently about such petty things. They do it because they are self-centered egotists. So we may say the play is about two people who sacrifice important concerns by asserting their egos in trifling ways. Such a statement augments and gives direction to the characters as we have discovered them. Furthermore, it may be easily reconciled with a basic theme in nearly all of Chekhov's work—the triviality of the lives of the Russian *bourgeoisie.* This is the meaning as it would be comprehended by the spectators seeing a proper production. And Stanislavski emphasized that the super-objective of the entire play is ultimately determined by the response of the audience. The final purpose is to provide an experience which makes the audience wiser, or happier, or better, or more compassionate. The final meaning is the effect upon the audience both as a group and as individuals. From this short play the spectators realize how ridiculous it is to get so excited about trivial matters.

The actors (and the director) need go further by determining how the dramatist has made his meaning clear through a basic action that constitutes the dramatic conflict. The action that embodies the meaning is what Harold Clurman refers to as the *spine.* It serves as a constant guide to the director and the actors because it is the unifying factor for all details of the performance. We may say the spine of *The Proposal* is "to stand up for one's rights in all matters."

It may help to illustrate further by examining *Romeo and Juliet*. The play opens with a violent outbreak of the rivalry between the Montagues and the Capulets. Starting with a comic quarrel between the servants of the two houses, it next involves Benvolio and Tybalt (the younger generation) and finally the old men themselves—old Capulet calling for his sword, old Montague calling Capulet a villain. They are restrained from combat only by the jibes and pleadings of their wives. The unseemly brawl is brought to an end by the Prince of Verona. It is a nasty fight and it sickens us with its violence and its pointlessness.

In following scenes we see the Capulets and the Montagues, not as enemies but as parents. We see they are not ogres. They are concerned with their children—the Montagues with finding the cause of Romeo's depression, the Capulets with finding a suitable husband for Juliet. We wonder about this mixture of filial concern and violent hatred. It is significant that we first see Romeo and Juliet in relation to their parents.

The conflict develops rapidly. There follow in quick succession the meeting of the lovers, the balcony scene (death to Romeo if he should be discovered), the marriage, the killing of Mercutio and Tybalt, Romeo's banishment, the death of the lovers in the tomb. We glory in the greatness of their love, but we loathe the senseless "canker'd hate" that brought about their tragedy. We are filled with wonder at their sacrifice and grateful that the ancient rivalry has ended. But how unnecessary! The parents are left with golden statues instead of living children, and they are faced with a realization of the awful price Romeo and Juliet have paid.

What meaning does the audience find? It is a feeling of protest against the hatred between the families, and a feeling of exultation for the love that overcame such bitterness. We know that cankered hate brings tragedy and suffering, but that it must ultimately yield to the force of love. The spine of *Romeo and Juliet* may be stated as "to overcome all obstacles in the path of love." This is the basic meaning which provides the audience with an unforgettable experience and which guides the actors and the director throughout the production.

Beginning actors sometimes have a mistaken notion that careful analysis destroys spontaneity. This attitude is difficult to defend. Acting, like any other art, is a conscious process. Spontaneity is fruitful only when it is fostered by careful study which directs it toward the accomplishment of a purpose. The resistance to analysis may be especially strong in the case of comedy, where the actor assumes there is no purpose other than to be comical. Actually the dramatist's basic intention is no different in comedy than in the so-called serious types of drama. The difference lies in the treatment. It is not a matter of whether to analyze; knowing the meaning of the play is essential in any case. The difference, as the actor goes from one type of play to another, is the attitude he assumes toward the character he is creating.

It is the actor's attitude toward the character and toward the play as a whole to which we now turn our attention.

Interpreting the Play: The Dual Personality of the Actor

In discharging his responsibility of communicating the play to an audience, the actor assumes a dual personality. Figuratively, he splits himself into two parts. One part is the actor in the character. Up to now we have been primarily concerned with this aspect of the actor's problem. The other part remains outside the character as a *commentator* continually pointing out the significance, in relation to the total meaning, of what the character is doing and saying.

It is a truism that the actor must not "lose himself in the part." A frequently quoted statement is George Bernard Shaw's maxim: "The one thing not forgivable in an actor is *being* the part instead of *playing* it." Shaw would have stated the case more accurately if he had said: "*In addition* to being the part, the actor must also *play* it." This statement warns against losing oneself and recognizes the necessity of the divided personality.

The dramatist has not written character sketches only as a means of acquainting an audience with a particular group of people. He has drawn his characters to make some observation about life which he believes is true. So the actor's twofold function is

1. to create the character, and
2. to use his creation to express the dramatist's observation.

In addition to creating the character, the actor must *comment* upon his creation to the extent of telling the audience what the dramatist, and very possibly what he himself, thinks and feels about the character's behavior.

Again *The Proposal* will serve as illustration. In playing Lomov, the actor devotes a part of himself to creating a character in which he and the audience can believe. The other part is devoted to saying that Lomov is an absurd egotist. The "comment" must point out that Lomov's evening clothes are ridiculous; that his quarreling is petty and pointless; that his concern about his health is a bid for attention that he may feel more self-important. In playing Natalya, the actress expresses a similar pettiness which is perhaps more ridiculous than Lomov's. Having the ability to manage her father's farm, she might be expected to refrain from a display of egotism. Together the actors suggest the inevitable outcome of the proposal. The "married bliss" is certain to be marred, indeed we might say permanently scarred, by the frequent occurrence of such upheavals.

In making his comment, the actor guides the audience in forming an opinion of the character and, thus, leads them to an understanding of the basic meaning. The comment may say that a character is weak but essentially good; that although it may not be possible to approve his actions, he is entitled to sympathetic understanding. It may say another character is vain and selfish, undeserving of sympathy. It may say still another is living fully and happily according to sound principles.

The comment comes from the omniscience of the actor who knows the character better than the character can know himself. Lomov doesn't recognize that he's ridiculous. The actor has to recognize it and tell it to the audience by emphasizing certain details of his characterization.

It is of great importance that the actor's comments express the dramatist's intention as nearly as it is possible to discover what the intention is. To make the audience dislike a character whom the playwright intended to be received with sympathy would alter essential values. Obviously it would be very wrong to interpret *Romeo and Juliet* in such a way that the long-standing feud seemed justified and the love between the two young people was a breach of family loyalty. The comment must set the beauty and rightness of love in contrast to the ugliness and wrongness of the obstacles against it—the hatred between the families, the pointlessness of the quarrel between the servants, the Nurse's bawdy practicality, Mercutio's mockery, Tybalt's sly malice, the hardness of Lord and Lady Capulet to Juliet's grief.

In the matter of the *dual personality* the actor must decide what the "comment" should be to express best the meaning of the play. He must also determine how obviously the comment should be made. The decision will be based upon the type of play the dramatist has written and the style of production the director has planned. Differences are occasioned by:

1. The period in which the play was written (a classic Greek play is not acted like a modern play).
2. The type of play (a farce is not acted like a tragedy).
3. The style of the play and the production (a naturalistic play is not acted like an absurd play).

It is not in order here to consider the differences between comedy and tragedy or between realism and expressionism. Books have been written on these differences, and the thoughtful actor will want to become acquainted with them. But since a beginning actor (especially in college or university) is as likely to be confronted with Elizabethan tragedy as with modern comedy, it is in order to recognize varying demands.

The approach is essentially the same for all periods, types, and styles. The differences lie in the *extent* to which the actor "comments" and the *manner* in which the comment is made. It is largely a matter of the degree to which he appears to be aware of the presence of the audience. Although "open staging" is becoming more and more common, our modern theatre for the most part is realistic or illusionistic. It is based on the tradition of the "fourth wall" through which the audience sees the actors, but through which the actor must not *appear* to see the audience. The impression which many modern plays aim to produce is that on the stage is an action which members of the audience have

A performance of the Free Street Theatre, directed by Patrick Henry, at Chicago's Civic Center Plaza. (Photo—Al Ashe.) In this improvisational situation notice how each actor in his own person is making direct contact with the audience.

the privilege of observing, but which would go on in the same way whether or not they were there. This concept of theatre is called *representational* because the actor is attempting to represent action as it happens in life. He makes no direct contact with his observers because to do so would destroy the illusion. Any adjustments he makes to the presence of the audience (speaking in a voice loud enough to be heard, holding his lines for the laughs, and performing actions so that everyone may see them) must appear "natural" or lifelike; they must be clearly motivated in terms of the desire of the character he is playing.

This duality constitutes the actor's paradox. He must forget the audience and yet he must always keep them in mind. He must develop a technique so that he can at one and the same time immerse himself in the imaginary world of the play and consciously adapt to the audience that is outside of this imaginary

A scene from the Harold Prince production of *Candide*. **(Photo—Martha Swope.) To accommodate this multilevel production, a floor of the Brooklyn Academy of Music was gutted, and the set was designed in a way that allowed the actors to surround part of the audience while other members of the audience surrounded the playing space.**

world. He makes direct contact with the other actors while he makes indirect contact with the audience, and his connection with both is reciprocal. The spectators are always a challenge because the real essence of theatre is what happens between the actors and the audience.

In earlier periods, and in an increasing number of modern plays, the approach is *presentational* or nonillusionistic. Instead of representing events as they would happen in life, the actor frankly accepts the contrived circumstances under which the plays are given. He *presents* the play directly to the audience without attempting to conceal the theatrical devices he is using.

The ultimate in presentationalism is the traditional Chinese theatre. The Chinese recognize that the conditions of the theatre are not real. Consequently, they find no necessity for creating an illusion of reality. They will accept an actor astride a pole as a general on horseback. The property man sits at the side in full view and provides hand "props" as the actor needs them. The magic of their theatre comes from the formal manner in which they present truthful observations of life without attempting to represent life. They distinguish to a much greater extent than we do the difference between *truth* and *actuality*.

In some respects the classic plays—the plays of Sophocles and Shakespeare and Sheridan and Molière—are closer to the Chinese theatre than to our modern illusionistic stage. They are *presentational* in that they don't attempt to represent life in a realistic environment. They aren't as theatrical as the Chinese plays with their visible property men, but they permit the actor a greater frankness in recognizing the presence of the audience. In the soliloquies he may tell the character's thoughts directly to the house, and in the "asides" he may comment directly upon the action of the play.

Some contemporary plays, especially some that have not yet found a place in the commercial theatre, are moving in directions that establish a still different relationship between the actor and the audience, both social and physical. This aspect of performance is currently a major area of investigation. One direction is "improvisational theatre" in which the actors create their own play, often attempting to include the audience in the improvisation. Outstanding work of this kind has been done by the Open Theater under the leadership of Joseph Chaikin. Sometimes the performers, advocating a social cause in which they strongly believe, do not create characters. Their technique, such as that used by the Living Theatre, is to reach the audience directly in their own persons—a method frequently called "non-acting." Physical relationships have changed in that these performers often come into the aisles, walk between the rows of spectators talking to them directly on a person-to-person basis. Often they work in large open rooms, "found spaces," in which performing and "watching" spaces are arranged to prevent any physical separation. A major objective is to break down any barrier between actor and audience. This concept minimizes the duality of the actor.

Summary

In these different types and styles there are, of course, differences in acting. But these different types are rarely mutually exclusive. In improvisational and "non-acted" theatre there are always some sequences in which the actors behave in accordance with imaginary circumstances. In the most realistic play the actor is always to some degree visible within the character, and the audience responds to the actor as a performer as well as to the behavior of the character he has created. In addition, the actor uses his role to express the total meaning of the play. He emphasizes the aspects of his character that point up this meaning. This emphasis is what we have been referring to as "commenting." In comedy he figuratively holds the character up to the audience for them to ridicule and enjoy. He himself enjoys the ridiculousness of the character, and he has a keen sense of sharing his enjoyment. Sometimes, as in realistic drama, the comment is subtle; the audience is never consciously aware of it. Sometimes, as in farce or in a nonrealistic production, the comment is very obvious.

Most of all, it is important to recognize that whether an actor is creating an imaginary character behaving logically in circumstances given by a dramatist, playing an absurd drama in which the behavior is illogical, or contacting the spectators directly in advocation of a social cause, his objective remains the same: to influence the audience through the carrying out of some specific tasks that will communicate a meaning.

At the end of Chapter 8, you chose a role from a standard play for detailed study.   **EXERCISE**

(1) Return to the same play to determine the basic meaning (the observation of life) which was the unifying factor in the dramatist's mind. State the meaning briefly and clearly.

(2) Now determine the *spine* from a study of how the dramatic action embodies the meaning. State it clearly in terms which can stimulate each actor to action and which will make clear how each character is related to the basic idea. (Remember when a group is working together on a production, general agreement is necessary. Obviously no unity would be possible if each actor were working toward a different purpose. The most desirable means of arriving at an agreement is through group discussion under the guidance of the director, each actor having prepared an independent analysis.)

(3) List the character traits upon which you would want to comment in your performance to point up the total meaning.

(4) Read a number of plays to increase your understanding of different types and styles of drama. Here is a suggested list for a beginning:

David Rabe: *The Basic Training of Pavlo Hummel* and *Sticks and Bones*
Joseph A. Walker: *The River Niger*
Peter Handke: *Insulting the Audience*
Lonne Elder III: *Ceremonies in Dark Old Men*
Sam Shepard: *Red Cross* and *The Tooth of Crime*
Jean-Claude van Itallie: *America Hurrah* and *The Serpent*
LeRoi Jones: *Dutchman* and *The Death of Malcolm X*

Peter Weiss: *Marat/Sade*
Lillian Hellman: *The Little Foxes*
Eugene O'Neill: *Long Day's Journey into Night*
Harold Pinter· *The Caretaker* and *The Homecoming*
Henrik Ibsen: *A Doll's House*
Anton Chekhov: *The Three Sisters*
Arthur Miller: *Death of a Salesman*
Tennessee Williams: *The Glass Menagerie*
Garcia Lorca: *Blood Wedding*
Bertolt Brecht: *Mother Courage*
Eugene Ionesco: *Rhinoceros* and *Exit the King*
Samuel Beckett: *Waiting for Godot*
Edward Albee: *The American Dream* and *The Zoo Story*
Elmer Rice: *The Adding Machine*
Sheridan: *The Rivals*
Goldsmith: *She Stoops to Conquer*
Molière: *The Imaginary Invalid*
Shakespeare: *King Lear* and *The Taming of the Shrew*
Euripides: *Alcestis*
Sophocles: *Antigone*
Antonin Artaud: *Jet of Blood*
William Gillette: *Sherlock Holmes*
David Mamet: *The Duck Variations*
e. e. cummings: *Him*
Tom Stoppard: *Travesties*
August Strindberg: *The Stronger*
George Lillo: *The London Merchant*

Interpreting the Lines

So far we have mentioned only in passing the problem of interpreting lines. The problem is, of course, important. In spite of such old adages as "Seeing is believing" and "Actions speak louder than words," one of the actor's prime responsibilities is to communicate the dramatist's lines to the audience.

The basis for effective interpretation is a good voice. It would be possible to quote a number of great actors to the effect that the voice is the most important of the actor's attributes. Again let us recognize that trying to estimate the relative importance of the various essentials is like trying to determine which of the four wheels is more vital to the automobile. Certainly an actor must speak. Certainly to the extent his voice is not as good as it could be, he is a less effective actor than he could be. His voice and his body are the instruments through which he reaches his audience. He will want them trained so he has the finest possible instruments at his command.

Anyone interested in achieving success in acting will seek instruction to improve his voice, and he will regularly practice exercises in diction and voice production. Assuming the absence of physiological defects, there is no voice so poor that it will not respond to proper training; and there is no voice so fine that it could not be better if it were given the advantage of proper exercise. The actor should seek to accomplish several objectives. He should seek to acquire:

1. *Volume,* so his voice may be heard without difficulty; even quiet intimate scenes must be heard in the rear of the balcony. Jerzy Grotowski gives great emphasis to this objective: "Special attention should be paid to the carrying power of the voice so that the spectator not only hears the voice

of the actor perfectly, but is also penetrated by it as if it were stereopho-nic." [1]

2. *Relaxation*, so that his voice will not tire unduly during a long perfor-mance and so he will not involuntarily raise his pitch during climactic scenes. Relaxation means that the column of air carrying the sound flows freely, unconstricted by tension in the throat or the jaw. Voice tension creates undesirable empathic responses in the audience, impairs the ac-tor's expressiveness, and can cause permanent damage to his vocal mech-anism.

3. *Quality* that is pleasant to hear and capable of expressing varying emo-tional states. A voice that is pleasant to hear is one of the actor's most prized attributes. Quality is to a large extent a matter of resonance.

4. *Articulation*, so that he can be readily understood even in passages requiring rapid speech. Good articulation is achieved through careful at-tention to forming the consonants. It is essential to clear speech. A story is told of a very great actress, now a Dame of the British Empire, who was evaluating the work of an aspiring student. Her comment was, "Poor dear, no consonants."

5. *Pronunciation* that is free from slovenliness and provincial influences. This objective is becoming increasingly important. Television and mo-tion pictures that reach audiences all over the country cannot use actors whose speech identifies them with a particular region unless regional speech is essential to the character they are playing. Absolute absence of colloquial speech is necessary for classic plays that must emphasize the universality of the characters, not their individual idiosyncracies.

6. *Flexibility*, so his voice is capable of variety of volume, quality, and pitch. A good voice is capable of adapting to a large range of demands with maximum ease.

7. *Energy*, so that the voice commands attention and makes others want to listen. It is especially important to guard against a habit (common among young actors) of "fading out"—letting the energy diminish—at the ends of grammatical units. In speaking, as in golf or tennis, one must learn to "follow through."

Although the voice responds to proper exercises and it is possible to notice improvement after a few weeks of practice, the accomplishment of the objec-tives entails extensive training. It is conservative to say that a normal voice requires two years of daily exercise before it is capable of meeting the demands imposed by a variety of roles. This is training that no actor can afford to forgo. And to accomplish its purpose, training in voice and speech must be carried over into everyday living. There is no such thing as "stage diction." The fact that a procedure is not described here is not intended to minimize its impor-

[1] Grotowski, *Towards a Poor Theatre*, p. 147.

tance. The development of the voice should be directed by the most competent teacher available. Here we are concerned with *what* the actor expresses and *why*, rather than with the training of his instrument.

In earlier chapters it has been established that a character *speaks* for the same reason that he *acts*—to aid the satisfaction of some basic desire. The question always in the actor's mind as he seeks to interpret his lines is "*Why* does the character say what he says at this particular moment?"

Finding the Undermeaning of the Lines

Finding the meaning of the lines is a matter of discovering what the character *wants to result* from what he is saying. It is a matter of finding the motivation beneath the speeches. In seeking the motivation the actor must consider:

1. how a line helps the character accomplish his intention,
2. how a line relates to its context, especially to the line that has just preceded it.

A line which doesn't help the character accomplish his purpose will be one of those details which Stanislavski said will stand out as "superfluous or wrong." A line which isn't related to its context will baffle the audience because it will seem pointless and illogical.

In looking for its meaning, we must understand that the real significance of a line rarely is in the meaning of the words themselves or in the literal information they convey. A line rarely serves solely to give information. It has more to express than its surface meaning. Such a simple dialogue as

A. What time is it?
B. It's eleven o'clock.

has no dramatic significance until the meaning beneath the lines is known. *Why* does one character ask the time? What is in the other character's mind when he answers?

These words can convey a number of different meanings depending on the circumstances under which they are spoken. In a melodrama, A might be in the death cell awaiting execution, and the line might mean

A. How much longer do I have to live?
B. Exactly an hour. You are to be executed at midnight.

The situation might be that the speakers are listening to a dull and seemingly endless lecture, and the lines might mean

A. When is this thing going to end?
B. The bell will ring any second.

Or, the speakers might be engaged in some engrossing activity, and the meaning might be

A. We've completely lost track of the time.
B. We're already late for our appointment with Mr. Higgins.

An actor must know and *think* his subtext. The subtext is what the line means to the character who is speaking, which frequently is not what the line says on the surface. Directors often admonish actors with "I know what you're saying, but I don't know what you mean by saying it." The subtext should always be clear to the audience, although not necessarily to the other characters (or to all of the other characters) onstage. Audience omniscience in this respect provides one of the pleasures of going to the theatre; and it is one of the principal devices of comedy and dramatic irony.

An actor's interpretation of a role lies to a very considerable extent in his choice of subtext. He must speak the text that the dramatist has written, but the subtext is his own contribution and demonstrates his insight and his sensitivity to the play. An example of how subtext affects meaning (in this case not just of a single speech but of an entire play) is Katharine's famous "advice" at the end of *The Taming of the Shrew* in which she describes the responsibilities of a dutiful wife. Katharine is a headstrong, willful girl who has been "tamed" and wed by Petruchio. He wants to complete the taming by having Katharine show her obedience at the wedding banquet. With one choice of subtext the speech makes clear that he has brought Katharine to submission. With another choice, we know she is not tamed at all but has learned to carry on the battle of the sexes in a more subtle way. For this second choice, Petruchio's response—his inner monologue while she is speaking—also has a significant effect upon the total meaning. If he does not understand her subtext but takes the words for their surface value, the tables have been turned completely and it is now Katharine who will dominate their relationship. If on the other hand he understands her subtext while the other characters do not, it is clear they are going to have a lively marriage.

In *The Zoo Story*, by Edward Albee, the confrontation between Jerry and Peter over a park bench leads to Jerry's suicide. The confrontation requires a clear subtext. As the play opens, Peter is seated on a bench reading a book. Jerry's opening line, "I've been to the zoo. I said I've been to the zoo. MISTER, I'VE BEEN TO THE ZOO!" is more than an attempt at being noticed by becoming louder. That would distort the author's intention and create a willful, self-centered hoodlum who might frighten Peter immediately and cause him to leave. The actor playing Jerry must keep Peter there, so his subtext must include the pain and desperation of a person at the end of his rope. What Jerry thinks is as important as what he says.

Stanley's subtext in the scene with Lulu from *The Birthday Party*, by Harold Pinter, prepares the audience for the visit by the mysterious Goldberg and

McCann. If his reason for refusing to leave the house is not specific and important, the word games with Lulu and his offer to take her anywhere lose all importance. The actor must know that Stanley is in danger, and his options of hiding in the house or running away are ways of avoiding a dreaded confrontation. The scene is mere mental gymnastics without the underpinning of fear.

In *Cat on a Hot Tin Roof*, Maggie is determined to have a child by Brick. The child is an economic necessity as well as a fulfillment of love. A Maggie whose subtext is only her own survival becomes a shrew, which is not the playwright's intention. Maggie is full of positive life-force, and behind her desire to achieve security is her caring for Brick. The actress who misses this love will not be able to play the pain of her rejection. If we are to care for Maggie, the subtext has to contain the love along with the ambition.

People go to the theatre to hear the subtext. They can read the text in greater comfort at home.

A helpful exercise is to find different subtexts for the same line, and to speak the subtext immediately after you have said the text. Here are examples of different possible subtexts:

EXERCISE

Don't go. (I command you to stay.)
Don't go. (Please stay if you care anything about me.)
Don't go. (It's not safe for you to go out now.)
Don't go. (I warn you, you'll be sorry if you leave me.)
I love you. (But not in the way you want me to.)
I love you. (If you force me to say it, I will.)
I love you. (How can you treat me this way?)
I love you. (I don't ever want you to doubt it.)

Find at least two possible subtexts for each of these lines. Speak the lines followed by the subtext. Then speak them without the subtext making clear their different meanings.

I'm going to do it.
That's just fine.
Thank you.
I'm dying.
What's the matter?
I'm an awful person.
Time goes so fast.
Don't cry.
It's so expensive.
Baby.
You've changed your mind.

I haven't seen him for a long time.
He's been gone twenty minutes.
It's easy to understand why.

Finding the Verbal Action

It is important to recognize that to find the undermeaning or *subtext* of a line is not to paraphrase it, or to restate the words of the author in the words of the actor. Paraphrasing may be necessary when surface meaning is not immediately clear; the actor may find it especially worthwhile to restate in his own words the lines of a verse play. But after the paraphrase, he *still* has the problem of finding what is beneath the line, how it is related to the dramatic action and to the motivating desire of the character. To find the undermeaning we must consider the character's purpose in saying the line. To emphasize that lines, as well as actions, serve a character in accomplishing his intention, we will call the purpose of each line a *verbal action*. Hamlet's famous "To be or not to be," for example, may be paraphrased as "To live or not to live." The verbal action is to decide whether or not to kill himself.

When A asks, "What time is it?" meaning "How much longer do I have to live?" the verbal action is to hold back the time. When he means "When is this thing going to end?" his verbal action is to get out of a dull lecture. When he means "We have completely lost track of the time," the inherent action is to break off what he is doing and go to his appointment.

The significance of a line is not on the surface but beneath it. The real meaning is the undermeaning or subtext. It is the undermeaning that makes the character say the words. The actor's interpretation is in the undermeaning. When speaking a line, he doesn't think only of the words he is saying, but also of the undermeaning and of the inherent action.

In Oscar Wilde's famous satire on snobbery, *The Importance of Being Earnest*, the haughty Lady Bracknell speaks slightingly of the family background of Cecily Cardew. Cecily's guardian, Jack Worthing replies,

> Miss Cardew is the granddaughter of the late Mr. Thomas Cardew of 149 Belgrave Square, S. W.; Gervase Park, Dorking, Surrey; and the Sporran, Fifeshire, N. B.

To give the addresses of Mr. Thomas Cardew's three residences is not Jack's purpose. The undermeaning is

> My ward is a person of excellent family connections which may be quite as acceptable in English society as your own, Lady Bracknell!

The verbal action is to put Lady Bracknell in her place.

Earlier, Jack has been informed that Lady Bracknell does not quite approve of him either. He *says*, "May I ask why not?" But the line *means*, "I am sure I don't see why she doesn't approve of me. I am every bit as good as she is." Here the verbal action is to assert his equality.

The choice of the subtext determines to a considerable degree the overall effect of a line—whether it will be comic, pathetic, melodramatic. The simple line "Don't shoot," read with varying subtexts, can produce a variety of effects. The lines from *The Importance of Being Earnest* are, of course, comic because they point up the ridiculous seriousness with which the characters take themselves.

Relating the Lines to the Motivating Desire

Even after the actor has found the undermeaning and the verbal action he has not fully realized the significance of the line. He still must relate the meaning to the motivating desire of the character he is playing. He must understand how the line serves to help the character to *get what he wants*, and he must make it clear to the audience.

In the situation where A is in the death cell, the motivating desire must be clearly in the actor's mind before he can give the line its full value. The behavior of a character in such a circumstance might be motivated in one of several ways. If the condemned man feels only the primal urge to live, if he is hoping for a reprieve from the governor or even hoping blindly for a miracle, his asking for the time is essentially a cry for help. If he has accepted his death as inevitable, his motivating desire might be to seek redemption, and his line might be a plea for more time in which to make atonement. Even at the point of death he might be filled with the same bitterness which led him to commit the crime, and he might want to give no one the satisfaction of seeing any sign of remorse. In this case, the line would be a declaration of his intention to refrain from making any repentance.

B's purpose must also be understood to realize the meaning of such a simple line as, "It's eleven o'clock." If she is A's devoted and loyal wife, her motivating desire will be to comfort her husband. Her line will be an expression of love and faith. If, to imagine a melodramatic situation, B is a rival spy with a basic wish to coerce A to reveal vital information before he dies, the line might be a threat to harm his family if he refuses the request.

To draw a further illustration from *The Importance of Being Earnest*: Jack Worthing wants to marry Lady Bracknell's daughter. When he asks why Lady Bracknell does not approve of him, he is attempting to assert his own sense of superiority against the onslaught of this overpowering dowager with whom he may have to cope as a mother-in-law. When he tells her of Mr. Cardew's three addresses, he is attempting to equalize the score between them by returning a bit of her own brand of snobbishness.

Examination of some passages from *The Proposal* (complete text in Appendix) may provide further help in understanding the problem of relating a character's line to his motivating desire. This dialogue is the beginning of the quarrel over the land:

LOMOV. . . . You will remember that my Oxen Meadows touch your birchwoods.

NATALYA. Excuse my interrupting you. You say, "My Oxen Meadows. . . ." But are they yours?

LOMOV. Yes, mine.

NATALYA. What are you talking about? Oxen Meadows are ours, not yours!

LOMOV. No, mine, honoured Natalya Stepanovna.

NATALYA. Well, I never knew that before. How do you make that out?

LOMOV. How? I'm speaking of those Oxen Meadows which are wedged in between your birchwoods and the Burnt Marsh.

NATALYA. Yes, yes. . . . They're ours.

Both of these characters, we must remember, want to preserve their own egotistical natures. Almost any subject of conversation would lead to a conflict of personalities. Although a little later Lomov presents his claim at some length, during this passage he is merely putting up a dogged resistance.

Natalya is making the attack here, and there is another meaning beneath her apparent politeness when she says, "Excuse my interrupting you." Actually she is saying, "If you think I am going to let you get away with calling Oxen Meadows yours, you certainly don't know me very well."

Beneath her line, "What are you talking about?" she means, "You are talking outrageous nonsense."

When she says, "Well, I never knew that before," she is taunting Lomov by implying, "And I don't know it now either."

Later Natalya's father becomes involved, and the quarrel reaches the abusive stage. Finally Lomov takes refuge in his "ill health and delicate nerves" and runs for home.

CHUBUKOV. Your grandfather was a drunkard, and your younger aunt, Natasya Mihailovna, ran away with an architect. . . .

LOMOV. And your mother was hump-backed. (*Clutches at his side*) Something pulling in my side. . . . My head. Help! Water!

CHUBUKOV. Your father was a guzzling gambler!

NATALYA. And there haven't been many gossips to equal your aunt.

LOMOV. My left foot has gone to sleep. . . . You're an intriguer. . . . Oh, my heart! And it's an open secret that before the last election you bri. . . . I can see stars. . . . Where's the door? Oh! . . . I think I'm dying. . . . My foot's quite numb. (*Goes to the door*)

CHUBUKOV. (*Following him*) And don't set foot in my house again.

NATALYA. Take it to court! We'll see!

LOMOV *staggers out.*

The verbal action of each of the characters is "to abuse his opponent." All of these lines directly serve Lomov and Natalya in satisfying their basic desire of maintaining their egos—a desire to which they are willing to sacrifice many other needs along with their personal dignity.

Confusion often arises from the use of a variety of terms to describe the actor's relationship to the role, and the relationship of the role to the whole play. For clarity, let us review the definitions of those terms. The actor must realize that the terms "motivating desire," "spine," and "through line of action" are not synonymous:

(1) *Motivating desire* is the addition of justification, or "why," to the intention. It gives the character a sufficient reason to pursue a course of action. In *Death of a Salesman*, Willy's intention in the scene with his boss Howard could be, "I want to get an inside selling job." The "why" is "Because I can't succeed on the road—I want a way out." The two combine to create the motivating desire.

(2) *Spine* is the theme or basic line of the play. It is synonymous with the *super-objective* of the play. In this context it is a directional term. In addition, each role has a spine that must be compatible with the overall spine of the play. If the spine of *Cat on a Hot Tin Roof* is the study of mendacity, all the roles must be related to this objective. The actress playing Maggie should have as the super-objective of her role, "I want to strip away the lies that prevent Brick from fathering our child."

(3) The *through line of action* is the progressive movement from one unit of the play to the next. It assumes a series of consistent and logical actions, a pattern of behavior. It is the route an actor takes to the super-objective. The attempt to fulfill the objectives of the character against a series of obstacles moves the play to a conclusion. The through line of action is the thread that links all the character's actions.

Relating the Lines to the Dramatist's Meaning

The actor must also be aware of how the lines serve the dramatist's basic intention and how they aid in communicating the central idea to the audience. This problem has been anticipated in such previous steps as (1) finding the character's motivating desire—a process in which the lines were an important consideration, (2) relating this fundamental desire to the meaning of the play as a whole, and (3) finding the *undermeaning* and the *verbal action*, which, as we have seen, may be accomplished only by relating the lines to other elements.

Once these steps have been completed, it is likely the actor will understand how the dramatist intended each line to aid in expressing his meaning. We have said that the central idea of *The Proposal* has to do with people who sacrifice important things by asserting their egos in trivial ways. It is important, then, that the pettiness of the quarrel be emphasized. No one in the audience must be in doubt that "Oxen Meadows" is of little value. It must also be made clear that there is no advantage to either Natalya or Lomov in settling which hunting dog is superior. At the same time, the lines must be related to the basic purpose by indicating the seriousness with which the quarrel is waged. It begins with polite restraint:

NATALYA. Excuse my interrupting you.

and

LOMOV. No, mine, honoured Natalya Stepanovna.

Both quarrelers become indignant:

NATALYA. No, you're simply joking, or making fun of me. . . . What a surprise. We've had the land for three hundred years, and then suddenly we are told that it isn't ours. I can hardly believe my own ears.

and

LOMOV. Then you make out that I'm a land-grabber? Madam, never in my life have I grabbed anybody else's land, and I shan't allow anyone to accuse me of having done so. . . .

Later, as they become outraged, the lines further point up the triviality of the quarrel, the seriousness of the quarrelers, and the ridiculousness of the whole situation:

LOMOV. . . . Oxen Meadows are mine!
NATALYA. It's not true, they're ours!
LOMOV. Mine!
NATALYA. It's not true! I'll prove it! I'll send my mowers out to the Meadows this very day!
LOMOV. What?
NATALYA. My mowers will be there this very day!
LOMOV. I'll give it to them in the neck!
NATALYA. You dare!
LOMOV. Oxen Meadows are mine! You understand? Mine!
NATALYA. Please don't shout! You can shout yourself hoarse in your own house, but here I must ask you to restrain yourself.

LOMOV. If it wasn't, madam, for this awful excruciating palpitation, if my whole inside wasn't upset, I'd talk to you in a different way. (*Yells*) Oxen Meadows are mine!

NATALYA. Ours!

LOMOV. Mine!

NATALYA. Ours!

LOMOV. Mine!

The Importance of Being Earnest is another play about people who are concerned with trivialities. It is a satire on the snobbish upper classes at the close of the last century who sought to relieve their boredom by concentrating upon inconsequentials. Oscar Wilde saw the comic possibilities in the affectations of such people, and he ridiculed them good-naturedly in this farce. The plot has to do with two young ladies whose practically sole requirement for a husband is that his name be Ernest—a requirement that compels both Jack and Algernon to arrange to be rechristened.

The lines must continually serve Wilde's purpose of having fun at the expense of these people. The following dialogue indicates Jack's boredom and the eagerness with which Algernon engages in trivial pursuits:

ALGERNON. . . . may I dine with you tonight at Willis's?

JACK. I suppose so, if you want to.

ALGERNON. Yes, but you must be serious about it. I hate people who are not serious about meals. It is so shallow of them.

and later

ALGERNON. . . . Now, my dear boy, if we want to get a good table at Willis's, we really must go and dress. Do you know it is nearly seven?

JACK. Oh! it is always nearly seven.

ALGERNON. Well, I'm hungry.

JACK. I never knew you when you weren't.

ALGERNON. What shall we do after dinner? Go to a theatre?

JACK. Oh, no! I loathe listening.

ALGERNON. Well, let's go to the Club.

JACK. Oh, no! I hate talking.

ALGERNON. Well, we might trot around to the Empire at ten?

JACK. Oh, no! I can't bear looking at things. It is so silly.

ALGERNON. Well, what shall we do?

JACK. Nothing!

ALGERNON. It is awfully hard work doing nothing. However, I don't mind hard work where there is no definite object of any kind.

The verbal actions of the two characters are in conflict. Algernon's action is "to get ready for dinner." Jack's action is "to remain inert."

Many times a dramatist makes his basic intention clearer and stronger through the use of contrasting elements. In such cases, the relationship of the lines of certain characters to the total meaning is one of contrast to the central theme. The meaning is thus pointed more sharply, just as colors appear brighter when contrasted with other colors.

Romeo and Juliet is a play about young people in love. We found its theme to be the triumph of young love over "canker'd hate." Although Romeo and Juliet both meet a tragic death, their love is triumphant. Because of it, the Montagues and the Capulets end their ancient feud, and civil brawls no longer disturb the quiet of Verona's streets. Triumphant love is expressed throughout the play in Juliet's and Romeo's lines,

> My bounty is as boundless as the sea,
> My love as deep; the more I give to thee,
> The more I have, for both are infinite.

and

> O my love! my wife!
> Death, that has suck'd the honey of thy breath,
> Hath had no power yet upon thy beauty:
> Thou art not conquer'd; beauty's ensign yet
> Is crimson in thy lips and in thy cheeks,
> And death's pale flag is not advanced there.

Their love is made a thing of still greater beauty because it stands out in relief against the hatred of old Montague and old Capulet, the Nurse's vulgarity, Mercutio's mockery, Tybalt's malice, and Lady Capulet's coldness. The lines of these characters are related to the total meaning through contrast. It is important that the actors understand this relationship.

Mercutio's mocking lines emphasize the nature of Romeo's romantic love which rises above jibes and cynicism. Tybalt's malicious lines put Romeo's new-found love to a test and bring about the duel that causes Romeo's banishment. Lady Capulet rejects Juliet with

> Talk not to me, for I'll not speak a word:
> Do as thou wilt, for I have done with thee.

Throughout the play, Juliet's warmth and generosity stand out against her mother's unyielding practicality. These particular lines emphasize the desperation of Juliet's predicament and propel her toward her final course of action.

Although the Nurse's character is vastly different from that of Lady Capulet, she serves a similar purpose in providing dramatic contrast. Juliet's sweetness and purity stand out against the Nurse's bawdiness. Her advice to marry the Count of Paris for practical reasons, when Juliet is already secretly married to the banished Romeo, is revolting to a person of Juliet's innocence:

I think it best you married with the County.
O, he's a lovely gentleman!
Romeo's a dishclout to him: an eagle, madam,
Hath not so green, so quick, so fair an eye
As Paris hath. Beshrew my very heart,
I think you are happy in this second match,
For it excels your first: or if it did not,
Your first is dead, or 'twere as good he were
As living here and you no use of him.

In such instances, relating the lines to the dramatist's intention means making them provide dramatic contrasts.

Study carefully the lines of the character on which you are working. For **EXERCISE** each line determine

(1) its *undermeaning*
(2) its *verbal action*
(3) its relationship to the character's motivating desire (that is, what the character *wants as a result* of having said the line, and how the satisfaction of this immediate want would help him in realizing his basic motivating desire)
(4) its relationship to the meaning of the play as a whole.

Write out this information. It will complete your score of physical actions.

Choose a play from the list at the end of Chapter 9 and make a similar **EXERCISE** study of the lines of one or more of the characters.

Believing the Character's Manner of Speaking

The lines are composed of two elements both of which are vitally important:

1. the content—what the lines say including both the surface and the under-meanings.
2. the form—the manner in which the content is expressed.

We have spent some time considering how the actor finds the *content* of the lines. We shall now consider the problem of believing the *manner* in which the character speaks.

The same meaning may be expressed in a variety of manners:

I hope it ain't gointa rain an' spoil the picnic we was plannin' fer so long.

I trust inclement weather will not mar the outing we have been anticipating for such a time.

These two lines are alike in content. The surface meanings are identical. The undermeanings could be the same, and both lines could bear the same relation to the speaker's motivating desire. Neither is expressed in a manner that the average actor will find "natural."

The actor's problem is to understand the background of the character's speech so that he can *believe* the manner of speaking in the same way that he believes in the character's actions. For our purposes, we shall say that the manner of speaking includes vocabulary, grammar, pronunciation, and articulation.

For the most part, these are imposed by the dramatist. The actor must accept the vocabulary the playwright provides. The same is substantially true of the grammar. Occasionally the actor may introduce variations in pronunciation and articulation, such as playing a character with a dialect, or with a stammer, or with "baby talk." Such variations may externalize inner traits and help both the actor and the audience in believing them. "Baby talk" might be helpful in characterizing a woman who had been pampered by her parents and whose motivating desire is to get the same attention from her husband. Such variations, however, are justified only if they enable the actor to realize the intentions of the dramatist.

In attempting to understand a speech background, the actor is concerned with finding circumstances given by the dramatist which justify the character's manner of speaking. In addition, as in justifying actions, it is usually necessary to supply "imaginary circumstances" which, being truthful to the playwright's conception, provide a more thorough knowledge of the character (see Chapter 9).

If the manner of speaking is similar to the actor's, or if he has frequently heard others speak in a similar way, he will have little difficulty. The speech background of Joe Bonaparte and Lorna Moon in *Golden Boy*, by Clifford Odets, is so immediately comprehensible that it presents no problem to an American actor. The following dialogue is typical. Lorna is trying to persuade Joe to become a professional prizefighter.

LORNA. . . . . Joe, listen: be a fighter! Show the world! If you made your fame and fortune—and you can—you'd be anything you want. Do it! Bang your way to the lightweight crown. Get a bank account. Hire a great doctor with a beard—get your eyes fixed—

JOE. What's the matter with my eyes?

LORNA. Excuse me, I stand corrected. (*After a pause*) You get mad all the time.

JOE. That's from thinking about myself.

LORNA. How old are you Joe?

JOE. Twenty-one and a half, and the months are going fast.

LORNA. You're very smart for twenty-one and a half "and the months are going fast."

JOE. Why not? I read every page of the Encyclopaedia Britannica. My father's friend, Mr. Carp, has it. A shrimp with glasses had to do something.[2]

In John Steinbeck's *Of Mice and Men* the speech presents a problem. George and Candy are hired hands on a farm in California.

GEORGE. (*. . . steps to the front door, and looks out*) Say, what you doin', listenin'?

CANDY. (*Comes slowly into the room . . .*) Naw . . . I wasn't listenin'. . . . I was just standin' in the shade a minute, scratchin' my dog. I jest now finished swamping out the washhouse.

GEORGE. You was pokin' your big nose into our business! I don't like nosey guys.

CANDY. (*Looks uneasily from* GEORGE *to* LENNIE *and then back*) I jest come there. . . . I didn't hear nothing you guys was sayin'. I ain't interested in nothing you was sayin'. A guy on a ranch don't never listen. Nor he don't ast no questions.

GEORGE. . . . Not if the guy wants to stay workin' long. . . .[3]

The problem for the average actor is believing the manner of speaking in terms of his own experience. The actor may have no doubt that the speech is right for the character. He may understand the lack of education which has produced this semi-illiteracy. His difficulty arises from an awareness that his own speech is quite different, and such a difference is not always easy to reconcile.

Beginning efforts toward believing a variation from the actor's normal speech must often be largely mechanical or imitative. The actor may listen to himself as he forms the sounds in accordance with the dramatist's attempt to represent the character's speech on the printed page. Some playwrights are very skillful in their use of phonetic spellings to indicate speech variations. George Bernard Shaw was adept in representing Cockney English in this way. The actor, also, may listen to recordings or imitate actual models if he is fortunate enough to know someone whose speech is similar.

If this external approach is to serve its purpose, however, it must lead the actor to believe the character's speech. And believing the speech should, in turn, increase his belief in the character. In other words, as the actor becomes convinced he has developed a true manner of speaking, he will have a greater conviction in his total characterization. Diction—the manner of vocal expression—is one of the actor's principal resources in creating a character.

[2] Clifford Odets, *Golden Boy* (New York: Random House, 1937).

[3] John Steinbeck, *Of Mice and Men* (New York: Viking Press, 1937).

Joe and Lorna and Candy are modest folk who use their meager abilities to express their thoughts and feelings as best they can. In *The Importance of Being Earnest* we meet people with quite a different background. Algernon Moncrieff is, by his own admission, "immensely overeducated." He speaks not only to express his ideas, but also to impress his hearers with his cleverness and his aptness of phrasing. All of the characters exhibit a kind of "speech embroidery" indicative of their elegance and earnest artificiality. The following lines of Gwendolen Fairfax are an example. She is talking to Cecily Cardew whom she has learned is Jack Worthing's ward. Gwendolen and Jack have recently become engaged.

GWENDOLEN. Oh! It is strange he never mentioned to me that he had a ward. How secretive of him! He grows more interesting hourly. I am not sure, however, that the news inspires me with feelings of unmixed delight. (*Rising and going to her*) I am very fond of you, Cecily; I have liked you ever since I met you. But I am bound to state that now that I know you are Mr. Worthing's ward, I cannot help expressing a wish you were—well, just a little older than you seem to be—and not quite so very alluring in appearance. In fact, if I may speak candidly—

CECILY. Pray do! I think that whenever one has anything unpleasant to say, one should always be quite candid.

GWENDOLEN. Well, to speak with perfect candour, Cecily, I wish that you were fully forty-two, and more than usually plain for your age. Ernest has a strong upright nature. He is the very soul of truth and honor. Disloyalty would be as impossible to him as deception. But even men of the noblest possible moral character are extremely susceptible to the influence of the physical charms of others. Modern, no less than Ancient History, supplies us with many most painful examples of what I refer to. If it were not so, indeed, History would be quite unreadable.

Such speech is the result of ostentation and snobbery which is evident both in the vocabulary and in the structure. Understanding of such a background is necessary if the actors are to believe the speech and actions of the characters, and if they are to make an adequate "comment" upon their ridiculousness.

Believing a character's manner of speaking is a matter of understanding the influences in his background that have determined his way of speech. It is a matter of *justifying* the character's speech in terms of his background. It is a matter of finding specific answers to such questions as

Why does one character have such an extensive vocabulary whereas another speaks almost entirely in words of one syllable?

Why does one character speak in long involved sentences whereas another speaks in halting fragments?

Why does one character speak with faultlessly correct grammar whereas another says "he don't" and "we was"?

Why does one character say "you gentlemen" whereas another says "you guys"?

Why does a character say "jist" and "git" and "goin' "?

Why does a character say "poosh" for push and "haouse" for house?

EXERCISE

(1) Make a careful study of the speech of the character on which you are working. *Justify* the manner of speaking in terms of background. Continue your study until there is no detail that does not seem right and true.

(2) From another play choose at least one character whose manner of speaking shows a variation from your own. Make a careful study of the speech. Practice the lines until you believe you are truthfully reproducing the character's manner of speaking. If possible make use of actual models, phonograph records, or phonetic transcriptions.

Motivating the Longer Speech

Throughout this discussion of line interpretation we have been especially concerned with the problem of *motivation*—with relating the lines to the character's basic desire and with making each line help the character to get what he wants. Long speeches frequently appear difficult and frequently fail to serve their purpose because not enough time is given to breaking such speeches into small parts, finding the undermeaning of each, and relating it to the character's motivating desire. The tendency of the beginning actor is to attempt to motivate an entire speech as a single unit.

The longer speech must be broken into structural units in much the same way we have been working on the exercises, and each unit should have a clearly stated verbal action. Many speeches will be "classically" developed. Although intrinsic to the entire scene, they will have a completeness in themselves accomplished through the familiar three-part structure—the beginning, the middle, and the end. Other speeches may have only two parts. Some may have five, or seven. A speech should not be broken into so many units that the actor cannot keep the pattern in his mind. Sometimes speeches are broken off, either by the speaker or by another character, before they reach a structural ending.

A speech from *Golden Boy* will serve to illustrate this process. Joe Bonaparte, on the eve of his twenty-first birthday, is telling his father he wants to break away from the restraints of home so he may have "wonderful things from life." He thinks he can find what he wants by becoming a prize fighter. Mr. Bonaparte, a humane and kindly man, has hopes of Joe's finding happiness as a violinist. He has spent a good part of his savings to buy a fine violin that he plans to give Joe for his birthday. Frank, Joe's older brother who travels about a good deal, is present. Also there is Mr. Carp, a neighbor who owns an *Encyclopaedia Britannica*.

MR. BONAPARTE. Sit down, Joe—resta you'self.

JOE. Don't want to sit. Every birthday I ever had I sat around. Now'sa time for standing. Poppa, I have to tell you—I don't like myself, past, present, and future. Do you know there are men who have wonderful things from life? Do you think they're better than me? Do you think I like this feeling of no possessions? Of learning about the world from Carp's encyclopaedia? Frank don't know what it means—he travels around, sees the world! (*Turning to Frank*) You don't know what it means to sit around here and watch the months go ticking by! Do you think that's a life for a boy my age? Tomorrow's my birthday! I change my life!

Joe's purpose in this speech is to inform his father that he is going to change his way of life and that the change will mean a difference in their relationship. His verbal action is to break away from his home and his father. In spite of being excited and resentful, he doesn't find it easy to say, and he can't say it all at once. Furthermore, he feels that it is necessary to defend his decision. His relationship with his father creates a psychological obstacle. Each unit serves a different purpose in accomplishing his intention.

The speech may be divided into three structural units.

1. Verbal action: *to assert his independence from his father*.

Don't want to sit. Every birthday I ever had I sat around. Now'sa time for standing.

2. Verbal action: *to defend his decision to break away from his father*. This is the middle part—the development leading to the climax. He gives several reasons for his decision, and he plays each reason with increasing intensity.

Poppa, I have to tell you—I don't like myself, past, present, and future. Do you know there are men who have wonderful things from life? Do you think they're better than me? Do you think I like this feeling of no possessions? Of learning about the world from Carp's encyclopaedia? Frank don't know what it means—he travels around, sees the world! (*Turning to Frank*) You don't know what it means to sit around here and watch the months go ticking by! Do you think that's a life for a boy my age?

3. Verbal action: *to make a final statement of defiance*. This is the climax of the speech.

Tomorrow's my birthday! I change my life!

The following speeches provide material for practice in interpreting lines. **EXERCISES** Work successively on several of them. Read the plays from which they have been selected because the significance of any speech lies in its relationship to the play. Determine the motivating desire of the character. Break the speech into units. Find the verbal actions. Make a score of physical actions. Memorize the speech. Rehearse it for the purpose of motivating each unit separately and clearly relating the meaning to the intention of the speech as a whole. If the language is different from your own, make a study of the speech background of the character.

(1) Trepleff in *The Sea Gull*, by Anton Chekhov.[4]

(*Constantin Trepleff is an idealistic young man whose ambition to write for the theatre is constantly thwarted by his mother, a vain and frivolous actress. He is talking to a kindly and understanding uncle.*)

TREPLEFF. (*Picking petals from a flower*) Loves me—loves me not, loves me— loves me not, loves me—loves me not. (*Laughing*) You see, my mother doesn't love me, of course not. I should say not! What she wants is to live, and love, and wear pretty clothes; and here am I twenty-five years old and a perpetual reminder that she is no longer young. You see when I'm not there she's only thirty-two, and when I am she's forty-three—and for that she hates me. . . . I love my mother—I love her very much—but she leads a sense- less life, always making a fuss over this novelist, her name forever chucked about in the papers—it disgusts me. It's just the simple egotism of an ordi- nary mortal, I suppose, stirring me up sometimes that makes me wish I had somebody besides a famous actress for a mother, and fancy if she'd been an ordinary woman I'd been happier. Uncle, can you imagine anything more hopeless than my position in her house? It used to be she'd entertain, all famous people—actors and authors—and among them all I was the only one who was nothing, and they put up with me only because I was her son. Who am I? What am I? I left the university in my third year, owing to circum- stances, as they say, for which the editors are not responsible; I've no talent at all, not a kopeck on me; and according to my passport I am—a burgher of Kiev. My father was a burgher of Kiev, though he was also a famous actor. So when these actors and writers of hers bestowed on me their gracious at- tentions, it seemed to me their eyes were measuring my insignificance. I guessed their thoughts and felt humiliated.

[4] Anton Chekhov, *The Sea Gull*, translated by Stark Young. Charles Scribner's Sons.

(2) Biff Loman in *Death of a Salesman*, by Arthur Miller.[5]

(*Biff has returned home after knocking aimlessly about the country for a number of years. He has no object in life and no certain sense of values. He is talking to his brother.*)

BIFF. I tell ya, Hap, I don't know what my future is. I don't know—what I'm supposed to want. . . . I spent six or seven years after high school trying to work myself up. Shipping clerk, salesman, business of one kind or another. And it's a measly manner of existence. To get on that subway on the hot mornings in summer. To devote your whole life to keeping stock, or making phone calls, or selling or buying. To suffer fifty weeks of the year for the sake of a two-week vacation, when all you really desire is to be outdoors, with your shirt off. And always to have to get ahead of the next fella. And still— that's how you build a future. . . . Hap, I've had twenty or thirty different kinds of jobs since I left home before the war, and it always turns out the same. I just realized it lately. In Nebraska when I herded cattle, and the Dakotas, and Arizona, and now in Texas. It's why I came home now, I guess, because I realized it. This farm I work on, it's spring there now, see? And they've got about fifteen new colts. There's nothing more inspiring or— beautiful than the sight of a mare and a new colt. And it's cool there now, see? Texas is cool now, and it's spring. And whenever spring comes to where I am, I suddenly get the feeling, my God, I'm not getting anywhere! What the hell am I doing, playing around with horses, twenty-eight dollars a week! I'm thirty-four years old, I oughta be makin' my future. That's when I come running home. And now, I get here, and I don't know what to do with myself. (*A pause*) I've always made a point of not wasting my life, and every time I come back here I know that all I've done is to waste my life.

(3) Mrs. Lincoln in *Abraham Lincoln*, by John Drinkwater.[6]

(*The scene is the parlor of Abraham Lincoln's house in Springfield, Illinois, in 1860. Mrs. Lincoln is speaking to a group of men who have come to offer her husband the nomination to the Presidency of the United States.*)

MRS. LINCOLN. You have said this was a great evening for me. It is, and I'll say more than I mostly do, because it is. I'm likely to go into history now with a great man. For I know better than any how great he is. I'm plain looking and I've a sharp tongue, and I've a mind that doesn't always go in his easy, high way. And that's what history will see, and it will laugh a little, and say, "Poor Abraham Lincoln." That's all right, but it's not all. I've always known when he should go forward, and when he should hold back. I've watched, and watched,

---

[5] Arthur Miller, *Death of a Salesman*. Viking Press.
[6] John Drinkwater, *Abraham Lincoln*. Houghton Mifflin Co.

and what I've learnt America will profit by. There are women like that, lots of them. But I'm lucky. My work's going farther than Illinois—it's going farther than any of us can tell. I made things easy for him to think and think when we were poor, and now his thinking has brought him to this. They wanted to make him Governor of Oregon, and he would have gone and come to nothing there. I stopped him. Now they're coming to ask him to be President, and I've told him to go.

(4) Christy Mahon in *The Playboy of the Western World*, by John Millington Synge.[7]

(A *young Irishman named Christy Mahon, having run away from home, is befriended by Pegeen Mike and her father, who owns a public house. Up early in the morning, Christy is polishing Pegeen's boots and counting the jugs behind the bar. He is speaking to himself.*)

CHRISTY. Half a hundred beyond. Ten there. A score that's above. Eighty jugs. Six cups and a broken one. Two plates. A power of glasses. Bottles, a schoolmaster'd be hard set to count, and enough in them, I'm thinking, to drunken all the wealth and wisdom of the County Clare. (*He puts the boot down carefully*) There's her boots, nice and decent for her evening use, and isn't it grand brushes she has? (*He puts them down and goes by degrees to the looking-glass*) Well, this'd be a fine place to be my whole life talking out with swearing Christians, in place of my old dogs and cat, and I stalking around, smoking my pipe and drinking my fill, and never a day's work but drawing a cork an odd time, or wiping a glass, or rinsing out a shining tumbler for a decent man. (*He takes the looking-glass from the wall and puts it on the back of a chair; then sits down in front of it and begins washing his face*) Didn't I know rightly I was handsome, though it was the divil's own mirror we had beyond, would twist a squint across an angel's brow; and I'll be growing fine from this day, the way I'll have a soft lovely skin on me and won't be the like of the clumsy young fellows do be ploughing all times in the earth and dung. (*He starts*) Is she coming again? (*He looks out*) Stranger girls. God help me, where'll I hide myself away and my long neck naked to the world. (*He looks out*) I'd best go to the room maybe till I'm dressed again. (*He gathers up his coat and looking-glass, and runs into the inner room*)

(5) Abbie Putnam in *Desire Under the Elms*, by Eugene O'Neill.[8]

(*Abbie is a young woman who has married an old farmer named Ephraim Cabot. She is talking to Eben, Ephraim's grown-up son. He is strongly resentful of her.*)

---

[7] John Millington Synge, *The Playboy of the Western World*. Modern Library.
[8] Eugene O'Neill, *Desire Under the Elms*. Random House.

ABBIE. (*Calmly*) If cussin' me does ye good, cuss all ye've a mind t'. I'm all prepared t' have you agin me—at fust. I don't blame ye nuther. I'd feel the same at any stranger comin' t' take my Maw's place. (*He shudders. She is watching him carefully*) Yew must've cared a lot fur yewr Maw, didn't ye? My Maw died afore I'd growed. I don't remember her none. (*A pause*) But yew won't hate me long, Eben. I'm not the wust in the world—an' ye an' me've got a lot in common. I kin tell that by lookin' at ye. Waal—I've had a hard life, too—oceans o' trouble an' nuthin' but wuk fur reward. I was an orphan early an' had t' work fur others in other folks' hums. Then I married an' he turned out a drunken spreer an' so he had to wuk fur others an' me too agen in other folks' hums, an' the baby died, an' my husband got sick an' died too, an' I was glad sayin' now I'm free fur once, on'y I diskivered right away all I was free fur was t' wuk agen in other folks' hums, doin' other folks' wuk till I'd most give up hope o' ever doin' my own wuk in my own hum, an' then your Paw comes. . . . .

(6) Edmund in *Long Day's Journey into Night*, by Eugene O'Neill.[9]

(*Even though he has tuberculosis and is soon to go to a sanatorium, Edmund has been walking late at night on the beach. He has also been drinking, and his father has just told him he should have more sense. Edmund is bitter because he blames his father for an intensely unhappy family situation.*)

EDMUND. To hell with sense! We're all crazy. What do we want with sense? (*He quotes from Dowson sardonically.*)

"They are not long, the weeping and the laughter,
Love and desire and hate:
I think they have no portion in us after
We pass the gate.

They are not long, the days of wine and roses:
Out of a misty dream
Our path emerges for a while, then closes
Within a dream."

(*Staring before him.*) The fog was where I wanted to be. Halfway down the path you can't see this house. You'd never know it was here. Or any of the other places down the avenue. I couldn't see but a few feet ahead. I didn't meet a soul. Everything looked and sounded unreal. Nothing was what it is. That's what I wanted—to be alone with myself in another world where truth is untrue and life can hide from itself. Out beyond the harbor, where the

---

[9] Eugene O'Neill, *Long Day's Journey into Night*. Yale University Press.

road runs along the beach, I even lost the feeling of being on land. The fog and the sea seemed part of each other. It was like walking on the bottom of the sea. As if I had drowned long ago. As if I was a ghost belonging to the fog, and the fog was the ghost of the sea. It felt damned peaceful to be nothing more than a ghost within a ghost. (*He sees his father staring at him with mingled worry and irritated disapproval. He grins mockingly.*) Don't look at me as if I'd gone nutty. I'm talking sense. Who wants to see life as it is, if they can help it? It's the three Gorgons in one. You look in their faces and turn to stone. Or it's Pan. You see him and you die—that is, inside you—and have to go on living as a ghost.

(7) Juanita in *Blues for Mister Charlie*, by James Baldwin.[10]

(*Juanita is a black student whose lover has been senselessly murdered by a white man.*)

JUANITA. (*Rises from bed; early Sunday morning.*) He lay beside me on that bed like a rock. As heavy as a rock—like he'd fallen—fallen from a high place—fallen so far and landed so heavy, he seemed almost to be sinking out of sight—with one knee pointing to heaven. My God. He covered me like that. He wasn't at all like I thought he was. He fell on—fell on me—like life and death. My God. His chest, his belly, the rising and the falling, the moans. How he clung, how he struggled—life and death! Life and death! Why did it all seem to me like tears? That he came to me, clung to me, plunged into me, sobbing, howling, bleeding, somewhere inside his chest, his belly, and it all came out, came pouring out, like tears! My God, the smell, the touch, the taste, the sound, of anguish! Richard! Why couldn't I have held you closer? Held you, held you, borne you, given you life again? Have made you be born again! Oh, Richard. The teeth that gleamed, oh! when you smiled, the spit flying when you cursed, the teeth stinging when you bit—your breath, your hands, your weight, my God, when you moved in me! Where shall I go now, what shall I do? . . . Mama was frightened. Frightened because little Juanita brought her first real lover to this house. I suppose God does for Mama what Richard did for me. Juanita! . . . Mama is afraid I'm pregnant. Mama is afraid of so much. I'm not afraid. I hope I'm pregnant. I *hope* I am! One more illegitimate black baby—that's right you jive mothers! And I'm going to raise my baby to be a man. A *man*, you dig? . . . Did this happen to Mama sometime? Did she have a man sometime who vanished like smoke? And left her to get through this world as best she could? Is that why she married my father? . . . You're going crazy, Juanita. Oh, Lord, don't let me go mad. Let me be pregnant! Let me be pregnant!

---

[10] James Baldwin, *Blues for Mister Charlie*. Dial Press.

(8) Orestes in *The Prodigal,* by Jack Richardson.[11]

(Orestes, son of Agamemnon, tells why he refuses to respect his father and to emulate him as a great king and warrior. He is speaking to Penelope who is scornful of his way of life, which keeps him uninvolved with the affairs of his country.)

ORESTES. . . . who knows my father better than I? True, he left when I was a boy and has been gone for some ten years, but this has only served to make him more familiar to me. For when he set off to mutilate Trojans he left his legend behind, and how is a man known but through his legend? Can laughter, can intimacy, can touch tell more about a man, especially a king, than a personal myth he bequeaths to us in death or absence? For example, when the war was still going badly for us at Troy, I was brought stories of my father's past epic accomplishments. I was told how he, acting under the indubitable and humane principle that the seas should be free and orderly, took it upon himself to clear the Mediterranean of pirates, and how nearly a thousand of our citizens sank, as immortal heroes, of course, to its bottom putting this principle into effect. Was it not also related to me, in great detail by yourself, Penelope, how, when he heard a small island, I forget the name, was being ruled by a petty tyrant with unsavory whims, he set off to bring them a more liberal and morally antiseptic government? I won't bother you with what principles he used there—they seemed rather muddled when I heard them the first time—but you must know their worth since a good five thousand lives were paid for them. Then, when the war turned in our favor, the pleasant story was brought to me of how my sister, Iphigenia, was sacrificed by her father so that his men, inspired by such a sacrifice, would fight better for the principle which had set them off again, sword in hand. This time it had to do with a national insult and Helen's chastity. Helen's chastity! A contradiction in terms. But the score is still not in on the numbers who died substantiating that poor judgment of character. Not know my father? Why, I even have a copybook filled with the trenchant sayings he uttered while cracking Trojan heads. Not know my father? All I need is the binder to wrap around his principles and he is a closed, memorized, and understood book. No, Penelope, I know my father only too well.

(9) Blanche in *A Streetcar Named Desire,* by Tennessee Williams.[12]

(Blanche DuBois is telling her sister Stella why the family home Belle Reve has been lost because of debts.)

BLANCHE. I, I, *I* took the blows in my face and my body! All of those deaths! The long parade to the graveyard! Father, mother! Margaret, that dreadful

---

[11] Jack C. Richardson, *The Prodigal.* E. P. Dutton & Co.

[12] Tennessee Williams, *A Streetcar Named Desire.* New Directions and Curtis Brown, Ltd.

way! So big with it, it couldn't be put in a coffin! But had to be burned like rubbish! You just came home in time for the funerals, Stella. And funerals are pretty compared to deaths. Funerals are quiet, but deaths—not always. Sometimes their breathing is hoarse, and sometimes it rattles, and sometimes they even cry out to you, "Don't let me go!" Even the old, sometimes, say, "Don't let me go." As if you were able to stop them! But funerals are quiet, with pretty flowers. And, oh, what gorgeous boxes they pack them away in! Unless you were there at the bed when they cried out, "Hold me!" you'd never suspect there was the struggle for breath and bleeding. You didn't dream, but I saw! *Saw! Saw!* And now you sit there telling me with your eyes that I let the place go! How in hell do you think all that sickness and dying was paid for? Death is expensive, Miss Stella! And old Cousin Jessie's right after Margaret's, hers! Why, the Grim Reaper had put up his tent on our doorstep! . . . Stella. Belle Reve was his headquarters! Honey—that's how it slipped through my fingers! Which of them left us a fortune? Which of them left a cent of insurance even? Only poor Jessie—one hundred to pay for her coffin. That was all, Stella! And I with my pitiful salary at the school. Yes, accuse me! Sit there and stare at me, thinking I let the place go! *I* let the place go? Where were *you!* In bed with your—Polack!

(10) Ardell in *The Basic Training of Pavlo Hummel*, by David Rabe.[13]

(A *black soldier in Vietnam watches as Private Pavlo Hummel, a victim of a hand grenade, is placed on a stretcher by the body detail.*)

ARDELL. He don't die right off. Take him four days, thirty-eight minutes. And he don't say nothin' to nobody in all that time. No words; he just kinda lay and look up, and when he die he bitin' his lower lip, I don't know why. So they take him, they put him in a blue rubber bag, zip it up tight, and haul it off to the morgue in the back of a quarter-ton, where he get stuck naked into the refrigerator 'long with the other boys killed that day and the beer and cheese and tuna and stuff the guys who work in the morgue keep in the refrigerator except when it inspection time. The bag get washed, hung out to dry on a line out back a the morgue. (*Slight pause.*) Then . . . lemme see, well, finally he get shipped home, and his mother cry a lot, and his brother get so depressed he gotta go out and lay his chippie he so damned depressed about it all. And Joanna, she read his name in the paper, she let out this little gasp and say to her husband across the table, "Jesus, Jimmy, I used to go with that boy. Oh, damn the war, why can't we have peace? I think I'll call his mother." Ain't it some kinda world? (*And he is laughing.*) Soooooooo . . . that about it. That about all I got to say. Am I right, Pavlo? Did I tell you true? You got anything to say? Oh, man, I know you do, you say it out.

---

[13] David Rabe, *The Basic Training of Pavlo Hummel.* Viking Press.

Speaking the Lines

12

There is an assumption among many actors that, if they understand the general meaning of a line and have an idea of its overall purpose, their line reading will be correct without further conscious effort. This assumption is only partially tenable. An intelligent actor speaking dialogue in straightforward prose will probably need to give only occasional attention to the mechanics of language. But many plays (all classics and a considerable number of contemporary works) are not written in simple prose. They employ rhetorical and poetic devices, and frequently a vocabulary, that demand attention to both content and form if the actor is to communicate their full value to an audience.

A comprehensive study of the uses of prose and poetry is a matter of great complexity, and it is not in order to attempt it here. We need, however, to explore the more common means that dramatists use to make their dialogue effective. A knowledge of them should stimulate you to a closer examination of the dramatist's lines, revealing subtlety of meaning and aptness of form of which you might otherwise be unaware. Since communication is the actor's primary responsibility and since language is a major means of communication, it goes without saying that an actor's success depends considerably upon his sensitivity to words and his ability to communicate their meaning.

Understanding the Words

It is essential that an actor know what the words he is speaking mean! This is so obvious you may resent having it said. Yet it is not an uncommon occurrence for an actor to speak lines at rehearsal not only not knowing what they mean, but not realizing that he doesn't know. The actor's greatest help in this area is a good standard dictionary. He should have one, and he should use it frequently. He needs, besides, to have access to some special sources, such as dictionaries of slang and colloquial speech. And for almost all period plays he needs a glossary and a well-annotated edition of the text. The study of such sources to discover the meaning of the words is *homework* that many young actors fail to do with any degree of thoroughness. Another example from *Romeo and Juliet* will illustrate this point.

Juliet's first line in the Balcony Scene (Act II, Scene 2), spoken to herself after she has just met Romeo at the Capulet ball and fallen deeply in love with him, is

O Romeo, Romeo! wherefore art thou Romeo?

Almost all young actresses misread the line. They place the emphasis on *art* making it mean "Where are you, Romeo?" with some such subtext as "I yearn to know where you are, what you are doing, whether you are longing for me as I am longing for you."

Checking a dictionary will disclose that *wherefore* does not mean *where*, it means *why*. *Wherefore* then becomes the emphatic word, and the correct subtext is "Why do you, whom I have come to love, have to be called Romeo, the son of our great enemy?" This reading leads logically to the next line

Deny thy father, and refuse thy name;
Or, if thou wilt not, be but sworn my love,
And I'll no longer be a Capulet.

In searching for the meaning of Juliet's first line, a careful actress will also note that there is no comma between *thou* and *Romeo* indicating that here Romeo is not being addressed. Attention to punctuation helps greatly in finding the meaning of a line.

Juliet uses *wherefore* in the same sense in expressing her alarm when Romeo reveals his presence in the Capulet orchard:

How cam'st thou hither, tell me, and *wherefore*?

She means *how* did you manage to get in here and *why* did you come.

Several other usages in the same scene further illustrate the necessity of close attention to the meaning of the words. After Juliet has said her famous ". . . that which we call a rose/ By any other name would smell as sweet," she continues:

So Romeo would, were he not Romeo call'd,
Retain that dear perfection which he *owes*
Without that title.

A few lines later, fearing Romeo will think she is too forward in declaring her love, she says:

In truth, fair Montague, I am too *fond*.

It is important to know that *owes* in Shakespeare usually means *owns*, and that *fond* usually means *foolish*. Juliet is not saying "I love you too much," she is saying "I am foolish to declare my love to someone I have known only an hour and whose family is an enemy to my family." This feeling is expressed more fully later in the lines:

I have no joy of this contract tonight:
It is too rash, too unadvis'd, too sudden;

Words that look familiar, but that the dramatist uses with an unfamiliar meaning, can be particularly deceiving.

After Juliet has warned Romeo that he will be killed if any of her kinsmen find him in their orchard, he says:

My life were better ended by their hate,
Than death *prorogued*, wanting of thy love.

The word *prorogued* is not likely to be in the average student's vocabulary. It means *postponed* or *delayed*. Romeo is saying, "It is better to be killed at once by your kinsmen, than to endure a living death without your love." To make this meaning clear, six words must have some degree of emphasis.

My *life* were better *ended* by their *hate*,
Than *death prorogued*, wanting of thy *love*.

Selecting the word or words to be emphasized is an important factor in interpreting the lines. The selection is determined by the meaning of the words and by the context in which they are used. We will call these words the *operative* words. Operative means "exerting force that produces an appropriate effect," and we choose this term because it suggests the *active* influence that certain words have in communicating a meaning. Think of the simple sentence "I gave him the revolver." If we exclude the article, any one of the four words might be chosen as operative, depending upon the meaning intended. Speak the sentence in four ways with four different operative words, and write an appropriate subtext for each reading.

Finding the operative words is not, of course, an arbitrary matter. Different actors will make different choices. The choice the actor makes, however, will reveal his understanding of the playwright's text and his sensitivity to the uses of language.

We must notice that it is not only in verse plays of other periods that vocabulary needs attention. Not every actor will be immediately familiar with the term "jive," used frequently by some black playwrights, nor the full connotation of their use of "cat." Nor this Cockney dialogue in Edward Bond's *Early Morning*:

LEN. We'd bin stood there 'ours, and me guts starts t' rumble. 'Owever, I don't
let on. But then she 'as t' say "I ain arf pecky."
JOYCE. Thass yer sense a consideration, ain it! I'd 'eard your gut.
LEN. I 'ad an empty gut many times, girl. That don't mean I'm on the danger
list. But when you starts rabbitin' about bein' pecky I . . . . You're a rabbitin' ol' git! 'Ear that? [1]

Practically every play demands close examination of its particular idiom. Michael Weller's *Moonchildren* depends heavily on the audience's familiarity with
college slang of the 1960s; *Short Eyes*, by Miguel Pinero, makes heavy use of
ethnic and prison slang, especially the term "short eyes," which is prison slang
for a child molester; and one would have to know a whole range of homosexual
terms—straight, gay, in the closet, queen, and so on—in order to extract nuances of meaning from many of the lines in Mart Crowley's *The Boys in the
Band*.

Handling the Sentence

Academic as it may sound, an actor who is ignorant of the basic rules of
grammar is quite helpless in discovering and communicating a playwright's
lines. He must know the way words are put together to form sentences. He
must be able to recognize subjects and predicates, as well as modifying words,
phrases, and clauses; and he must understand the principles of subordination
and pronoun reference. Jerzy Grotowski wrote:

The ability to handle sentences is important and necessary in acting. The sentence
is an integral unit, emotional and logical, that can be sustained by a single expiratory
and melodic wave. It is a whirlwind concentrated on an epicentrum [focal center—we
need a dictionary here] formed by the logical accent or accents. The vowels at this
epicentrum should not be shortened but rather prolonged slightly in order to give
them a special value, taking good care not to break up the unity of the sentence with
unjustified pauses. . . .
In poetry too, the sentence must be considered as a logical and emotional entity to
be pronounced in one single respiratory wave. Several lines (one and a half, two, or
more) often constitute the sentence. [2]

Understanding the sentence as a structural *unit*, recognizing the relationship
and relative importance of its different parts, determining the operative words
(or logical accents as Grotowski calls them), and keeping the sentence moving

[1] Edward Bond, *Early Morning*. Calder and Boyars, Ltd.
[2] Grotowski, *Towards a Poor Theatre*, p. 171.

toward its "epicentrum" is one of the actor's principal concerns in dealing with the language of a play. Grotowski's warning against unjustified pauses should be heeded very carefully. Unnecessary pauses, for an intake of breath or for any other reason, obscure the relationship of the parts that must be made clear to communicate the meaning, and destroy the rhythmic flow that is essential to the form. Good actors handle sentences so that the words are constantly moving forward toward a focal point. The problem can be more complex than Grotowski suggests. In *The Tempest*, Prospero's "Farewell to his Art" (Act V, Scene 1) has a sentence that is seventeen and a half lines long, and Juliet's Potion Speech (Act IV, Scene 3) has a sentence of eighteen lines. Here are some sentences, less complex than those just mentioned, that will illustrate the problem.

In *Major Barbara*, by George Bernard Shaw, Lady Britomart is answering the protest that she treats her grown-up offspring like children.

> I have always made you my companions and friends, and allowed you perfect freedom to do and say whatever you liked, so long as you liked what I could *approve* of.[3]

Here is a sentence of thirty-one words that can be handled as a "single melodic wave," culminating in the operative word *approve*. It should be noted that to select *approve* as operative does not mean that other words in the sentence do not have a degree of importance and should not receive some manner of emphasis. But *approve* is a correct choice. It is logical because in Lady Britomart's mind her approval is more important than the freedom she claims to allow. It is appropriate to reveal her dominating character. It points the comic contradiction of the line by indicating she is blameworthy of the very charge she is denying.

This line from Arthur Kopit's *Indians* presents a similar, but more difficult, problem. John Grass, a young Indian, is testifying before a group of senators sent by the President of the United States, the Great Father, to investigate charges of mistreatment. He is talking about the futile and bungling attempts of a missionary bishop to help the situation.

> But when we told him we did not wish to be Christians but wished to be like our fathers, and dance the sundance, and fight bravely against the Shawnee and the Crow, and pray to the Great Spirits who made the four winds, and the earth, and made man from the dust of the earth, Bishop Marty *hit* us! [4]

This is a group of fifty-nine words constituting a logical and *emotional* entity, always moving toward the operative word *hit*. Grammatically, "Bishop Marty hit us" is the principal clause, and *hit* is the main verb of the entire unit. Logically, it is John Grass' purpose to impress upon the senators the mistreat-

---

[3] George Bernard Shaw, *Major Barbara*. Dodd, Mead and Co.
[4] Arthur Kopit, *Indians*. Hill & Wang.

ment the Indians have received, in spite of what (to them, at least) has been a reasonable attitude. Emotionally, he feels very deeply about the physical abuse they have suffered. Kopit's choice of the word *hit* is peculiarly expressive of John Grass' childlike earnestness and naïveté.

In *Blues for Mister Charlie*, a mature white man tells about his youthful love for a black girl.

> I used to look at her, the way she moved, so beautiful and free, and I'd wonder if at night, when she might be on her way home from someplace, any of those boys at school had said *ugly things* to her.[5]

The speaker realized that, at the school that they attended, a black girl in permitting any kind of relationship with a white boy subjected herself to a good deal of cruel comment. This is the concern he is expressing, and, consequently, the whole sentence must move forward to *ugly things*. It is also necessary here to observe the principles of subordination, to pick out the main structure, the "skeleton," and to relate the less important parts to it. Here is the skeleton of this sentence:

> I used to look at her . . . . and I'd wonder if . . . . any of those boys . . . . had said ugly things to her.

The other parts must be made properly subordinate.

Following is a passage of dramatic dialogue in verse, the opening lines of *Love's Labour's Lost*, spoken by the young King of Navarre to three attending Lords.

Let fame, that all hunt after in their lives,
Live register'd upon our brazen tombs,
And then grace us in the disgrace of death;
When, spite of cormorant devouring Time,
Th' endeavour of this present breath may buy
That honour which shall bate his scythe's keen edge,
And make us heirs of all eternity.
Therefore, brave conquerors,—for so you are,
That war against your own affections
And the huge army of the world's desires,—
Our late edict shall strongly stand in force:
Navarre shall be the wonder of the world;
Our court shall be a little Academe,
Still and contemplative in living art.

[5] James Baldwin, *Blues for Mister Charlie*. Dial Press.

These fourteen lines constitute two sentences of seven lines each. The sentences are not unusually complex, but fully to appreciate their meaning recourse to a dictionary or glossary is necessary, as is some examination of their grammatical structure. You may need help to understand these words:

brazen: made of brass

grace: honor

disgrace: disfigurement, decay (This is not a customary use of the word even in Shakespeare, but the contrast between *grace* and *disgrace* is poetically effective.)

cormorant: ravenous, rapacious (A cormorant is a rapacious bird that catches fish in its beak. It also means a greedy person. Shakespeare uses the noun as an adjective.)

bate: blunt (*Bate* means to reduce the intensity of, used in such terms as "with bated breath"—when we catch our breath in fear—or "the fire raged unabated." We must see the familiar picture of Father Time with an hourglass in one hand and a scythe in the other.)

Academe: a place of learning, coming from the name of the grove where Plato and his students met to discuss philosophy.

A prosaic line-by-line paraphrase would be:

We will allow fame, that all men seek to achieve during their lives,
To come to us through the inscriptions on the brass plates on our tombs,
So that we will be honored, not during our lives but after we have decayed in
    death,
When (that is, after death), in defiance of the way time obliterates men's
    fame,
What we are going to do during our lives will assure us
An honor that will defeat the usual effects of time,
And perpetuate our memory forever.
Therefore, valiant fighters—for you are valiant
In your struggle to overcome your lustful desires
And to resist the many temptations the world offers—
The proclamation I have recently issued * will be enforced:
All the world will be impressed with what is taking place in our country;
Our court will become a center of learning comparable to Plato's academy,
Where we will quietly study the art of living.

EXERCISE   Find the operative words in this speech. There will be more than one in each sentence, but remember that each sentence should be unified into a

* The terms of the edict are described in the succeeding lines. For three years they are to live apart from the world, giving attention only to their studies, and without the company of women.

single structure with its parts related to the whole through the proper use of subordination. Notice that "Therefore, brave conquerors," with the following subordinate clause, is a transition between the terminal point at the end of the first sentence and a new attack on the second. Memorize this speech and rehearse it until you have control of both its meaning and its form. This kind of hard work is essential. It demonstrates the truth of the saying: "Art is 90 percent perspiration and 10 percent inspiration."

Looking Forward

In the previous section on *Handling the Sentence* we have stressed the importance of finding the operative words and directing the rest of the sentence toward them—if not like a whirlwind, as Grotowski suggests, at least in some form of progression. We must feel when an actor is speaking that his lines are "going somewhere," and it is following this progression of thought and feeling that keeps the audience listening. The actor, like the traveler, must keep moving in some predetermined direction, and he has to structure his dialogue with this direction in mind.

Besides the examples already cited, dramatists have other ways of giving direction and forward movement to their lines. The simplest is a series of two or more members in which each member receives increasing emphasis as the series progresses. One of the best-known lines in dramatic literature is the series with which Antony begins his funeral oration for Julius Caesar.

Friends, Romans, countrymen, lend me your ears;
                    (Act III, Scene 2)

The Prince of Verona uses a similar construction in breaking up the street brawl between the Montagues and the Capulets.

Rebellious subjects, enemies to peace,
Profaners of this neighbour-stained steel,—
Will they not hear? What, ho! you men, you beasts . . .
                    (Act I, Scene 1)

In *The Lady's Not for Burning*, by Christopher Fry, Jennet has told how her father, an alchemist, once accidentally turned base metal into gold, and how he died trying to rediscover the formula. The cynical Thomas Mendip answers that if he had been successful

                    . . . you
Would be eulogised, lionised, probably
Canonised for your divine mishap.[6]

---

[6] Christopher Fry, *The Lady's Not for Burning*.

Effective handling of such structures requires looking forward to the end and building the series to a climax.

There is also a *ladder* device in which the idea is "stepped-up," like ascending the rungs of a ladder, by a careful progression of words. Starting at the bottom, one must look forward to the top rung. Claudius makes this toast to Hamlet before the duel he has plotted between Hamlet and Laertes.

> And let the *kettle* to the *trumpet* speak,
> The *trumpet* to the *cannoneer* without,
> The *cannons* to the *heavens*, the *heavens* to the *earth*,
> "Now the king drinks to Hamlet!"
>
> (Act V, Scene 2)

Hamlet's mother is overcome with grief when he makes her aware of her guilty behavior.

> Be thou assur'd, if words be made of *breath*,
> And *breath* of *life*, I have no *life* to *breathe*
> What thou hast said to me.
>
> (Act III, Scene 4)

In *As You Like It*, Rosalind tells Orlando how Celia and Oliver fell in love.

> . . . for your brother and my sister no sooner *met* but they *looked*; no sooner *looked* but they *loved*; no sooner *loved* but they *sighed*; no sooner *sighed* but they asked one another the *reason*; no sooner knew the *reason* but they sought the *remedy*: and in these degrees have they made a pair of stairs to marriage which they will *climb incontinent*, or else *be* incontinent before marriage.
>
> (Act V, Scene 2)

Polixenes in *The Winter's Tale* has been wrongly accused of misconduct with the wife of his good friend King Leontes. He ponders his fate when he hears of the accusation.

> This jealousy
> Is for a *precious* creature: as she's *rare*
> Must it be *great*, and as his person's *mighty*
> Must it be *violent*, and as he does conceive
> He is dishonour'd by a man *which ever*
> *Profess'd to him*, why, his revenges must
> In that be made more *bitter*.
>
> (Act I, Scene 2)

EXERCISE   Study and rehearse these examples of progressive structure. Memorize them. Work on them until you have complete control of the form as a way of expressing the meaning.

Another way in which dramatists "progress" the lines is by piling, one on top of another, details that accumulate to create a total effect. This is called *periodic* structure. Periodic means "consisting of a series of repeated stages," which well describes this method. The repeated stages build to a climax with no trailing subordinate elements afterward to minimize their effectiveness. Again, it is a structure that requires careful handling. From the very beginning, the actor must look forward to the end and keep moving toward it. Shakespeare often used periodic structure. A classic example is John of Gaunt's description of England in *Richard II*.

> This royal throne of kings, this scept'red isle,
> This earth of majesty, this seat of Mars,
> This other Eden, demi-paradise,
> This fortress built by nature for herself
> Against infection and the hand of war,
> This happy breed of men, this little world,
> This precious stone set in a silver sea,
> Which serves it in the office of a wall,
> Or as a moat defensive to a house,
> Against the envy of less happier lands,
> This blessed plot, this earth, this realm, this England . . .
> (Act II, Scene 1)

There actually are several more "stages" before the final climax.

Periodic structure is not always so formal. Sean O'Casey uses it in *Juno and the Paycock* when Mrs. Madigan describes how "her man" used to court her.

> "That'll scratch your lovely, little white neck," says he, ketchin' hould of a danglin' bramble branch, holdin' clusters of the loveliest flowers you ever seen, an' breakin' it off, so that his arm fell, accidental like, roun' me waist, an' as I felt it tightenin', an tightenin', an tightenin', I thought me buzzom was every minute goin' to burst out into a roystherin' song about
>> "The little green leaves that were shakin' on the threes,
>> The gallivantin' buttherflies, an' buzzin' o' the bees!" [7]

Arthur Kopit uses this structure in *Indians* when Wild Bill Hickok is standing over the beautiful Teskanjavila.

> Hickok, fastest shooter in the West, 'cept for Billy the Kid, who ain't as accurate; Hickok, deadliest shooter in the West, 'cept for Doc Holliday, who wields a sawed-off shotgun, which ain't fair; Hickok, shootinest shooter in the West, 'cept for Jesse James, who's absolutely indiscriminate; this Hickok, strong as an eagle, tall as a mountain, swift as the wind, fierce as a rattle-snake—a legend in

---

[7] Sean O'Casey, *Juno and the Paycock*. Macmillan and Co., Ltd.

his own time, or any other—this Hickok stands now above an Indian maiden . . .[8]

It is interesting to note how, for comic effect, Kopit has Teskanjavila ruin the climax of Hickok's splendid speech, and he is forced to weaken it by adding subordinate elements.

TESKANJAVILA. I'm not an Indian and I'm not a maiden!
HICKOK. Who's not an Indian and not a maiden, but looks pretty good anyhow. . . .

EXERCISE   Work on these selections. Find other examples of periodic structure for study and practice.

Looking Backward

Paradoxically, though the actor needs constantly to be looking forward building toward a culminating point, he must also at times look backward referring to what has already been said. We will call this particular usage *back reference*. Actors frequently miss this construction. Consequently, they choose to "operate" on a word or phrase that has already been emphasized, rather than selecting words that will advance the idea. In Hamlet's soliloquy "To be, or not to be" (Act III, Scene 1) he says

Whether 'tis nobler in the mind to suffer
The slings and arrows of outrageous fortune,
Or to take arms against a sea of troubles,
And by opposing end them?

"Sea of troubles" refers back to, in this case is synonymous with, "outrageous fortune." The operative words that carry the idea forward are *take arms*.

Portia's famous Mercy Speech in *The Merchant of Venice* (Act IV, Scene 1) begins with a back reference. After all legal recourses to save Antonio's life have been fruitless, she declares Shylock must be merciful. He retorts with

On what compulsion must I? tell me that.

And Portia answers

The quality of mercy is not strained,
It droppeth as the gentle rain from heaven
Upon the place beneath . . .

[8] Arthur Kopit, *Indians*. Hill & Wang.

Strained means *forced* or *compelled*; it is a back reference to Shylock's *compulsion*.

A back reference may be to something that has been said sometime before. In George Bernard Shaw's *Major Barbara*, the spineless Stephen Undershaft, who after an expensive education has lived always on his mother's income, declares he may go into politics. Later after claiming that he is unequipped for almost every profession, but that he does know the difference between right and wrong, his father says

. . . he knows nothing but thinks he knows everything. That points clearly to a political career.

The operative word, of course, is *clearly* referring back to Stephen's earlier declaration. Back reference is often used for comic effect.

Making Contrasts

The choice of operative words is often determined by the playwright's use of *contrast emphasis*. This is a practice in which emphasis is placed on the difference between two terms, or on the possibility of two or more alternatives. The words expressing these differences, or stating the alternative choices of action, are always emphasized. It is a pithy mode of expression as is apparent in such well-known sayings as "It is more blessed to *give* than to *receive*," or by the double contrast emphasis in "To *err* is *human*; to *forgive*, *divine*." The lines quoted from the "To be, or not to be" soliloquy as an example of back reference are also an example of contrast emphasis. The emphatic contrasting words are *suffer* and *take arms*. The alternatives are whether it is better to endure the slings and arrows of outrageous fortune or to take a positive stand against them.

The actor should be alert to the frequent occurrence of contrast emphasis in dramatic dialogue, and he should always handle the words so that the contrast is clearly made. A few examples will be sufficient to make this usage plain. All of these examples are from contemporary or classic plays.

It is not only *unusual*, madam. I might even say it is *suspicious*.[9]

An investigation of *my* affairs would lead to an investigation of *his* affairs. . . .[10]

ALICE. Kurt, we're *leaving*.
EDGAR. You're *staying*.[11]

[9] Luigi Pirandello, *Right You Are If You Think You Are*.
[10] Friedrich Duerrenmatt, *Play Strindberg*.
[11] Friedrich Duerrenmatt, *Play Strindberg*.

I pray you, father, *being* weak, *seem* so. [12]

I have *hope* to *live*, and am *prepared* to *die*. [13]

And let my *liver* rather *heat* with *wine*
Than my *heart cool* with mortifying *groans*. [14]

Let that fool *kill hisse'lf*. Ain't no call for *you to he'p him*. [15]

OL' CAP'N. Who's been putting these integrationary ideas in my boy's head? Was it you—I'm asking you a question, dammit! Was it *you*?
IDELLA. Why don't you ask *him*? [16]

EXERCISES   (1) Find the contrast emphases in the following selections. Rehearse them so you can clearly communicate the meanings.

In *The Tempest*, Ferdinand, much in love with Miranda, is forced by her father to do menial labor. He must "remove some thousand logs and pile them up."

FERDINAND. (*Bearing a log.*)
There be some sports are painful, and their labour
Delight in them sets off: some kinds of baseness
Are nobly undergone and most poor matters
Point to rich ends. This my mean task
Would be as heavy to me as odious, but
The mistress which I serve quickens what's dead
And makes my labours pleasures: O, she is
Ten times more gentle than her father's crabbed,
And he's composed of harshness.

In *Othello*, Desdemona, having eloped with Othello, is confronted by her father as to "where most she owes obedience."

DESDEMONA.   My noble father,
I do perceive here a divided duty:
To you I am bound for life and education;
My life and education both do learn me
How to respect you; you are the lord of duty;

12 William Shakespeare, *King Lear*.
13 William Shakespeare, *Measure for Measure*.
14 William Shakespeare, *The Merchant of Venice*.
15 Charles Gordone, *No Place to Be Somebody*.
16 Ossie Davis, *Purlie Victorious*.

I am hitherto your daughter. But here's my husband,
And so much duty as my mother showed
To you, preferring you before her father,
So much I challenge that I do profess
Due to the Moor my lord.

(2) Find in the plays you are reading ten examples of contrast emphasis.

Sharing the Imagery

In Chapter 7 we discussed the technique of relating to images—pictures that the actor supplies from his imagination. Dramatists also make extensive use of images in their dialogue, and communicating these images to the audience through the dramatist's words is one of the actor's major tasks in handling language. Peter Brook says:

> The exchange of impressions through images is our basic language: at the moment when one man expresses an image at that same instant the other man meets him in belief. The shared association is the language—if the association evokes nothing in the second person, if there is no instance of shared illusion, there is no exchange. . . . The vividness and fulness of this momentary illusion depends on his [the speaker's] conviction and skill.[17]

Imagery is defined as "the representation through language of sense experience." And, of course, sensory experience is one of the pleasures derived from going to the theatre. The definition continues:

> The word *image* perhaps most often suggests a mental picture, something seen in the mind's eye—and *visual* imagery is the most frequently occurring kind. . . . But an image may also represent a sound; a smell; a taste; a tactile experience, such as hardness, wetness, or cold; an internal sensation, such as hunger, thirst, or nausea; or movement or tension in the muscles or joints.[18]

Although they both serve the same purpose of providing a vivid sensory experience, images are of two kinds: *literal* and *figurative*. A figurative image expresses something in terms ordinarily used for expressing something else; thus some comparison is either stated or implied. A literal image is a direct description of whatever is intended to stimulate the sensory response. "The russet dawn colors the eastern sky" and "She talks about her secret as she sleeps upon her pillow" are literal images. But in *Hamlet* and *Macbeth*, Shakespeare says in figurative language:

But look, the morn in russet mantle clad
Walks o'er the dew of yon high eastern hill,

[17] Peter Brook, *The Empty Space* (New York: Atheneum, 1968), pp. 77–78.
[18] Laurence Perrine, *Sound and Sense* (New York: Harcourt Brace Jovanovich, 1956), p. 40.

and

Infected minds
To their deaf pillows will discharge their secrets.

The terminology relating to imagery can be very complex. More than two hundred kinds of figurative speech have been identified. It is neither necessary nor desirable for the actor to become entangled in such subtlety. It *is* essential that for both literal and figurative images he appreciate the sensory experience the dramatist is expressing, and that in figurative language he understand the aptness of the comparison. And he must respond to imagery with *all* his senses. Consider Sam Shepard's description in *Red Cross* of swimming in the rain.

JIM. . . . Your body stays warm inside. It's just the outside that gets wet. It's really neat. I mean you can dive under the water and hold your breath. You stay under for about five minutes. You stay down there and there's nothing but water all around you. Nothing but marine life. You stay down as long as you can until your lungs start to ache. They feel like they're going to burst open. Then just at the point where you can't stand it anymore, you force yourself to the top. You explode out of the water gasping for air, and all this rain hits you in the face. You ought to try it.[19]

Consider these figurative images from *Macbeth* and *King Lear*:

Now does feel
His secret murders sticking on his hands.

Thou art a boil,
A plague-sore, an embossed carbuncle
In my corrupted blood.

Imagery has particular power to move both the actor and the audience emotionally. Consider Constance's lament for her lost son in *King John*:

Grief fills the room up of my absent child,
Lies in his bed, walks up and down with me,
Puts on his pretty looks, repeats his words,
Remembers me of all his gracious parts,
Stuffs out his vacant garments with his form.

Imagery can be gorgeously beautiful, as in Romeo's response when he first sees Juliet:

O, she doth teach the torches to burn bright!
It seems she hangs upon the cheeks of night
As a rich jewel in an Ethiop's ear.

[19] Sam Shepard, *Red Cross*. Bobbs-Merrill Co.

It can be folksy, as in *The Shadow of a Gunman*:

MRS. HENDERSON. I'm afraid he'll never make a fortune out of what he's sellin'.
. . . Every time he comes to our place I buy a package of hairpins from him
to give him a little encouragement. I 'clare to God I have as many pins now
as ud make a wire mattress for a double bed.[20]

It can be earthy, as in *Purlie Victorious*:

OL' CAP'N. You don't know, boy, what a strong stomach it takes to stomach
you. Just look at you sitting there—all slopped over like something the horses
dropped; steam, stink and all! [21]

Practice the examples of imagery. Work to communicate as fully as possible the sensory experience the playwright intended to evoke.

EXERCISE

Work on several of the following speeches exploring the language and using it fully to communicate the meaning. Do whatever research is necessary to understand the words, the structures and the images.

EXERCISE

(1) First Voice in *Under Milk Wood*, a Play for Voices, by Dylan Thomas. (*The Voice is describing a small town in Wales.*)

FIRST VOICE. (*Very softly.*) It is Spring, moonless night in the small town, starless and bible-back, courters'-and-rabbits' wood limping invisible down to the sloeblack, slow, black, crowblack, fishingboat-bobbing sea. The houses are blind as moles (though moles see fine to-night in the snouting, velvet dingles) or blind as Captain Cat there in the muffled middle by the pump and the town clock, the shops in mourning, the Welfare Hall in widows' weeds. And all the people in the lulled and dumbfound town are sleeping now.

Hush, the babies are sleeping, the farmers, the fishers, the tradesmen and pensioners, cobbler, school-teacher, postman and publican, the undertaker and the fancy woman, drunkard, dressmaker, preacher, policeman, the web-foot cocklewomen and the tidy wives. Young girls lie bedded soft or glide in their dreams, with rings and trousseaux, bridesmaided by glowworms down the aisles of the organ-playing wood. The boys are dreaming wicked or of the bucking ranches of the night and the jollyrodgered sea. . . . You can hear the dew falling, and the hushed town breathing.[22]

[20] Sean O'Casey, *The Shadow of a Gunman*. Macmillan and Co., Ltd.
[21] Ossie Davis, *Purlie Victorious*. Samuel French.
[22] Dylan Thomas, *Under Milk Wood*. New Directions.

(2) Carol in *Red Cross*, by Sam Shepard.

(She stands on the bed and acts out the speech as though she were skiing on a mountain slope.)

CAROL. . . . I'll be at the top of this hill and everything will be all right. I'll be breathing deep. In and out. Big gusts of cold freezing air. My whole body will be warm and I won't even feel the cold at all. I'll be looking down and then I'll start to coast. Very slowly. I'm a good skier. I'll be halfway down and then I'll put on some steam. A little steam at first and then all the way into the egg position. The Europeans use it for speed. I picked it up when I was ten. I'll start to accumulate more and more velocity. The snow will start to spray up around my ankles and across my face and hands. My fingers will get tighter around the grips and I'll start to feel a little pull in each of my calves. Right along the tendons and in front, too. Everything will be working at once. All my balance and strength and breath. The whole works in one bunch. There'll be pine trees going past me and other skiers going up the hill. They'll stop and watch me go past. I'll be going so fast everyone will stop and look. They'll wonder if I'll make it. I'll do some jumps and twist my body with the speed. They'll see my body twist, and my hair and my eyes will water from the wind hitting them. My cheeks will start to sting and get all red. I'll get further and further into the egg position with my arms tucked up. I'll look down and see the valley and the cars and houses and people walking up and down. I'll see all the cabins with smoke coming out the chimneys.[23]

(3) Johnny in *No Place to Be Somebody*, by Charles Gordone.

(Johnny is a young Negro who runs a bar. He is talking to a white college girl who is agitating for the black cause.)

JOHNNY. Know what's in the daiquiri, baby? . . . Jizzum juice. A triple dose of jizmistic juice. Any minute you gonna turn into a depraved sex maniac! A teenage Jeckle an' Hide. Yo' head is gon' sprout fuzzy like somebody from the Fee-gee Eye-lan's. Yo' hot tongue'll roll out'a your mouth like a fat snake. You'll pant like'a go-rilla in heat. Yo' buzzooms will blow up like gas balloons an' the nipples will swell an' hang like ripe purple plums. Yo' behin' will begin to work like an ol' gray mare an' you'll strut aroun' flappin' yo' wings like'a raped duck. Then you'll suck me up with one mighty slurp an' fly out'a here a screamin' vampire. They'll finally subdue an' slay you on top'a the Empire State Buildin', with ray guns where you'll be attemptin' to empale yo'self astride that giant antenna. An' nobody will ever know that you, li'l Mary

[23] Sam Shepard, *Red Cross*.

Lou Bolton, who jus' graduated from Elmira College, was lookin' to lay down in front of a big, black bulldozer, to keep America safe for democracy.[24]

(4) Miss Amelia in *The Ballad of the Sad Cafe*, by Edward Albee.

(*Miss Amelia Evans, a woman of independent mind and habits, runs a general store and a cafe in a small Southern town. Since her father's death, she has lived a lonely life. She speaks of her father and her past only to Cousin Lymon whom she has recently befriended.*)

MISS AMELIA. (*With a remembering smile.*) Law, I remember when I was little, I slept and slept. I'd go to bed just as the lamp was turned on and sleep—why, I'd sleep like I was drowned in warm axle grease. Then come daybreak Papa would walk in and put his hand on my shoulder. "Get stirring, Little," he would say. Then later he would holler up the stairs from the kitchen when the stove was hot. "Fried grits," he would holler. "White meat and gravy. Ham and eggs." And I'd run down the stairs and dress by the hot stove while he was washing up out at the pump. Then off we'd go to the still. . . . And when Papa would run off liquor in those days . . . or when he would take me with him when he buried the barrels . . . an' we would go, an . . . I loved my poppa. Momma dyin' as she did, birthin' me . . .[25]

(5) Juliet in *Romeo and Juliet*, by William Shakespeare.

(*To prevent her having to marry Paris, Friar Laurence has given Juliet a potion which will make her appear as dead. She will then remain in the family vault until Romeo comes from banishment to rescue her. She has said goodnight to her mother and her nurse, and is now alone realizing she must drink the potion.*)

JULIET. Farewell! God knows when we shall meet again.
I have a faint cold fear thrills through my veins,
That almost freezes up the heat of life:
I'll call them back again to comfort me:
Nurse? What should she do here?
My dismal scene I needs must act alone.
Come, vial.
What if this mixture do not work at all?
Shall I be married then tomorrow morning?
No, no; this shall forbid it. Lie thou there.
  (*Laying down a dagger*)

---

[24] Charles Gordone, *No Place to Be Somebody*. Bobbs-Merrill Co.

[25] Edward Albee, *The Ballad of the Sad Cafe*. A dramatization of a novel by Carson McCullers. Copyright 1936, 1951, by Carson McCullers; reprinted by permission of Robert Lantz on behalf of the Estate of Carson McCullers.

What if it be a poison, which the friar
Subtly hath minister'd to have me dead,
Lest in this marriage he should be dishonor'd,
Because he married me before to Romeo?
I fear it is: and yet, methinks, it should not,
For he hath still been tried a holy man.
How, if, when I am laid into the tomb,
I wake before the time that Romeo
Come to redeem me? there's a fearful point!
Shall I not then be stifled in the vault,
To whose foul mouth no healthsome air breathes in,
And there die strangled ere my Romeo comes?
Or, if I live, is it not very like,
The horrible conceit of death and night,
Together with the terror of the place,
As in a vault, an ancient receptacle,
Where, for this many hundred years, the bones
Of all my buried ancestors are pack'd;
Where bloody Tybalt, yet but green in earth,
Lies fest'ring in his shroud; where, as they say,
At some hours in the night spirits resort;
Alack, alack! is it not like that I
So early waking, what with loathsome smells,
And shrieks like mandrakes' torn out of the earth,
That living mortals hearing them run mad:
O! if I wake, shall I not be distraught,
Environed with all these hideous fears,
And madly play with my forefathers' joints,
And pluck the mangled Tybalt from his shroud?
And, in this rage, with some great kinsman's bone,
As with a club, dash out my desperate brains?
O! look, methinks I see my cousin's ghost
Seeking out Romeo, that did spit his body
Upon a rapier's point. Stay, Tybalt, stay!
Romeo, I come! this do I drink to thee.
    (*Falls upon the bed*)

(6) Romeo in *Romeo and Juliet*, by William Shakespeare.

(*Romeo, believing Juliet is dead, comes to the tomb to say farewell and to die at her side.*)

ROMEO. How oft when men are at the point of death
    Have they been merry! which their keepers call

A lightning before death: O! how may I
Call this a lightning? O my love! my wife!
Death, that has suck'd the honey of thy breath,
Hath had no power yet upon thy beauty:
Thou art not conquer'd; beauty's ensign yet
Is crimson in thy lips and in thy cheeks,
And death's pale flag is not advanced there.
Tybalt, liest thou there in thy bloody sheet?
O! what more favor can I do to thee
Than with that hand that cut thy youth in twain
To sunder his that was thine enemy?
Forgive me, cousin! Ah, dear Juliet,
Why art thou yet so fair? shall I believe
That unsubstantial Death is amorous,
And that the lean abhorred monster keeps
Thee here in dark to be his paramour?
For fear of that I still will stay with thee,
And never from this palace of dim night
Depart again; here, here will I remain
With worms that are thy chambermaids; O! here
Will I set up my everlasting rest,
And shake the yoke of inauspicious stars
From this world-wearied flesh. Eyes, look your last!
Arms, take your last embrace! and, lips, O you
The doors of breath, seal with a righteous kiss
A dateless bargain to engrossing death!
Come, bitter conduct, come, unsavory guide!
Thou desperate pilot, now at once run on
The dashing rocks thy sea-sick weary bark!
Here's to my love! (*He drinks*) O true apothecary!
Thy drugs are quick. Thus with a kiss I die.

PART 3 THE ACTOR AND THE PRODUCTION

Learning the Lingo

13

When the actor starts rehearsals for a production, he has the advantage of working under the guidance of a director. The director, equipped with a thorough knowledge of the values of the play and the technical resourcefulness to realize them on the stage, will be concerned with developing the characterizations of the individual actors to make the greatest possible contribution to the play's total meaning. He will be eager to help the actor create a character which is true to the dramatist's intentions. He will be concerned with making each actor an effective part of his master plan—a plan often intricately complicated in its detail—for coordinating all aspects of the production into an artistic whole. To bring each actor to "performance level," he will work for clear speech, good projection, precise movement, rhythm, and energy. During the rehearsal period, he will give many directions using a standard terminology with which the actor must be familiar.

Like every profession, the theatre has its special vocabulary. Partly technical, partly slang, it is generally standardized on the English-speaking stage. It is as necessary for the actor to be familiar with it as for a mechanic to know the names of his tools or a surgeon the names of his instruments.

No effort will be made to provide here an exhaustive list of terms. At this point we need only those the actor is likely to encounter in the process of receiving directions. For convenience they are grouped into categories.

Stage Directions

Stage right The actor's right as he stands onstage facing the audience.
Stage left The actor's left as he stands onstage facing the audience.
Downstage Toward the audience.

STAGE AREAS. These abbreviations stand for: up right, up right center, up center, up left center, up left; right, right center, center, left center, left; down right, down right center, down center, down left center, down left.

Upstage Away from the audience.

Below Toward the audience. Same as "downstage of."

Above Away from the audience. Same as "upstage of."

(An actor who walks *below* a piece of furniture walks between the furniture and the audience; an actor who walks *above* a piece of furniture walks between the furniture and the upstage wall of the setting.)

In Toward the center of the stage.

Out Away from the center of the stage.

(The direction to *move in three feet* means to move three feet closer to the center of the stage; to move *out three feet* means to move three feet farther away from the center of the stage.)

Stage Areas

In order that a director may designate an actor's position onstage precisely, the acting portion of the stage is divided into fifteen areas.

Onstage That part of the stage enclosed by the setting which is visible to the audience in any particular scene.

Offstage All parts of the stage not enclosed by the setting.

Backstage Usually the entire stage portion of the theatre building in contrast to the auditorium which is designated as *out front*.

Wings Offstage space at right and left of the acting areas.

Body Positions

In order to designate the position the actor is facing in relation to the audience, there are eight *body positions*.

Open An "open" position is one in which the actor is facing toward the audience, or nearly so. To "open" is to turn toward the audience. Since effective communication requires that the actor be seen and heard, he must—without sacrificing believability—keep himself as "open" as possible. Although there are frequent exceptions, you should follow these practices unless there is reason for doing otherwise:

1. Play shared scenes in a quarter position.
2. Make turns downstage.
3. Do not cover yourself or other actors in making gestures or passing objects. In other words, use the upstage arm.
4. Kneel on the downstage knee.

Closed A "closed" position is one in which the actor is turned away from the audience. To "close in" is to turn away from the audience.

Actor's Positions in Relation to Each Other

Actors' positions in relation to each other are considered with regard to the relative emphasis each actor receives.

Share Two actors *share* a scene when they are both "open" to an equal degree, allowing the audience to see them equally well.

Give, take When two actors are not equally "open" and one receives a greater emphasis than the other, the actor emphasized is said to *take* the scene. The other is said to *give* the scene.

Upstaging The term applied when one actor takes a position above another actor which forces the second actor to face upstage, or away from the audience. Since the downstage actor is put at a disadvantage, "upstaging" has an unpleasant connotation and is generally to be avoided. You should take positions on the exact level of the actor with whom you are playing. Learn neither intentionally nor unintentionally to upstage another actor unless you are directed to do so.

FULL BACK

THREE QUARTERS RIGHT

THREE QUARTERS LEFT

PROFILE RIGHT

PROFILE LEFT

ONE QUARTER RIGHT

ONE QUARTER LEFT

FULL FRONT

BODY POSITIONS

SHARED POSITIONS

GIVEN AND TAKEN POSITIONS

UPSTAGING

Stage Movement

Blocking The arrangement of the actors' movements on stage with respect to each other and the stage space. Some of the purposes of blocking are to tell the story, develop characterization, set mood and atmosphere, and create suspense.

Cross Movement from one area to another. In writing it is abbreviated by X.

Countercross A movement in the opposite direction in adjustment to the cross of another actor. The instruction usually given is "Counter to left" or "Counter to right." If only a small adjustment is necessary, the actor should make it without being told.

CURVED CROSSES

Curved cross In crossing to a person or an object above or below you, it is necessary to cross in a curve so you do not arrive either upstage or downstage of the person or object. Follow the solid lines in the drawings.

Cover An actor is said to be *covered* when another actor moves into a position between him and the audience, thus obstructing him from view. Covering is usually to be avoided. These principles and practices are generally to be observed:

1. The responsibility is on the downstage actor. In other words, do not stand in front of another actor.
2. If another actor *does* stand directly below you, make a small adjusting movement.

3. Since a moving actor usually should receive attention, make crosses *below* other actors so you are not covered. This rule does not apply if the moving actor should not receive attention.

Dress Stage   A direction requesting the actors to adjust their positions to improve the compositional effect of the stage picture.

Stage Business

Small actions, such as smoking, eating, slapping, falling, telephoning, crying, using a fan, and tying a necktie, are known on the stage as "business."

Properties

Business often involves the use of properties. *Props*, as they are commonly called, are divided into several categories.

Hand props   Small objects which the actors handle onstage such as teacups, letters, books, candies.

Personal props   Hand props which are carried on the actor's person and are used only by him—such as watches, spectacles, cigarette holders. An actor is usually responsible for taking care of his personal props during rehearsals and performances.

Costume props   Costume accessories used by the actor in executing business—such as fans, walking sticks, gloves, handbags.

Stage props   Objects for dressing the stage which are not used by the actors in executing their business. Vases of flowers, lamps, clocks, bric-a-brac might be stage props.

Prop table   Tables are usually placed offstage right and left to accommodate props which the actors carry on and off the set. The property master and the stage manager are responsible for placing props on the tables, but a careful actor checks his props before each performance. And it is the actor's responsibility to return immediately to the table all props he carries off the set.

Lines and Dialogue

Ad lib   Coming from the Latin *ad libitum* (at pleasure), the term applies to lines supplied by the actor wherever they may be required as in crowd scenes or to fill in where there would otherwise be an undesirable pause. "Ad libs" must be motivated and related to the character's intention as carefully as the playwright's dialogue. Mechanical or indifferent "ad libs" can destroy belief in an otherwise effective scene.

Aside A line which the other actors onstage are not supposed to be hearing. The aside was a regular convention in plays of the seventeenth, eighteenth, and nineteenth centuries. It is rarely used by modern dramatists.

Build To increase the tempo or the volume or both in order to reach a climax.

Cue The last words of a speech, or the end of an action, indicating the time for another actor to speak or act. An actor must memorize his cues as carefully as he memorizes his lines.

Drop Lines on which the actor does not project his voice sufficiently to be heard are said to be *dropped*. The direction in such a case is usually, "Don't drop your lines." The term is also used to mean unintentional omission of lines.

Pick up cues A direction for the actor to begin speaking immediately on cue without allowing any lapse of time. Beginning actors tend to be slow in picking up cues with the result that they often fail to maintain a tempo fast enough to hold the interest of the audience.

Pointing Giving special emphasis to a word or phrase. An actor may also be directed to "point" a movement or a piece of business.

Tag line The last line of a scene or an act. It usually needs to be "pointed."

Telescoping Overlapping speeches so that one actor speaks before another has finished. It is a technique for accelerating the pace and building a climax.

Top To "build" a line higher than the one that preceded it.

Miscellaneous Terms

Act drop A drop curtain lowered at the end of acts. Often it is a drop especially painted for a particular play.

Apron The part of the stage that extends toward the audience in front of the curtain. Also termed *forestage*.

Asbestos The fireproof curtain that closes the proscenium opening and separates the stage from the auditorium in case of fire.

Auditions Readings of specific roles before the director to determine casting. In both the professional and nonprofessional theatre, plays are usually cast through auditions.

Back drop The drop farthest upstage in any setting.

Backing A drop or flats used outside an opening in the setting such as a door or window.

Bit part A small part with few lines.

Call board A backstage bulletin board on which notices of concern to the actors are posted.

Center line An imaginary line running in the exact center of the stage from the edge of the apron to the upstage wall. Actors are sometimes directed to take positions in relation to the center line.

Cheating A term used without any derogatory meaning when an actor plays in a more open position, or performs an action more openly, than complete realism would permit.

Clear stage A direction given by the stage manager for everyone not immediately involved to leave the stage preparatory to the beginning of an act or to striking the setting.

Costume parade Prior to the first dress rehearsal, actors are sometimes requested to appear onstage wearing their costumes. This appearance permits the director and the designer to check each costume and make necessary alterations before the dress rhearsals.

Crowd scenes Scenes involving a number of extras or bit players. Crowd scenes are usually rehearsed separately and then integrated with the rest of the production.

Curtain call The appearance of actors onstage after the performance to acknowledge the applause of the audience. Curtain calls are carefully rehearsed. Actors are required to remain in costume and make-up and to take the calls as rehearsed without variation. The term applies whether or not a curtain has been used.

Curtain line The imaginary line across the stage floor which the front curtain touches when it is closed.

Ensemble scene A scene in which audience attention is focused on the characters as a group rather than as individuals. Actually all group scenes when well played are ensemble scenes.

Extra A small nonspeaking part: soldiers, townspeople, ladies-in-waiting, and so forth.

Faking Business which is not possible or practical actually to perform is "faked." For example, writing a letter realistically would take too much time; knocking an opponent to the floor might injure the actor.

Flats The canvas-covered frames that constitute the walls of a stage setting.

Flies The space above the stage in which scenery is suspended.

Freezing Mechanically holding a position or an expression. The nonspeaking actors at one time "froze" during an aside. It is not a common technique in the modern theatre.

Front curtain A curtain closing the proscenium opening which hangs immediately behind the asbestos. It is usually used as the act drop.

Green room A room located close to the stage in which the actors may await entrance cues and receive guests after the performance.

Gridiron A contrivance located in the flies for suspending scenery.

Ground plan The arrangement of doors, windows, steps, levels, furniture, and so forth for a stage setting; also a diagram showing the arrangements. The director usually explains the ground plan at an early rehearsal. Each actor should draw the diagram in his script and make sure that he thoroughly understands the arrangement.

Half-hour The time at which an actor is required to be in his dressing-room before a performance. It is usually, although not always, thirty minutes before curtain. On arriving at the theatre, each actor is required to "check in" with the stage manager, usually by initialing a cast list.

Indicating A term, derogatory in the psychologically motivated drama, for performing an action without an intention.

Mugging A derogatory term for exaggerated facial expression.

Pacing Although some directors attempt to distinguish between *pace* and *tempo*, for practical purposes they both mean the rate of speed at which the actors speak their lines, pick up their cues, perform their actions—the length and number of the pauses. Pace is a subtle, and *vital*, element in a performance. Frequently heard directions are "Pick up the pace" or "The pace is too slow (or too fast)."

Places A direction given by the stage manager for everyone to be in his proper position for the beginning of an act.

Proscenium The wall dividing the stage from the auditorium.

Proscenium opening The arched opening in the proscenium wall through which the audience sees the stage.

Run-through An uninterrupted rehearsal of a scene, an act, or the entire play. In contrast to the "running" rehearsal is the "working" rehearsal in which either the director or the actors may stop to work on details.

Stealing A director may ask an actor to "steal." He wants a movement which will not receive audience attention. The term is also used to mean taking audience attention when it should be elsewhere. Scene stealers, either intentional or unintentional, are not well-liked in any cast.

Strike The direction given by the stage manager to change the setting for another scene or to dismantle it at the end of a performance.

Trap An opening in the stage floor.

Try-outs Auditions.

Walk-on A small part without lines. An extra.

Acting in the Round

Theatre-in-the-round is also called "arena staging" or "central staging." An arena theatre is similar in arrangement to a sports arena. This method of production, in which a centrally located acting area is surrounded by the audience, demands in some instances its own terminology. The vocabulary of the picture-frame stage having to do with direction and position (stage right and left, up and down, one quarter right, and so forth) does not apply because the actor and the audience are in a different relationship.

The arena is possibly the oldest natural form of theatre and dance space, possibly prehistoric, but it is comparatively recent in the modern theatre. Following World War II, there was a sudden boom in arena theatres, partly because they represented a break with the formality of the proscenium stage, and partly because arena theatres are more economical to build and maintain than proscenium theatres. Today there are arena stages all over the United States: Buffalo, New York; Washington, D.C.; Houston, Texas; and Nashville, Tennessee.

Production of *Project Immortality* at the Arena Stage in Washington, D.C. (Photo—courtesy of the Arena Stage, Washington, D.C.) Arena theatres add a great deal of intimacy to the theatre-going experience, as well as providing a challenge to actors who have acted only on proscenium or thrust stages.

ACTING AREAS IN ARENA

So far no vocabulary for central staging has come into general use. There is a practice of designating acting areas in either one of two ways: according to the points of the compass or according to the hours of the clock. Thus, an actor may be directed to cross either to "northwest" or to "ten o'clock."

Theatre-in-the-round is truly an "actors' theatre." Since it cannot use standing scenery, nor make extensive use of many kinds of stage effects, the actor bears a greater responsiblity for communicating the play to the audience. There is, however, no basic difference in creating a character in the arena and on the proscenium stage. Such differences as exist are the result of the actor's having to make technical adjustments to different actor-audience relationships. The actor in arena must be heard and seen from all sides rather than from one. The closeness of the audience, the fact that spectators are sitting only a few feet from the acting area, may be distracting and add an additional complication to the problem of concentration. Furthermore, this same closeness makes an exacting demand for maintaining an unwavering belief throughout the performance.

There is an increasing popularity of the *thrust* or *peninsula* stage, sometimes called "three-quarter round." It provides a physical actor-audience relationship roughly comparable to the Elizabethan theatre. In fact, the modern thrust stage is a conscious modern adaptation of that form to modern theatre. The stage juts out, or thrusts, into the auditorium so that the audience sits on three sides. The fourth side is an architectural façade, often permitting some variation, which provides exits and entrances. It is a combination of proscenium and arena offering some of the best features of both. The terminology and the problems it presents to the actors are also a combination of the two methods.

The great plays of the Greek and Elizabethan theatres were written for the thrust stage. More recent plays such as Arthur Miller's *After the Fall*, David Rabe's *Streamers*, and Dale Wasserman's musical *Man of La Mancha* also were written to be performed on thrust stages. Among the most popular thrust

Production of *Design for Living* by Noel Coward at the Tyrone Guthrie Theatre in Minneapolis. (Photo—Robert Ashley Wilson.) The Guthrie is one of the world's most famous thrust stages. This unique, seven-sided thrust stage is surrounded by the audience in a 200-degree arc. No seat is more than 52 feet from the center of the stage. Built in 1963, the Guthrie auditorium was designed by Sir Tyrone Guthrie and Tanya Moiseiwitsch.

stages are the Tyrone Guthrie Theatre in Minneapolis and the Stratford Festival of Canada Theatre in Stratford, Ontario (see p. 257).

You will not be ready to work with a director until you are familiar with standard terminology and proficient in stage mechanics. Practice these exercises carefully. They are an important part of your training.

EXERCISES

GROUND PLAN

(1) Using the above ground plan, rehearse the directions given below:

Enter UR from L.
X L of desk to DRC.
Take position three-quarter L.
Turn downstage to one-quarter R.
Sit DR.
X above desk to below table UC.
Sit L of fireplace.
X R of ottoman to DLC.
X below desk, exit R.
Enter R.
X above desk to fireplace.
Take full back position.
X C.
Sit L of desk.
X below ottoman to DL.
X above ottoman, exit URC to R.
Enter URC from R.
X below desk to DC.

X above ottoman to cabinet L.
Take position half R.
Sit upstage side of ottoman.
X R of ottoman, sit DL.
X R of ottoman, exit UL.
Enter UL, X RC to above desk.
Sit upstage of desk facing L.
Open your position.
X R of desk to DLC.
Sit downstage side of ottoman facing front.
X DR.
X in 3 ft.
X up 3 ft.

(2) Work with a partner making crosses in relation to each other. Practice sharing, giving, and taking positions.

(3) Practice giving stage directions to your partner. Reverse roles and take directions from him.

(4) These exercises have provided practice in the mechanics of movement. In a production, mere mechanical movement is without dramatic interest. Everything the actor does must have a purpose. A movement is usually made in relation to some person or some object. For example, you move to the desk to answer the phone, to hide papers in the drawer. You cross to the fireplace to get warm, to place a vase of flowers on the mantel. You exit because you are secretly leaving home, because you are angry about what is happening in the room. Now repeat these movements providing from your imagination a motivation for each one.

Rehearsing the Play

14 Long before rehearsals begin, the actor encounters the director at that nerve-racking experience, the audition. The audition is a simple, time-saving way for a director to become familiar with numerous actors in an attempt to find those who most closely resemble the director's concept of the characters in the play being cast. The director uses the audition to find an actor fit to play a certain part who is also physically right for the part and will blend well with the other cast members.

In most auditions, whether for college, stock, or professional productions, an actor is called upon to read a scene from the play being cast. Actors may get the scene when they arrive for the audition and only have a short time to look it over. At other times, they simply may be interviewed by the director or asked to do a monologue or scene prepared for the occasion. The League of Regional Theatres (LORT) customarily auditions actors by allotting them a total of three minutes, asking that they prepare one dramatic and one comedic piece to perform within the allotted time.

There are as many ways to hold auditions as there are directors, and an actor should not be alarmed at a director who uses unusual methods to determine an actor's suitability for a role. In *A Chorus Line*, a musical about dancers auditioning for a Broadway musical, the "director" asks each dancer to talk about himself or herself as well as to dance. Some of the dancers rise to the occasion; others do not.

It is impossible to give sound advice that will cover all contingencies, but actors should maintain a variety of prepared pieces and avoid dialects that are "half-baked" and ring false. Be ready to improvise. Be honest. Present yourself and your abilities. Don't attempt to anticipate "what they want." Most important, do not blame yourself if you do not get the part. Competition is staggering for even the smallest parts, and soon you will learn to trust that most directors have a vision of the play, and their choices are rarely whimsical. Not being selected by a director is not necessarily a reflection of how you auditioned or how you act.

The pre-rehearsal period—after you have been cast, and before rehearsals begin—is a time for cast members to discover their roles and the structure of the play as a whole. It is a time to read about the period of the play, and, if appropriate, study the art and general history of the period. Do not be in a hurry to memorize lines and have your part blocked out. Study the play's structure, attempting to find out the part each character plays in the drama. Take a while to examine the play with fresh eyes—as if you had no role in it at all. Your flexibility toward your role early in rehearsals is just as important as your preparedness when rehearsals end.

During the rehearsal period the actor works with the director, the stage manager, the other actors, and, finally, with the various production crews. Everyone involved is working toward a single objective—the expression of the total meaning of the play. The actor must relate his performance to the production that the director has planned as a means of expressing the play to the audience. He must learn his proper relationship to the elements of modern theatre, including lights, scenery, costumes, sound, and many more. He must learn to fulfill his function in a demanding group enterprise. Producing a play is a fine example of cooperative effort—a process described by Harold Clurman as "the relating of a number of talents to a single meaning."[1] Although they often are not sharply defined, and there may be considerable overlapping, there are five principal phases in the process of rehearsal:

1. finding the meaning
2. developing the characters
3. creating the form
4. making technical adjustments
5. polishing for performance.

Finding the Meaning

If a production is to realize its possibilities, if it is to be the "relating of a number of talents to a single meaning," everyone working on the production must understand what that single meaning is. And everyone must understand how his particular part, small or large as it may be, contributes to the expression of it. That part of the rehearsal period devoted to finding the meaning is of fundamental importance.

[1] Harold Clurman, *The Fervent Years* (New York: Alfred A. Knopf, 1945), p. 41.

There are a number of ways in which the director, the actors, and the designers may come to an agreement. An understanding may be reached in group discussion, each person having analyzed the play beforehand and thus being ready to present his interpretation but being willing to modify it if necessary. The director, possibly having a more thorough knowledge of the play than anyone else, may teach his interpretation to the others. Or agreement may be reached through a combination of these approaches. A common procedure is a number of "reading rehearsals" in which actors sit in a circle reading aloud their individual parts and discussing the play with the director and with each other.

The important thing is that everyone clearly understands what the play means. Until this common understanding has been reached, the group is likely to be working at cross purposes and rehearsals cannot proceed effectively.

As soon as an interpretation has been agreed upon, each actor will search for the basic motivating desire of the character he is playing and its relationship to the total meaning. Here again discussion is in order. Agreement between the actor and the director is necessary. Usually, an understanding is reached during reading rehearsals. At the same time, the actor begins to consider the problem of line interpretation—of relating the lines to the character's motivating desire and to the meaning of the play as a whole.

The time given to finding the meaning through reading and discussion may vary from one rehearsal to as much as a third of the entire rehearsal period, depending upon the practice of the director and the subtleties of the play. It is a process that is rarely finished. New and deeper meanings are certain to reveal themselves during rehearsals and performances.

Although the actor and director are teammates, sharing the goal of excellence, they have different responsibilities. The director is the team captain who ultimately decides which particular actions move the play toward the desired effect. The director also interacts with other team members—set designer, lighting designer, costume designer, and property master—and most of all, with the playwright and the play. A play is not just an imitation of an action, but a work of art, requiring structure and focus that a director must create. The director guides actors in much the same way an acting teacher guides an acting class—supervising the production, inspiring an actor's own analysis, growth, and development, and serving as a formal friend.

College actors tend to expect directors to give them too much direction. Actors are creators. In addition to learning their roles, showing up at rehearsals, and adapting to different directorial methods and to their fellow actors, they should be self-reliant. The truly professional actor understands that the director's perspective is the totality, and that his or her word is final. The actor has a right to expect the director to help with some problems of nuance, style, and motivation, but not to teach acting or suffer tantrums from actors who have just had their their roles shaved by a line or two.

Developing the Character

With the meaning of the play in mind, the actor is ready to concentrate on characterization. It is at this time that he may find greatest satisfaction as a creative artist. He *explores* his inner resources to discover how he can use his experiences to understand the problems of the character. He *uses his imagination* to supply additional circumstances to round out the character's background and to aid him in believing the action. He *observes* people and objects to find helpful details. He reads, studies paintings, listens to music if he needs to enlarge his experience to understand any aspect of the play.

He makes a "breakdown" of his role into *beats*. He states the intention in each beat and relates it to the character's motivating desire. He makes a score of physical actions through which he can realize his intentions. He experiments in playing each beat both at home by himself and at rehearsals with the other actors.

At the same time the actor is working on his lines. He is studying them carefully to determine the motivation behind each line, to discover the under-meaning and the verbal action, and to relate them to the character's motivating desire. He is concerning himself with the background of the character's speech. If the background differs from his own, he is learning to reproduce the speech believably by listening to speakers with a similar background or to phonograph records. He is also memorizing his lines and cues.

Among professional actors practice in memorization varies widely. Lynn Fontanne has said that she has her lines memorized before she begins rehearsals so she is free to concentrate upon problems of character development. Alla Nazimova said she never memorized her lines. She "absorbed" them as she developed her character. She came finally to understand her role so thoroughly that she could *think* the lines as the playwright had written them without having actually committed them to memory.[2]

Both of these practices are extremes. There are dangers in memorizing the lines before the rehearsals begin. Without having had the opportunity of discussing the play with the director and other members of the cast, there is a possibility of forming opinions which are incorrect or, at least, at odds with the interpretation decided upon by the group. Once the actor has learned the lines, it may be difficult for him to modify the pattern that has become established. Gradual absorption is a time-consuming process. And anyone with a less superb technique than Mme. Nazimova's can hardly rely upon coming to think the lines without having memorized them—admirable as the theory may be. Granted adequate time for rehearsal, it is best not to memorize until you have completed your score—until you know your intentions, your physical and verbal actions, your structural units, your subtext, your monologues, your

---

[2] See Morton Eustis, *Players at Work* (New York: Theatre Arts Books, 1937).

images. Accurate memorization is another of the actor's responsibilities. He owes it to the dramatist who is dependent upon the actor for a truthful representation of his work. He owes it also to his fellow players whose own lines must be motivated by what has gone before.

As a general practice a policy of memorization somewhere between these two extremes is advisable. After the actor is familiar with the meaning of the play and with the motivating desire of his character, he will not establish incorrect interpretations. After the play has been blocked, the lines may be associated with the movement which is likely to clarify their meaning and make memorization easier. Circumstances may alter cases, but generally it is wise to have the lines memorized at the halfway point of the entire rehearsal period. This schedule allows the actor to gain advantage from the earlier rehearsals, and it insures his freedom from the burden of memorization during the final stage.

Creating the Form

In its narrowest and most practical application, creating the form means blocking the movement and inventing the business. There are many practical problems of blocking and business which must receive attention and which can be solved only by mechanical repetitions. But the form of a production is something more than blocking and business and mechanics. It is the external embodiment of the actor's inner characterization. Without it the actor can't convey either the dramatist's meaning or his own. It is his obligation not only to bring inner life to his characterization, but also to externalize this experience in a concrete form that is artistically valid. It is not enough that the form be lifelike. It must also be theatrically effective.

Creating the form is a rewarding, and sometimes agonizing, process. It does not spring full grown from the imaginations of either the actors or the director. It grows slowly. It comes in bits and pieces. It cannot be forced. It cannot be imposed from without. It comes from the combined imaginations of the actors and the director, stimulated initially by the playwright and later by the responses of the actors to each other and even to the props and setting. It must develop organically as the character develops. Form grows out of character and character out of form. What a character is determines what he does, and what he does determines what he is!

The actor's large movements (entrances and exits, crosses from one area to another) are to a great extent determined by the ground plan. They have, therefore, been carefully thought out by the director and the designer before rehearsals have begun, both of them being aware that the most important consideration in making the ground plan is the movement it will impose on the actors. The large movements become apparent as soon as the ground plan is explained. The actors accept and motivate them as they accept and motivate the dialogue provided by the dramatist. They accept, in fact, the director's concept, the scenic, costume, and light design as a part of the given circumstances.

There are always movements and other physical activities inherent in the lines, such as crossing to answer the doorbell or telephone, serving tea, or less obvious indications such as Kate's admonition to Hotspur, "In faith, I'll break thy little finger, Harry,/ An if thou wilt not tell me all things true," or Juliet's plea to Romeo, "Wilt thou be gone? It is not yet near day." Most modern dramatists also describe a part of the physicalization in their stage directions. But it is necessary to have additional movement and physical activity. The actor needs as many physical objectives as possible to give him belief in his character and, also, as a means of expressing the desires of the character in ways that the audience can *see* and understand. During this part of the rehearsal period actor and director are constantly using their imaginations to invent movement which will give outer form to inner characterization.

It is during this time that the actor decides what *externals* of manner, dress, action, and so forth will aid in characterization. These externals are vital because, as we recall from earlier chapters, *doing is believing*. The actor is likely to believe the character to the extent he can translate his desires into action. Such small things as using a handkerchief, eating a sandwich, rolling a cigarette, writing down an address, provide physical objectives on which the actor can concentrate his attention. Determining the amount and nature of the physical activity is a matter to be settled between actor and director. The director frequently makes suggestions. But the actor has both the opportunity and the responsibility for originating small actions which will help in creating form. Nowhere is the quality of the actor's imagination more evident than in this phase of his work. All business, like the lines and movement, must be justified in terms of the total meaning of the play and the production.

Costumes and properties are vastly important in creating the form. When properly related to, they become in themselves excellent "actors." And they are essential to the creation of a physical image. Stanislavski wrote:

> A costume or an object appropriate to a stage figure ceases to be a simple material thing, it acquires a kind of sanctity for an actor. . . . You can tell a true artist by his attitudes towards his costume and properties.[3]

Making Technical Adjustments

Somewhere toward the end of the rehearsal period the actors begin to work in the setting, with the properties that will be used in performance, in costume, and under the lights. At this time adjustments are always necessary. The furni-

[3] Stanislavski, *An Actor's Handbook*, p. 43.

ture may take up more space than the small chairs and tables the actors have been working with. Opening and closing actual doors may require more time than the actors have been allowing in pantomime. The position of a piano may have to be changed to improve the sight lines for the audience. The manipulation of the costumes may require more care than has been anticipated. A climactic scene may have to be played farther downstage in order that it may be lighted effectively. Certain actions may have to be repeated over and over to allow the lighting and sound crews to coordinate their timing with that of the actors.

Such adjustments are an inevitable part of rehearsal. They are necessary to realize fully the possibilities of the play. For a short time they may interfere with the actor's concentration and prevent him from believing the action he is performing. For the experienced actor, however, the period of discomfort is brief. He recognizes the necessity for the changes, and he immediately finds ways (sometimes by inventing additional "circumstances") to motivate them in terms of the desires of his character.

Polishing for Performance

The final rehearsals are devoted to polishing for performance. At this time experimentation ceases. Any feelings of tentativeness are eliminated. The actor has had opportunity during the earlier rehearsals to try different ways of bringing his character to life. He has experimented (always under the guidance and subject to the approval of the director) with details of business, movement, and line reading. Throughout the entire period he has been deciding what details will help him in believing his character. There has been, in fact, a continual process of selection and rejection. By the time the play is ready for polishing, choices must have been made. During the final rehearsals the actor needs to be confident that problems of characterization, as well as all technical problems, have been solved to the best of everyone's ability. Only then can he be comfortable and assured in his performance.

Although both will have been anticipated earlier, the principal considerations in the process of polishing are *timing* and *projection*.

Timing is a matter of pace and rhythm. It has to do with the tempo at which lines are spoken, at which business and movement are executed, and with the rapidity at which cues are picked up. A tempo cannot be established and maintained as long as the actors feel uncertain about the details of their performance.

A sense of timing is one of the most subtle elements of stage technique. It demands for its development that the actor have experience before an audience. Too slow a tempo will not hold interest. Too fast a tempo will obscure the meaning. Too consistent a tempo will become monotonous. Too varied a tempo will seem jerky and illogical. The beginning actor tends to be slow in picking up cues with the result that the rhythm falters between speeches. The actor must be both physically and mentally alert to his cues. Physical readiness is largely a matter of breathing. He must inhale before his partner has finished speaking so he has the necessary breath to begin his line. Otherwise, the time required to take a breath will make a gap in the rhythm of the dialogue. The young actor often tends to be too fast in speaking his lines with the result that the meaning is blurred—a clear indication that he is not using his lines to accomplish a verbal action. He tends to maintain too constant a tempo—an indication that he is not finding different tempo-rhythms for different structural units.

An important consideration in timing is the use of the *pause*. Many beginning actors tend to use the pause for their own convenience (because they aren't breathing correctly, because they aren't thinking fast enough, because they aren't sure of what they are doing) without regard to dramatic effect. The pause should be used sparingly, and only when silence is more effective than speech. As a general rule, the pause serves the actor best during a transition from one structural unit to another.

Timing varies from play to play, from scene to scene, from character to character, and from audience to audience. The thought-provoking play requires a slower tempo than the farce comedy. Expository scenes at the beginning require a slower tempo than climactic scenes at the end. One character moves and speaks more slowly than another. One audience is quicker at grasping meanings than another. During the final rehearsals, the director will guide the cast in establishing effective tempos for the play, for different scenes, for different characters. The actors alone have the responsibility of *feeling out* the audience and making such adjustments as may be necessary.

Projection is another variable element. The constant requirement is that the audience hear and understand the lines. This requirement may be satisfied in a variety of voices ranging from a shout to a whisper. Projection is not talking loud. It is a matter of the actor's effort to share the play with the audience. The degree of loudness which is most suitable must be determined by the play, the scene, the character, the size and acoustical qualities of the auditorium. Again, variety is necessary. Nothing is more tiresome than listening over a period of time to an unvaried voice. Too abrupt changes, on the other hand, are likely to startle the audience, to attract undue attention; and, of even greater importance, they may rarely be justified.

There must be visual projection, as well as auditory. The audience must *see* the action as clearly as they *hear* the lines. Three requirements of movement, business, and gesture are:

1. They must be suitable to the character, the scene, the play, and the general style of the production.

2. They must be clearly seen.
3. Their significance in terms of the total meaning must be readily comprehensible.

At final rehearsals, actors must be concerned with auditory and visual projection. The director will be careful to check its effectiveness. The final test can be made only by performing before an audience. It is to insure that the actors will meet the test on opening night that New York producers have out-of-town tryouts. It is for the same reason that noncommercial directors have preview performances or invite audiences to the final "run-throughs."

Working at Rehearsals

No attempt will be made to formulate a set of rules for conduct at rehearsals, but it may be helpful to comment upon proper attitudes and methods of work. For a talented actor, well trained in the techniques of his art, rehearsals are a happy time. Not that they are always filled with pleasant fun! Preparing a play for production is at best hard work, often fraught with frustration, in the efforts to reach desired goals. But during rehearsals the actor has the greatest opportunity for creative accomplishment. He should begin rehearsals resolved to use all of his resources for the good of the production. What is best for the production should be the single criterion by which choices are made, and nothing makes for a happier atmosphere than the sharing of this resolve by all members of the cast.

Of great importance is the actor's relation to the director and to the other actors. The words that describe the best relationship are *mutual respect*. The director determines the working methods, the rehearsal schedule, the distribution of rehearsal time among the different acts and scenes. The actor respects both the method and the schedule. He cooperates with the director in his way of working. Needless to say, he attends rehearsals regularly and punctually. He is *ready to work* at the scheduled times. He has an *obligation* to keep himself healthy, rested, and in good spirits, so that sickness, fatigue, or personal problems do not interfere. To the other actors he is generous and demanding. Demanding that they give their best. Generous in giving his best to them.

Throughout a rehearsal he is alert and committed to the work at hand. He gives his entire attention to what is going on both when he is in the scene and when he is waiting for an entrance. He marks directions in his script or in a notebook. Once movement has been given by the director, or worked out by the actor and director at rehearsal, the actor is responsible for retaining it. He indicates all movements in the margin of his script at the time they are blocked, using standard abbreviations:

BLOCKING DIAGRAMS

Sit ULC
X DRC below sofa
Exit DL

Drawing diagrams in the margin is also a practical way of recording blocking.

He does more, though, than keep track of his blocking. He writes down beats, intentions, undermeanings, comments and interpretations until he has a complete score for the playing of his role. The score becomes an invaluable source of reference during later rehearsals and performances.

The actor recognizes that early rehearsals must progress in bits and pieces. He recognizes the dangers of going too fast. Each moment of the play must be explored and the problems solved through trial and error. Rehearsals require countless new starts, changes, and repetitions. Early decisions can be only tentative. The production must develop organically, and each moment depends upon many others. Only late in the rehearsal period can solutions safely be relegated to some degree of permanence.

Working at Home

In addition to rehearsals the actor must work outside. "Home work" is too often neglected by the beginner. A creative actor uses rehearsals as an opportunity to test for the director and with the other actors what he has worked out by himself. The division of his role into beats, discovering and stating the intentions, finding additional circumstances, setting the sensory tasks, writing the subtext are all problems for the individual actor—subject to the guidance of the director. He must also work by himself on specific problems that arise during rehearsal, so that he comes each day bringing fresh imagination to the problems to be solved.

Playing the Part

15

From the consideration of rehearsal procedure, it is apparent that first the actor is concerned with discovering the total meaning of the play—a discovery made through a study of the script, an examination of other sources, and through discussions with the director and the other actors. In the kind of play that constitutes the great body of Western drama, both classic and contemporary, the kind of play in which the dramatist expresses his meaning by creating characters involved in some conflict, the actor must give immediate attention to understanding the character he is playing and to believing the character's speech and actions. Later he becomes increasingly concerned with projecting the character to the audience. During performance he is concerned with both characterization and projection. He must bring the character to life, not just by duplicating onstage the details of everyday living, but by creating a form that is theatrically effective. He must select, arrange, and heighten his speech and actions. He must also project the character with whatever "comment" the play and the production demand.

As the play is repeated in performance, the core—the super-objective, motivating desires, intentions of the beats, externals of character, physical form of the production—stays the same. And keeping it the same is one of the actor's responsibilities. He is required to perform the play as rehearsed. Actors Equity Association fines and ultimately suspends professionals who fail to respect their obligation. This does not mean that creativity ceases and that the actor repeats from memory what has been "set" in rehearsal. Each performance requires him to bring life to his character by committing himself to accomplishing the character's objectives and to establishing relations with objects and other actors. Performance demands continual adjustment to the stage life that is going on around him. To keep it the same it must always be subtly different. A mechanical repetition does not retain vitality.

Concentration is the keynote to success. And the actor concentrates throughout on *two levels*.

On one level he directs his attention to satisfying the desires of the character. Through his speech and action he attempts to get what the character wants. He attempts to influence the behavior of the other characters for the purpose of satisfying his objective. In concentrating on this objective he comes to have belief in his actions which produces, in turn, feelings similar to the feelings the character would have if the situations were in life. He also makes imaginative use of the feelings that arise from his relation to the other actors.

On another level the actor is concentrating on expressing the character in theatrical terms. The lines must be heard. The actions must be seen. A tempo must be maintained which will be suitable to the play, stimulating to the audience, and dramatically effective. Throughout the performance, all the elements must have enough variety to insure a continual renewal of interest. The character must be presented to draw forth the response intended by the dramatist. The actor must develop what Lynn Fontanne calls an "outside eye and ear" to guide him in the playing of his role. He has the dual function of being both character and interpreter.[1]

In some contemporary works the creation of character in imaginary circumstances is a minimal part of the actor's responsibility. He expresses his or the playwright's meaning directly to the audience in his own person. His task is to find every way he can of communicating the meaning clearly and forcefully.

The actor must serve his function with ease and authority. There is no pleasure watching a performer who is tense and strained, and there is no comfort watching one who does not appear confident in his ability to perform with some degree of credit to himself. Concentration, again, is the keynote to relaxation. When the actor can turn his full attention to doing a job he knows he is prepared to do, he forgets his fears and his self-consciousness. He "turns to" with the directness and energy which are requisite to his success.

It has been the purpose of this book to help the beginning actor acquire skills that will give him such ease and confidence.

[1] Funke and Booth, *Actors Talk About Acting*, p. 67.

APPENDIX

SHORT PLAYS
FOR STUDY
AND PRACTICE

THE PROPOSAL[1]
by Anton Chekhov

Characters

STEPAN STEPANOVITCH CHUBUKOV, a landowner.
NATALYA STEPANOVNA, his daughter, twenty-five years old.
IVAN VASSILEVITCH LOMOV, a neighbour of Chubukov, a large and hearty, but very suspicious landowner.

The scene is laid at CHUBUKOV'S *country house.*

LOMOV enters, wearing a dress-jacket and white gloves. CHUBUKOV *rises to meet him.*

CHUBUKOV. My dear fellow, whom do I see! Ivan Vassilevitch! I am extremely glad! (*Squeezes his hand*) Now this is a surprise, my darling. . . . How are you?

LOMOV. Thank you. And how may you be getting on?

CHUBUKOV. We just get along somehow, my angel, thanks to your prayers, and so on. Sit down, please do. . . . Now, you know, you shouldn't forget all about your neighbours, my darling. My dear fellow, why are you so formal in your get-up? Evening dress, gloves, and so on. Can you be going anywhere, my treasure?

LOMOV. No, I've come only to see you, honoured Stepan Stepanovitch.

CHUBUKOV. Then why are you in evening dress, my precious? As if you're paying a New Year's Eve visit!

LOMOV. Well, you see, it's like this. (*Takes his arm*) I've come to you, honoured Stepan Stepanovitch, to trouble you with a request. Not once or twice have I already had the privilege of applying to you for help, and you have always, so to speak. . . . I must ask your pardon, I am getting excited. I shall drink some water, honoured Stepan Stepanovitch. (*Drinks*)

CHUBUKOV. (*Aside*) He's come to borrow money! Shan't give him any! (*Aloud*) What is it, my beauty?

[1] From *The Plays of Anton Chekhov* (New York: World Publishing Co., 1935). Copyright by Illustrated Editions, Inc., 1935. Reprinted by permission of Avon Books.

LOMOV. You see, Honour Stepanitch. . . . I beg pardon, Stepan Honouritch.
. . . I mean, I'm awfully excited, as you will please notice. . . . In short,
you alone can help me, though I don't deserve it, of course . . . and haven't
any right to count on your assistance. . . .

CHUBUKOV. Oh, don't go round and round it, darling! Spit it out! Well?

LOMOV. One moment . . . this very minute. The fact is, I've come to ask the
hand of your daughter, Natalya Stepanovna, in marriage.

CHUBUKOV. (*Joyfully*) By Jove! Ivan Vassilevitch! Say it again—I didn't hear it
all!

LOMOV. I have the honour to ask . . .

CHUBUKOV. (*Interrupting*) My dear fellow . . . I'm so glad, and so on. . . .
Yes, indeed, and all that sort of thing. (*Embraces and kisses* LOMOV) I've
been hoping for it for a long time. It's been my continual desire. (*Sheds a
tear*) And I've always loved you, my angel, as if you were my own son. May
God give you both His help and His love and so on, and I did so much
hope. . . . What am I behaving in this idiotic way for? I'm off balance with
joy, absolutely off my balance! Oh, with all my soul. . . . I'll go and call
Natasha, and all that.

LOMOV. (*Greatly moved*) Honoured Stepan Stepanovitch, do you think I may
count on her consent?

CHUBUKOV. Why, of course, my darling, and . . . as if she won't consent!
She's in love; egad, she's like a love-sick cat, and so on. . . . Shan't be long!
(*Exit*)

LOMOV. It's cold . . . I'm trembling all over, just as if I'd got an examination
before me. The great thing is, I must have my mind made up. If I give
myself time to think, to hesitate, to talk a lot, to look for an ideal, or for real
love, then I'll never get married. . . . Brr! . . . It's cold! Natalya Stepanovna is an excellent housekeeper, not bad-looking, well-educated. . . .
What more do I want? But I'm getting a noise in my ears from excitement.
(*Drinks*) And it's impossible for me not to marry. . . . In the first place, I'm
already 35—a critical age, so to speak. In the second place, I ought to lead a
quiet and regular life. . . . I suffer from palpitations, I'm excitable and
always getting awfully upset. . . . At this very moment my lips are trembling, and there's a twitch in my right eyebrow. . . . But the very worst of
all is the way I sleep. I no sooner get into bed and begin to go off when suddenly something in my left side—gives a pull, and I can feel it in my
shoulder and head. . . . I jump up like a lunatic, walk about a bit, and lie
down again, but as soon as I begin to get off to sleep there's another pull!
And this may happen twenty times. . . .

NATALYA STEPANOVNA *comes in.*

NATALYA STEPANOVNA. Well, there! It's you, and papa said, "Go; there's a
merchant come for his goods!" How do you do, Ivan Vassilevitch!

LOMOV. How do you do, honoured Natalya Stepanovna?

NATALYA STEPANOVNA. You must excuse my apron and house dress . . . we're shelling peas for drying. Why haven't you been here for such a long time? Sit down. . . . (*They seat themselves*) Won't you have some lunch?

LOMOV. No, thank you, I've had some already.

NATALYA STEPANOVNA. Then smoke. . . . Here are the matches. . . . The weather is splendid now, but yesterday it was so wet that the workmen didn't do anything all day. How much hay have you stacked? Just think, I felt greedy and had a whole field cut, and now I'm not at all pleased about it because I'm afraid my hay may rot. I ought to have waited a bit. But what's this? Why, you're in evening dress! Well, I never! Are you going to a ball, or what?—though I must say you look better. . . . Tell me, why are you got up like that?

LOMOV. (*Excited*) You see, honoured Natalya Stepanovna . . . the fact is, I've made up my mind to ask you to hear me out. . . . Of course you'll be surprised and perhaps even angry, but a . . . (*Aside*) It's awfully cold!

NATALYA STEPANOVNA. What's the matter? (*Pause*) Well?

LOMOV. I shall try to be brief. You must know, honoured Natalya Stepanovna, that I have long, since my childhood, in fact, had the privilege of knowing your family. My late aunt and her husband, from whom, as you know, I inherited my land, always had the greatest respect for your father and your late mother. The Lomovs and the Chubukovs have always had the most friendly, and I might almost say the most affectionate, regard for each other. And, as you know, my land is a near neighbour of yours. You will remember that my Oxen Meadows touch your birchwoods.

NATALYA STEPANOVNA. Excuse my interrupting you. You say, "My Oxen Meadows. . . ." But are they yours?

LOMOV. Yes, mine.

NATALYA STEPANOVNA. What are you talking about? Oxen Meadows are ours, not yours!

LOMOV. No, mine, honoured Natalya Stepanovna.

NATALYA STEPANOVNA. Well, I never heard that before. How do you make that out?

LOMOV. How? I'm speaking of those Oxen Meadows which are wedged in between your birchwoods and the Burnt Marsh.

NATALYA STEPANOVNA. Yes, yes. . . . They're ours.

LOMOV. No, you're mistaken, honoured Natalya Stepanovna, they're mine.

NATALYA STEPANOVNA. Just think, Ivan Vassilevitch! How long have they been yours?

LOMOV. How long? As long as I can remember.

NATALYA STEPANOVNA. Really, you won't get me to believe that!

LOMOV. But you can see from the documents, honoured Natalya Stepanovna. Oxen Meadows, it's true, were once the subject of dispute, but now everybody knows that they are mine. There's nothing to argue about. You see, my aunt's grandmother gave the free use of these Meadows in perpetuity to the peasants of your father's grandfather, in return for which they were to make bricks for her. The peasants belonging to your father's grandfather had the free use of the Meadows for forty years, and had got into the habit of regarding them as their own, when it happened that . . .

NATALYA STEPANOVNA. No, it isn't at all like that! Both my grandfather and great-grandfather reckoned that their land extended to Burnt Marsh—which means that Oxen Meadows were ours. I don't see what there is to argue about. It's simply silly!

LOMOV. I'll show you the documents, Natalya Stepanovna!

NATALYA STEPANOVNA. No, you're simply joking, or making fun of me. . . . What a surprise! We've had the land for nearly three hundred years, and then we're suddenly told that it isn't ours! Ivan Vassilevitch, I can hardly believe my own ears. . . . These Meadows aren't worth much to me. They only come to five dessiatins,[2] and are worth perhaps 300 roubles,[3] but I can't stand unfairness. Say what you will, but I can't stand unfairness.

LOMOV. Hear me out, I implore you! The peasants of your father's grandfather, as I have already had the honour of explaining to you, used to bake bricks for my aunt's grandmother. Now my aunt's grandmother, wishing to make them a pleasant . . .

NATALYA STEPANOVNA. I can't make head or tail of all this about aunts and grandfathers and grandmothers. The Meadow are ours, and that's all.

LOMOV. Mine.

NATALYA STEPANOVNA. Ours! You can go on proving it for two days on end, you can go and put on fifteen dress-jackets, but I tell you they're ours, ours, ours! I don't want anything of yours and I don't want to give up anything of mine. So there!

LOMOV. Natalya Stepanovna, I don't want the Meadows, but I am acting on principle. If you like, I'll make you a present of them.

NATALYA STEPANOVNA. I can make you a present of them myself, because they're mine. Your behaviour, Ivan Vassilevitch, is strange, to say the least! Up to this we have always thought of you as a good neighbour, a friend; last year we lent you our threshing-machine, although on that account we had to put off our own threshing till November, but you behave to us as if we were gipsies. Giving me my own land, indeed! No, really, that's not at all neighbourly! In my opinion, it's even impudent, if you want to know. . . .

LOMOV. Then you make out that I'm a land-grabber? Madam, never in my life have I grabbed anybody else's land, and I shan't allow anybody to accuse me of having done so. . . . (*Quickly steps to the carafe and drinks more water*) Oxen Meadows are mine!

[2] 13½ acres.
[3] 30 pounds.

NATALYA STEPANOVNA. It's not true, they're ours!

LOMOV. Mine!

NATALYA STEPANOVNA. It's not true! I'll prove it! I'll send my mowers out to the Meadows this very day!

LOMOV. What?

NATALYA STEPANOVNA. My mowers will be there this very day!

LOMOV. I'll give it to them in the neck!

NATALYA STEPANOVNA. You dare!

LOMOV. (*Clutches at his heart*) Oxen Meadows are mine! You understand? Mine!

NATALYA STEPANOVNA. Please don't shout! You can shout yourself hoarse in your own house, but here I must ask you to restrain yourself!

LOMOV. If it wasn't, madam, for this awful, excruciating palpitation, if my whole inside wasn't upset, I'd talk to you in a different way! (*Yells*) Oxen Meadows are mine!

NATALYA STEPANOVNA. Ours!

LOMOV. Mine!

NATALYA STEPANOVNA. Ours!

LOMOV. Mine!

Enter CHUBUKOV.

CHUBUKOV. What's the matter? What are you shouting at?

NATALYA STEPANOVNA. Papa, please tell this gentleman who owns Oxen Meadows, we or he?

CHUBUKOV. (*To* LOMOV) Darling, the Meadows are ours!

LOMOV. But, please, Stepan Stepanovitch, how can they be yours? Do be a reasonable man! My aunt's grandmother gave the Meadows for the temporary and free use of your grandfather's peasants. The peasants used the land for forty years and got as accustomed to it as if it was their own, when it happened that . . .

CHUBUKOV. Excuse me, my precious. . . . You forget just this, that the peasants didn't pay your grandmother and all that, because the Meadows were in dispute, and so on. And now everybody knows that they're ours. It means that you haven't seen the plan.

LOMOV. I'll prove to you that they're mine!

CHUBUKOV. You won't prove it, my darling.

LOMOV. I shall!

CHUBUKOV. Dear one, why yell like that? You won't prove anything by just yelling. I don't want anything of yours, and don't intend to give up what I have. Why should I? And you know, my beloved, that if you propose to go on arguing about it, I'd much sooner give up the Meadows to the peasants than to you. There!

LOMOV. I don't understand! How have you the right to give away somebody else's property?

CHUBUKOV. You may take it that I know whether I have the right or not. Because, young man, I'm not used to being spoken to in that tone of voice, and so on: I, young man, am twice your age, and ask you to speak to me without agitating yourself, and all that.

LOMOV. No, you just think I'm a fool and want to have me on! You call my land yours, and then you want me to talk to you calmly and politely! Good neighbours don't behave like that, Stepan Stepanovitch! You're not a neighbour, you're a grabber!

CHUBUKOV. What's that? What did you say?

NATALYA STEPANOVNA. Papa, send the mowers out to the Meadows at once!

CHUBUKOV. What did you say, sir?

NATALYA STEPANOVNA. Oxen Meadows are ours, and I shan't give them up, shan't give them up, shan't give them up!

LOMOV. We'll see! I'll have the matter taken to court, and then I'll show you!

CHUBUKOV. To court? You can take it to court, and all that! You can! I know you; you're just on the look-out for a chance to go to court, and all that. . . . You pettifogger! All your people were like that! All of them!

LOMOV. Never mind about my people! The Lomovs have all been honourable people, and not one has ever been tried for embezzlement, like your grandfather!

CHUBUKOV. You Lomovs have had lunacy in your family, all of you!

NATALYA STEPANOVNA. All, all, all!

CHUBUKOV. Your grandfather was a drunkard, and your younger aunt, Nastasya Mihailovna, ran away with an architect, and so on. . . .

LOMOV. And your mother was hump-backed. (*Clutches at his heart*) Something pulling in my side. . . . My head. . . . Help! Water!

CHUBUKOV. Your father was a guzzling gambler!

NATALYA STEPANOVNA. And there haven't been many backbiters to equal your aunt!

LOMOV. My left foot has gone to sleep. . . . You're an intriguer. . . . Oh, my heart! . . . And it's an open secret that before the last elections you bri . . . I can see stars. . . . Where's my hat?

NATALYA STEPANOVNA. It's low! It's dishonest! It's mean!

CHUBUKOV. And you're just a malicious, double-faced intriguer! Yes!

LOMOV. Here's my hat. . . . My heart! . . . Which way? Where's the door? Oh! . . . I think I'm dying. . . . My foot's quite numb. . . . (*Goes to the door*)

CHUBUKOV. (*Following him*) And don't set foot in my house again!

NATALYA STEPANOVNA. Take it to court! We'll see!

LOMOV *staggers out.*

CHUBUKOV. Devil take him! (*To table for drink*)

Walks about in excitement.

NATALYA STEPANOVNA. What a rascal! What trust can one have in one's neighbours after that!

CHUBUKOV. The villain! The scarecrow! (*Down L.*)

NATALYA STEPANOVNA. The monster! First he takes our land and then he has the impudence to abuse us.

CHUBUKOV. And that blind hen, yes, that turnip-ghost has the confounded cheek to make a proposal, and so on! (*Down R.C. Stuttering. Front to door R.*)

NATALYA STEPANOVNA. What proposal?

CHUBUKOV. Why, he came here so as to propose to you. (*L.*)

NATALYA STEPANOVNA. To propose? To me? Why didn't you tell me so before?

CHUBUKOV. So he dresses up in evening clothes. (*R.C.*) The stuffed sausage! The wizen-faced frump! (*L.*)

NATALYA STEPANOVNA. To propose to me? Ah! (*Falls into an easy chair and wails*) Bring him back! Back! Ah! Bring him here.

CHUBUKOV. Bring whom here?

NATALYA STEPANOVNA. Quick, quick! I'm ill! Fetch him! (*Hysterics*)

CHUBUKOV. What's that? (*To her*) What's the matter with you? (*Clutches at his head*) Oh, unhappy man that I am! I'll shoot myself! I'll hang myself!

NATALYA STEPANOVNA. I'm dying! Fetch him!

CHUBUKOV. At once. Don't yell!

Runs out. A pause. NATALYA STEPANOVNA *wails.*

NATALYA STEPANOVNA. What have they done to me! Fetch him back! Fetch him.

A pause.

CHUBUKOV *runs in. Comes down L.C.*

CHUBUKOV. He's coming, and so on, devil take him! Ouf! Talk to him yourself; I don't want to. (*To R.*)

NATALYA STEPANOVNA. (*Wails*) Fetch him!

CHUBUKOV. (*Yells*) He's coming, I tell you. Oh, what a burden, Lord, to be the father of a grown-up daughter! I'll cut my throat! I will, indeed! (*To her*) We cursed him, abused him, drove him out, and it's all you . . . you!

NATALYA STEPANOVNA. No, it was you!

CHUBUKOV. I tell you it's not my fault. (LOMOV *appears at the door*) Now you talk to him yourself. (*Exit*)

LOMOV *enters, exhausted.*

LOMOV. My heart's palpitating awfully. . . . My foot's gone to sleep. . . . There's something keeps pulling in my side. . . .

NATALYA STEPANOVNA. Forgive us, Ivan Vassilevitch, we were all a little heated. . . . I remember now: Oxen Meadows really are yours.

LOMOV. My heart's beating awfully. . . . My Meadows. . . . My eyebrows are both twitching. . . .

NATALYA STEPANOVNA. The Meadows are yours, yes, yours. . . . Do sit down. . . . (*They sit*) We were wrong. . . .

LOMOV. I did it on principle. . . . My land is worth little to me, but the principle . . .

NATALYA STEPANOVNA. Yes, the principle, just so. . . . Now let's talk of something else.

LOMOV. The more so as I have evidence. My aunt's grandmother gave the land to your father's grandfather's peasants . . .

NATALYA STEPANOVNA. Yes, yes, let that pass. . . . (*Aside*) I wish I knew how to get him started. . . . (*Aloud*) Are you going to start shooting soon?

LOMOV. I'm thinking of having a go at the blackcock, honoured Natalya Stepanovna, after the harvest. Oh, have you heard? Just think, what a misfortune I've had! My dog Guess, whom you know, has gone lame.

NATALYA STEPANOVNA. What a pity! Why?

LOMOV. I don't know. . . . Must have got twisted, or bitten by some other dog. . . . (*Sighs*) My very best dog, to say nothing of the expense. I gave Mironov 125 roubles for him.

NATALYA STEPANOVNA. It was too much, Ivan Vassilevitch.

LOMOV. I think it was very cheap. He's a first-rate dog.

NATALYA STEPANOVNA. Papa gave 85 roubles for his Squeezer, and Squeezer is heaps better than Guess!

LOMOV. Squeezer better than Guess? What an idea! (*Laughs*) Squeezer better than Guess!

NATALYA STEPANOVNA. Of course he's better! Of course, Squeezer is young, he may develop a bit, but on points and pedigree he's better than anything that even Volchanetsky has got.

LOMOV. Excuse me, Natalya Stepanovna, but you forget that he is overshot, and an overshot dog always means the dog is a bad hunter!

NATALYA STEPANOVNA. Overshot, is he? The first time I heard it!

LOMOV. I assure you that his lower jaw is shorter than the upper.

NATALYA STEPANOVNA. Have you measured?

LOMOV. Yes, he's all right at following, of course, but if you want him to get hold of anything . . .

NATALYA STEPANOVNA. In the first place, Squeezer is a thoroughbred animal, the son of Harness and Chisels, while there's no getting at the pedigree of your dog, at all. . . . He's old and as ugly as a worn-out cab-horse.

LOMOV. He is old, but I wouldn't take five Squeezers for him. . . . Why, how can you? Guess is a dog; as for Squeezer, well, it's too funny to argue. . . . Anybody you like has a dog as good as Squeezer . . . you may find them under every bush almost. Twenty-five roubles would be a handsome price to pay for him.

NATALYA STEPANOVNA. There's some demon of contradiction in you today, Ivan Vassilevitch. First you pretend that the Meadows are yours; now, that Guess is better than Squeezer. I don't like people who don't say what they mean, because you know perfectly well that Squeezer is a hundred times better than your silly Guess. Why do you want to say he isn't?

LOMOV. I see, Natalya Stepanovna, that you consider me either blind or a fool. You must realize that Squeezer is overshot!

NATALYA STEPANOVNA. It's not true.

LOMOV. He is!

NATALYA STEPANOVNA. It's not true!

LOMOV. Why shout, madam?

NATALYA STEPANOVNA. Why talk rot? It's awful! It's time your Guess was shot, and you compare him with Squeezer!

LOMOV. Excuse me; I cannot continue this discussion, my heart is palpitating.

NATALYA STEPANOVNA. I've noticed that those hunters argue most who know least.

LOMOV. Madam, please be silent. . . . My heart is going to pieces. . . . (*Shouts*) Shut up!

NATALYA STEPANOVNA. I shan't shut up until you acknowledge that Squeezer is a hundred times better than your Guess!

LOMOV. A hundred times worse! Be hanged to your Squeezer! His head . . . eyes . . . shoulder . . .

NATALYA STEPANOVNA. There's no need to hang your silly Guess; he's half-dead already!

LOMOV. (*Weeps*) Shut up! My heart's bursting!

NATALYA STEPANOVNA. I shan't shut up.

Enter CHUBUKOV.

CHUBUKOV. What's the matter now?

NATALYA STEPANOVNA. Papa, tell us truly, which is the better dog, our Squeezer or his Guess.

LOMOV. Stepan Stepanovitch, I implore you to tell me just one thing; is your Squeezer overshot or not? Yes or no?

CHUBUKOV. And suppose he is? What does it matter? He's the best dog in the district for all that, and so on.

LOMOV. But isn't my Guess better? Really, now?

CHUBUKOV. Don't excite yourself, my precious one. . . . Allow me. . . . Your Guess certainly has his good points. . . . He's pure-bred, firm on his feet, has well-sprung ribs, and all that. But my dear man, if you want to know the truth, the dog has two defects: he's old and he's short in the muzzle.

LOMOV. Excuse me, my heart. . . . Let's take the facts. . . . You will remember that on the Marusinsky hunt my Guess ran neck-and-neck with the Count's dog, while your Squeezer was left a whole verst behind.

CHUBUKOV. He got left behind because the Count's whipper-in hit him with his whip.

LOMOV. And with good reason. The dogs are running after a fox, when Squeezer goes and starts worrying a sheep!

CHUBUKOV. It's not true! . . . My dear fellow, I'm very liable to lose my temper, and so, just because of that, let's stop arguing. You started because everybody is always jealous of everybody else's dogs. Yes, we're all like that! You too, sir, aren't blameless! You no sooner notice that some dog is better than your Guess than you begin with this, that . . . and the other . . . and all that. . . . I remember everything!

LOMOV. I remember too!

CHUBUKOV. (*Teasing him*) I remember, too. . . . What do you remember?

LOMOV. My heart . . . my foot's gone to sleep. . . . I can't . . .

NATALYA STEPANOVNA. (*Teasing*) My heart. . . . What sort of a hunter are you? You ought to go and lie on the kitchen oven and catch black-beetles, not go after foxes! My heart!

CHUBUKOV. Yes, really, what sort of a hunter are you, anyway. You ought to sit at home with your palpitations, and not go tracking animals. You could go hunting, but you only go to argue with people and interfere with their dogs and so on. Let's change the subject in case I lose my temper. You're not a hunter at all, anyway!

LOMOV. And are you a hunter? You only go hunting to get in with the Count and to intrigue. . . . Oh, my heart! . . . You're an intriguer!

CHUBUKOV. What? I an intriguer? (*Shouts*) Shut up!

LOMOV. Intriguer!

CHUBUKOV. Boy! Pup!

LOMOV. Old rat!

CHUBUKOV. Shut up or I'll shoot you like a partridge! You fool!

LOMOV. Everybody knows that—oh my heart!—your late wife used to beat you. . . . My feet . . . temples . . . sparks. . . . I fall, I fall!

CHUBUKOV. And you're under the slipper of your housekeeper!

LOMOV. There, there, there . . . my heart's burst! My shoulder's come off. . . . Where is my shoulder? . . . I die. (*Falls into an armchair*) A doctor! (*Faints*)

CHUBUKOV. Boy! Milksop! Fool! I'm sick! (*Drinks water*) Sick!

NATALYA STEPANOVNA. What sort of a hunter are you? You can't even sit on a horse! (*To her father*) Papa, what's the matter with him? Papa! Look, papa! (*Screams*) Ivan Vassilevitch! He's dead!

CHUBUKOV. I'm sick! . . . I can't breathe! Air!

NATALYA STEPANOVNA. He's dead. (*Pulls* LOMOV's *sleeve*) Ivan Vassilevitch! Ivan Vassilevitch! What have you done to me? He's dead. (*Falls into an armchair*) A doctor, a doctor! (*Hysterics*)

CHUBUKOV. Oh! . . . What is it? What's the matter?

NATALYA STEPANOVNA. (*Wails*) He's dead . . . dead!

CHUBUKOV. Who's dead? (*Looks at* LOMOV) So he is! My word! Water! A doctor! (*Lifts a tumbler to* LOMOV's *mouth*) Drink this. . . . No, he doesn't drink. . . . It means he's dead, and all that. . . . I'm the most unhappy of men! Why don't I put a bullet into my brain? Why haven't I cut my throat yet? What am I waiting for? Give me a knife! Give me a pistol! (LOMOV *moves*) He seems to be coming round. . . . Drink some water! That's right. . . .

LOMOV. I see stars . . . mist. . . . Where am I?

CHUBUKOV. Hurry up and get married and—well, to the devil with you! She's willing! (*He puts* LOMOV's *hand into his daughter's*) She's willing and all that. I give you my blessing and so on. Only leave me in peace!

LOMOV. (*Getting up*) Eh? What? To whom?

CHUBUKOV. She's willing! Well? Kiss and be damned to you!

NATALYA STEPANOVNA. (*Wails*) He's alive. . . . Yes, yes, I'm willing. . . .

CHUBUKOV. Kiss each other!

LOMOV. Eh? Kiss whom? (*They kiss*) Very nice, too. Excuse me, what's it all about? Oh, now I understand . . . my heart . . . stars . . . I'm happy. Natalya Stepanovna. . . . (*Kisses her hand*) My foot's gone to sleep.

NATALYA STEPANOVNA. I . . . I'm happy too. . . .

CHUBUKOV. What a weight off my shoulders . . . Ouf!

NATALYA STEPANOVNA. But . . . still you will admit now that Guess is worse than Squeezer.

LOMOV. Better!

NATALYA STEPANOVNA. Worse!

CHUBUKOV. Well, that's a way to start your family bliss! Have some champagne!

LOMOV. He's better!

NATALYA STEPANOVNA. Worse! worse! worse!

CHUBUKOV (*Trying to shout her down*) Champagne! Champagne!

CURTAIN

THE TYPISTS[1]
by Murray Schisgal

THE TIME: *At twenty-odd years of age.*
THE SCENE: *An office: forward, center, a pair of simple metal typewriter tables, with leaves extended, on which there are two old standard typewriters, stacks of postcards, and a bulky telephone directory on each; rear, a large window, two tall green steel file cabinets, a desk between them on which there are a great many telephone directories and a telephone, a door to the restroom; at the right wall, forward, a water cooler, a wooden coat hanger, the entrance door; in the left wall, the door to the employer's office.*
The sun streams through the window; as the play progresses it fades imperceptibly until, at the end, the room is almost in complete darkness.
The same clothes are worn throughout by the actors, although altered to suit the physical changes—subtle, almost unnoticed when they occur—that take place during the course of the play.
Sylvia Payton enters from R. *She is late for work. She throws her coat on the hanger, rushes across the room, deposits her lunch bag in the top drawer of a cabinet, removes cover from her typewriter and begins typing rapidly, glancing anxiously at the employer's door. In a moment she relaxes; she types slowly and hums to herself; she takes her comb and mirror from her pocketbook and fixes her hair. The front door opens,* R. *She puts everything away and without turning to see who has entered she starts to type rapidly again. Paul Cunningham approaches, passing his lunch bag from hand to hand.*

PAUL. Good morning. I'm Paul Cunningham. I was hired yesterday by . . . (*Laughing uneasily.*) That's funny. I forgot his name. You'll have to excuse

---

The Typists, printed here in its entirety, provides exercise materials of several kinds. It may be studied for the purpose of analyzing each of the characters, of discovering the meaning of the play as a whole, and of relating each character to the total meaning. The dialogue is excellent for work in line interpretation. The actor may work by himself on the longer speeches. The play may readily be broken into short scenes for study and rehearsal, or it may be used in its entirety for rehearsal and performance in class. The aging of the characters provides opportunities for both internal and external characterization.

me. First day on the job . . . I'm a little nervous. It was the boss who hired me, though; at least that's what he said.

SYLVIA. I know. He told me. (*Rising, shaking his hand.*) Sylvia. Miss Sylvia Payton. Glad to meet you, Mr. Cunningham. If you'll hang up your coat I'll show you what you have to do.

PAUL. I'm sorry I'm late, Miss Payton. I got on the wrong train by mistake. Generally you'll find that I'm a pretty prompt person.

SYLVIA. Oh, that's all right. Just make sure it doesn't happen too often. He's very strict when it comes to being here on time. And now that he's made me responsible for this whole department . . . Of course I won't say anything to him about this morning.

PAUL. I'd appreciate that a lot.

SYLVIA. Don't even mention it. Believe me, I didn't ask him to be made a supervisor. I don't like telling anyone what to do; that's part of my nature, I guess. You give me your lunch bag, Mr. Cunningham. I'll put it in the file cabinet; that's where I keep mine.

PAUL. Thanks. I was sure lucky to get this job. I go to school at night and a lot of firms don't hire you if they know that.

SYLVIA. You must be a very ambitious person. What are you studying?

PAUL. (*Proudly.*) Law. Another three years and I should get my degree. Boy, that's one day I'm looking forward to.

SYLVIA. It must be extremely difficult to have a job and go to school at the same time.

PAUL. It's been real rough so far. But it has its advantages. When I get out, I'm going to have the satisfaction of knowing I did it myself, with my own sweat and my own money; that's more than most fellows my age can say.

SYLVIA. How true that is.

PAUL. Listen, I have an uncle who's a lawyer, a pretty darn famous lawyer, too. Francis T. Cunningham. You ask anybody in the legal field about Francis T. Cunningham and they'll tell you how much he's worth. Well, if I wanted to, I just have to pick up that phone, give him a ring and my worrying days would be over. But that's not for me; no, sir. I'll do it alone or I'm not doing it at all.

SYLVIA. (*Uncovers Paul's typewriter, opens directory for him.*) I think you're a hundred percent right. You know, I once went with a boy—it was nothing serious, it could have been, but . . . I won't go into that now. Anyway, his father was helping him through medical school. He didn't have to earn a penny of his own. Do you think he finished? What happened was that his father remarried and stopped giving him money. He fell completely apart; you never saw anything like it.

PAUL. There's no substitute for character.

SYLVIA. That's exactly the point. Well, we'd better get to work before he starts screaming. We're on a promotion campaign now and it's a very important job. I suppose that's why you were hired. What we do is type out the names and addresses of prospective customers on these postcards. The advertisement is printed on the back. We get the information we want straight from the telephone book. Don't leave out any names; go right down the line. He checks everything and he can be awfully mean if he wants to. I've just started on the A's, so you'll start with the . . .

PAUL. B's.

SYLVIA. Right. That way we'll be sure to get everyone.

PAUL. It sounds easy enough.

SYLVIA. It is. And after awhile you can do it without even thinking. (*They are both seated, typing.*)

PAUL. Ooops! My first card and my first mistake. I'm afraid I'm a little rusty. I haven't been doing much typing lately. (*He is about to throw card into basket.*)

SYLVIA. No, don't throw it away. If he sees it, he'll raise the roof. At the beginning you ought to type more slowly. Lean back in your chair. Posture's very important. And strike each key with the same steady rhythm.

PAUL. Like this?

SYLVIA. Better, much better; don't move your head; keep your eyes on the material you're typing.

PAUL. (*Sitting rigidly, uncomfortably.*) It's really nice of you to help me this way.

SYLVIA. I'm only too glad to, Mr. Cunningham.

PAUL. Paul.

SYLVIA. (*Staring at him, warmly.*) Paul. (*The buzzer rings once.*) That's for me. (*Quickly tidying herself.*) He doesn't usually call me in this early. You go on with your work, Paul. He gets furious when he doesn't hear these typewriters going. He probably wants to know why it took us so long to get started this morning. Don't worry. I'll cover up for you.

PAUL. (*Holding her arm.*) Thanks for everything, Sylvia.

SYLVIA. You're welcome . . . Paul. (*Paul watches her as she swings her hips self-consciously and exits L. to employer's office. He then starts to type, makes an error, crumples card and is about to throw it into basket; on second thought he slips the card into his pocket. Again he types and makes an error, looks guiltily toward the employer's office and slips card into his pocket. All the while he whistles to the tune of "Way Down Upon The Swanee River. . . ." Sylvia re-enters L., angrily.*) He's got some goddamn nerve! What does he think I am, a child? I see it doesn't pay to be nice to people. Well, he can just go and look for someone else to do his dirty work. I'm leaving! (*Gathers her things together.*)

PAUL. What happened?

SYLVIA. Bawling me out for being five minutes late; that's nerve, believe me.

PAUL. (*Laughing.*) So you were late this morning, too?

SYLVIA. There's nothing funny about it, Paul. When you've devoted as much time and energy as I have to this firm, giving them the best you're capable of, then maybe you'll see things differently. Where are my gloves?

PAUL. (*Rising, gives them to her.*) Here they are. Listen, Sylvia; you're excited. Why don't you think about it, huh?

SYLVIA. There's nothing to think about. When he asks you where I went, you just tell him for me that I don't care to associate with a firm that has no feelings for its employees. (*She struggles with coat; he helps her put it on.*)

PAUL. It's not easy finding a job now, I can tell you that.

SYLVIA. With my experience? You must be joking. I've been made many many offers in the past that I've refused out of a sense of loyalty to that . . . to that sex maniac in there. This is my reward.

PAUL. I wouldn't give him the satisfaction; no, sir.

SYLVIA. What satisfaction?

PAUL. Well, it stands to reason that he wanted you to quit, doesn't it? He knows you're a sensitive girl. By leaving you're doing just what he wants.

SYLVIA. You think he deliberately . . .

PAUL. Why else would he have bawled you out?

SYLVIA. (*Slight pause; takes off coat, puts it on hanger.*) I'd die before I gave him the satisfaction. If that's what he has in mind, he's got another guess coming. I'm leaving at my convenience, not his.

PAUL. Now you're talking.

SYLVIA. Believe me, there'll come a day when he'll really need me. "Miss Payton, won't you please help me get this job through in time?" Then it'll be my turn. I'll just laugh right in his stupid face and walk out.

PAUL. Boy, I'd like to be here to see it. Is he married?

SYLVIA. Who would marry him? Ugly as sin, that's what he is. (*They type, laugh over the noise of their typing, then suddenly stop.*) We had a girl working here once, she was a riot. She used to draw these caricatures and mail them to him; anonymously, of course. But you should have seen them; they were the funniest thing. (*They type, laugh, stop suddenly.*)

PAUL. The last job I had was for this woman, Mrs. Jameson. She was as blind as a bat without her glasses. You know what we used to do? Whenever we got the chance we hid her glasses somewhere in the office. For two or three days until she'd find them, we didn't have to do anything, not a single piece of work. We just sat around talking all day.

SYLVIA. I was with an insurance company when I graduated from high school. There was this man in charge there, Mr. Williams, his name was, and he used to have loose hands, if you know what I mean.

PAUL. I know.

SYLVIA. Well, one day he was telling me how to type a policy and he let his hands fall—very, very casually—on my shoulder. So I turned around and looked up at him and spat right in his face.

PAUL. You were fired, I bet.

SYLVIA. As a matter of fact we got along very well after that. (*They type, stop suddenly, turn to one another.*)

PAUL. Have you read any good books lately?

SYLVIA. I read a very good detective novel last week. It was called *Murder in Bombay*.

PAUL. I'm a science fiction man myself. (*They type; stop suddenly; turn to one another.*)

SYLVIA. Can I ask you something?

PAUL. Sure. What is it?

SYLVIA. If you had to choose between getting a million dollars or losing a leg which would you take?

PAUL. Right leg or left leg?

SYLVIA. Any leg.

PAUL. (*Pause.*) I'd take the million dollars.

SYLVIA. I wouldn't. I'd keep my legs. (*They type; stop suddenly. They both stare at the audience, Paul leaning forward, Sylvia back in her chair, her face expressionless, her hands in her lap.*)

PAUL. I was born in a poor section of Brooklyn. My parents were at each other's throat most of the time. It was a miserable childhood. I had no brothers or sisters; there was only the three of us living in this old run-down house, with cats crying and screaming all night in the alley. Why my parents ever got married, I don't know, and why they stayed together for as long as they did I don't know that either. They're separated now. But it doesn't much matter any more. They were as unlike as any two people could be. All my father wanted was to be left alone to smoke his pipe and listen to the radio. My mother—she was a pretty woman, she knew how to dress, all right—she liked to go out and enjoy herself. I was stuck between the two of them and they pulled on both sides. I couldn't talk to one without the other accusing me of being ungrateful; I couldn't touch or kiss one of them without being afraid that the other one would see me and there would be a fight. I had to keep my thoughts to myself. I had to grow up wishing for some kind of miracle. I remember coming home from school one afternoon. I must have been twelve or thirteen. There was this man in the living room with my mother. They weren't doing anything; they were just sitting and talking. But I felt that something was going on. I seemed to stop breathing and I ran out of the house and threw up on the curbstone. Later on I swore to myself that I would make a miracle happen; that I wouldn't ever have to be where I didn't want to be and I wouldn't have to do what I didn't want to do; that I could be myself, without being afraid. But it's rough. With a background like mine you're always trying to catch up; it's as if you were born two steps behind the next fellow. (*They type; stop suddenly. They both stare at the audience, Sylvia leaning forward, Paul back in his chair, etc.*)

SYLVIA. My family never had money problems. In that respect we were very fortunate. My father made a good living, while he was alive, that is. He passed away when I was seventeen. You could say he and my mother had a fairly happy marriage. At least we never knew when they were angry with one another, and that's a good thing for children. I have a sister. Charlotte. She's older than I am. She's married now and we don't bother much with each other. But when we were younger you wouldn't believe what went on. Every time we quarreled, according to my parents she was right; I was always wrong. She got everything she wanted, no matter what, and I had to be content with the leftovers. It was just unbearable. Anyway, my father was sick for a long time before he passed away. He had this ring, it was a beautiful ring, with a large onyx stone in it, and when I was a girl I used to play with it. I'd close one eye and I'd look inside of it and I'd see hundreds and hundreds of beautiful red and blue stars. My father had always promised me that ring; he always said it belonged to me. I thought for certain he'd give it to me before he passed away, but he didn't say anything about it; not a word. Well, afterward, I saw it. You know where I saw it? On my sister's finger. He had given it to her. Now I don't think that's a background that leaves many possibilities for development. I don't forgive my father; definitely not. And I don't forgive my sister. My mother, whom I now support with my hard work, still says I'm wrong. (*They type; stop suddenly; turn to one another.*)

PAUL. Do you go to the movies?

SYLVIA. Not too often.

PAUL. Me neither.

SYLVIA. Do you like to watch television?

PAUL. I never get the chance. Don't forget I go to school five nights a week. But my wife watches it a lot; that's all she does.

SYLVIA. (*Surprised.*) I didn't know you were married.

PAUL. (*Types.*) This machine's full of errors. I'm getting nowhere fast. (*He is about to crumple card.*)

SYLVIA. (*Rising.*) Let me see that, please. (*Examines card, incommensurate anger.*) Now this could be erased. We don't approve of wasting material when it can be saved. That isn't the policy of this office.

PAUL. Okay. You don't have to be mad. I'll do it.

SYLVIA. I'm not mad. But I am responsible for what goes on in this department. I'm sick and tired of covering up for your mistakes. Everyone must think I'm a piece of rag to be stepped on. First him and now you.

PAUL. Do you mind telling me what you're talking about!

SYLVIA. You know very well what I'm talking about. This is my thanks; this is what I get for trying to be helpful and nice to people. I'm wrong, I know. I'm always wrong. Everything I do is wrong. Well, Mr. Cunningham, I've had enough, quite enough, and I won't take any more from you or anyone else. I won't! I won't! (*She flees U. to the restroom. Paul slaps the typewriter, goes to telephone, dials.*)

PAUL. (*Loudly.*) Let me speak to Mr. Francis T. Cunningham, please. Who's calling? Paul Cunningham! (*Softly.*) Hello, Uncle Frank. It's me again. Paul. How . . . how are you? Everything all right? That's good. Oh, everything's fine with me; still plugging away. I got a new job; yeah, typing, office work; just enough for bread. Uhuh. Uncle, can't you give me a hand? It's too rough for me. I can't hold down a job and go to school five nights a week; it's killing me. I know, I know. But I thought if you could give me a part-time job in your office, or maybe one of your friends, if you spoke to them . . . Yeah, sure. I understand. It's okay. Yeah. Send my regards. (*Paul returns to typewriter. Sylvia enters, exchanges her directory. Her appearance is that of a woman in her thirties.*)

SYLVIA. I'm sorry for losing my temper, Paul. It won't happen again.

PAUL. Forget it. (*He types.*)

SYLVIA. You've become an expert at that machine.

PAUL. (*Glumly.*) At least I'm an expert at something.

SYLVIA. Is anything the matter?

PAUL. No, but I was just thinking. What am I knocking myself out for? School almost every night, weekends I'm home studying, I can't remember the last time I took a decent vacation. What for? You're young only once; this is the time to enjoy yourself.

SYLVIA. (*At typewriter.*) I don't know how true that is. You probably could enjoy yourself a great deal more if you were a lawyer; that's why some sacrifices have to be made now.

PAUL. That's the kind of logic that leads nowhere. By your reasoning all lawyers should be happy men. No, sir; that isn't the way life is. You could be a ditch-digger and be happy if you know how to live. I tell you, I've had it. A fellow in my position has to take advantage of what's offered to him. He's got to be practical and look the facts right in the eye. (*Tapping table.*) This here is what's offered to me. This is my chance and from now on I start concentrating on this job. I'll show him I'm on the ball and maybe he'll find something else for me, give me a promotion, a better salary. Why not? An outfit this big always needs men who aren't afraid to work. Listen, I've got two kids at home. I've got to start thinking of them, too.

SYLVIA. (*Stiffly.*) You have two children?

PAUL. Sure. I don't waste any time. Look, I've got their pictures here. We took these last summer. (*He shows her photographs inside wallet.*) Well, what do you think?

SYLVIA. (*Coldly.*) They're beautiful. Paul. What's their names?

PAUL. Frank and Sally. But we call the boy Buddy; he hates it when we call him Frank; funny rascal. They're not bad for a character like me, are they? You know what I'm going to do, Syl? I'm going right in to him and ask him what my chances for advancement are. I might as well get all this settled now. Frankly I can use a little more money, too. The expenses are killing me. If we had a union in this place, we'd get some action. I may do something about that yet. (*He heads* L. *for employer's office, turns.*) What . . . what would you say is the best way to approach him?

SYLVIA. I honestly don't know, Paul. He changes from one minute to the next. But if he isn't wearing his glasses, that's a bad sign; I know that much.

PAUL. Glasses . . . I got it. Wish me luck?

SYLVIA. I hope you get something good. (*After Paul exits* L., *she goes to phone, dials.*) Ma? Sylvia. No, I'm all right. Did the lamp come? Well, just make sure when it comes that it isn't damaged; you'll have to sign for it and that means you inspected it. Look at it carefully; if there isn't any damage you can sign, but if there's anything wrong with it, the smallest thing, refuse to sign and tell the man to take it back. Do you understand? I hope so. Did I . . . get any calls? I didn't say I was expecting any, don't put words in my mouth, I merely asked you if I got any. Never mind. It's not important. Did Charlotte call? How is she? (*Paul enters* L. *He has the appearance of a man in his thirties. Sylvia carries on the remainder of her call as though talking to a boyfriend.*) Oh, stop being silly. I really couldn't. I have something this Saturday. I mean it. (*Laughing.*) No, no. Well, perhaps Sunday. Call me at home. All right. Bye.

PAUL. (*At typewriter.*) It looks good, real good. He's considering it. He says they may need someone on the sales staff. I'm first on the list.

SYLVIA. That does sound good. What about the raise?

PAUL. I'll have to wait awhile, he said. But I'll get it. He was impressed, especially when I told him I had some legal experience. You should have seen his eyes open up. It's only a question of time, and once I start moving, you watch, it's going to take a pretty fast man to keep up with me.

SYLVIA. You certainly have ambition, Paul.

PAUL. (*Rises to exchange directory.*) Listen, I don't intend to spend the rest of my life working here or any place else. I'll make my bundle and that's it. There's a world outside that window, a world with a thousand different things to see and do, and I'm going to see and do every last one of them; you watch.

SYLVIA. There's a million different things to do in the world.

PAUL. Lie in the sun . . .

SYLVIA. Dance . . .

PAUL. Travel . . .

SYLVIA. Wear pretty clothes . . .

PAUL. Visit places . . .

SYLVIA. Meet interesting people . . .

PAUL. Mountains. A place with mountains . . .

SYLVIA. (*Grabs Paul's lapels, her emotions soaring.*) Oh, Paul, I'm so filled with the desire to live, to experience things, to laugh . . . . Oh, I want to laugh, Paul. (*Silence. Paul stares dumbly at her, clears his throat. Stiffly they return to their chairs, type energetically.*)

PAUL. (*In a moment, calmly.*) When do we have lunch?

SYLVIA. We can have it any time we want. But I usually have it at one. The later you have it the shorter the afternoon is.

PAUL. How about waiting until one-thirty?

SYLVIA. That isn't easy.

PAUL. I know, but then we'd only have a couple of more hours to go. The afternoon would fly. What do you say?

SYLVIA. I'm willing, if you are.

PAUL. It's a deal, then. One-thirty lunch. (*They shake hands.*)

SYLVIA. One-thirty.

PAUL. Right. (*They both type.*)

SYLVIA. You know, I'm getting hungry already.

PAUL. So am I. I didn't have any breakfast.

SYLVIA. I had a cup of coffee, that's all.

PAUL. What have you got for lunch?

SYLVIA. A tuna-fish sandwich with tomatoes and mayonnaise, an orange and a piece of layer cake. What did you bring?

PAUL. Two turkey sandwiches and an apple, I think.

SYLVIA. One-thirty. (*They shake hands.*)

PAUL. That's the deal. (*They both type.*) We went down to Chinatown last weekend. What a meal we had.

SYLVIA. I'm crazy about Chinese food. I once went with a fellow who knew how to speak Chinese and you should have seen the things he ordered; the most fantastic dishes, with chicken livers and mushrooms and almonds . . .

PAUL. The Chinese people can cook, all right, but when it comes to *real* cooking you can't beat the Italians. There's a place we go to on the West Side; you should taste their veal parmesan or their chicken cacciatore. And they make a spaghetti sauce, you could . . .

SYLVIA. (*Goes to file cabinet.*) I think I'll eat now.

PAUL. (*Rising, furiously.*) We made a deal, didn't we?

SYLVIA. Don't be childish. If I want to eat now, I'll eat now, and that's all there is to it.

PAUL. You women are all alike. No backbone. No self-discipline. Go ahead and eat, I'm not going to stop you. But I'm sticking to my word.

SYLVIA. I didn't say I was going to eat, Mr. Cunningham. I merely said I was thinking of eating; listen before you speak. (*She waves at him blank postcards which she has taken from cabinet.*) And if you want to know something else, I could probably wait longer than you; I could probably go without lunch, which is more than some people can say.

PAUL. (*At typewriter.*) Is that so?

SYLVIA. (*At typewriter.*) That's so exactly.

PAUL. We'll see, Miss Supervisor.

SYLVIA. You're jealous. It's coming out all over you. I am supervisor . . .

PAUL. (*Waving his arm.*) Of this whole department. Boy, I'll never forget that as long as I live. (*Mimicking her in a small voice.*) "Believe me, Mr. Cunningham, I didn't ask him to be made supervisor. I don't like telling anyone what to do; that's part of my nature . . ." (*He falls on typewriter in a fit of laughter.*)

SYLVIA. You just keep that up and you won't be working here much longer, I assure you of that, Mr. Cunningham.

PAUL. Tell him. Go ahead and tell him. You'd be doing me a favor!

SYLVIA. What? You mean a man with your legal experience, with your plans and ambitions, requires a favor from me?

PAUL. Miss Payton, I loathe you!

SYLVIA. That, Mr. Cunningham, would be a gross understatement to describe my feelings for you. You make me sick!

PAUL. Why don't you quit, then?

SYLVIA. Why don't you?

PAUL. I wouldn't give you the satisfaction.

SYLVIA. And I wouldn't give you the satisfaction! (*They both type, loudly, rapidly.*)

PAUL. (*Slaps keys.*) What the hell am I doing? This isn't what I want. No, goddamn it!

SYLVIA. (*Without looking at him.*) I wonder if the man knows what he wants.

PAUL. (*Almost ominously.*) You bet I do. And do you know what it is? You know what I'd really like to do? Now, right here in this office? (*Rises, moves around Sylvia's chair.*) I'd like to rip the clothes right off your back, piece by piece. I'd like to dig my fingers into your flesh and feel your body break and sweat under mine. Do you understand me, Miss Payton?

SYLVIA. (*Rises, softly.*) Paul.

PAUL. It's been eating me up, ever since I first saw you. I want you, Miss Payton. Now! Now! This minute! Here, on the floor, screaming your lungs out and with your legs kicking up in the air. That's all I've been thinking of at that stupid typewriter; that's all that's been on my mind. (*Pause.*) Now you know.

SYLVIA. And what do you think I've been thinking of? My body aches with wanting you, Paul. (*Turning, pointing to his typewriter.*) How many times have I closed my eyes, just hoping you'd do something instead of sitting there like a stone statue! (*She falls back into him; he embraces her around the waist, standing behind her.*)

PAUL. Sylvia.

SYLVIA. I'll have to tell my mother, Paul. And you should tell your wife. Oh, I'll be good to the children. I promise you that.

PAUL. (*Stunned.*) Tell my wife?

SYLVIA. We will get married, won't we?

PAUL. Sylvia, listen . . .

SYLVIA. (*Turning to face him.*) We will get married, won't we?

PAUL. Aw, the hell with it! I'm going to eat. (*Gets lunch bag, throws coat over arm.*)

SYLVIA. (*At typewriter.*) It's my fault I know; you don't have to tell me.

PAUL. It's nobody's fault. It's . . . the way things are. (*At door* R.) Can I get you anything?

SYLVIA. I'm not eating.

PAUL. Suit yourself. (*Paul exits* R. *Sylvia runs to cabinet, takes out lunch bag, she eats her sandwich ravenously. The door is suddenly thrown open. Quickly Sylvia turns, clutching the sandwich to her chest, hiding it.*) Are you sure you don't want anything?

SYLVIA. (*With a mouthful of food.*) Positive.

PAUL. All right. (*Paul exits* R. *Sylvia goes to the phone, slowly, lethargically, dials.*)

SYLVIA. Ma? Sylvia. Nothing's wrong. I'm having my lunch now. The sandwich is fine. Did the table come? How is it? Are you sure? Sometimes they get damaged in shipping. Did you look carefully? Well, I hope so. Yes. Did I get any calls? No, I wasn't expecting any; I just asked. (*Pause.*) What did Charlotte say? That's just like her. She could come at least once a week to see how you are. All right, have it your own way. I'm too tired to argue with you. How are the children? That's nice. (*Pause.*) An eighty-five average doesn't mean he's a genius; no, not by any stretch of the imagination. I'm not saying she has stupid children; that isn't what I said, but I can't stand it when you raise them to the sky. I repeat, an eighty-five average is not in the genius class, and if you want proof ask anyone in the educational field. Oh, all right, all right; let's just drop it. I'll see you later. Of course I'm coming home. Where do you think I'd go? Fine. Good-bye. (*Sylvia throws the remainder of her sandwich into basket, reluctantly sits down at typewriter. As she types and swings the carriage across—for want of something to do—she sings the material she is typing with the lilting intonation of a small girl bouncing a ball on the sidewalk while reciting doggerel. Typing.*) Mrs. Anna Robinson, of 4 East 32nd Street, in the city and state of New York. (*Taking card out, putting new card in, forlornly.*) How are you today, Mrs. Anna Robinson? It has been so nice talking to you. Who have we here? Oh, it's (*Typing.*) Mr. Arnold Robinson, of 1032 Lexington Avenue, in the city and state of New York. (*Taking card out, putting new card in.*) It was so pleasant talking to you, Mr. Robinson. Send my regards to the family. Why, if it isn't (*Typing.*) Mrs. Beatrice Robinson, who lives no less on Park Avenue, in the city and state of New York. (*Taking card out, putting new card in.*) Must you leave so soon, Mrs. Robinson? (*Sylvia takes a gumdrop from a bag of candy, continues typing. Paul enters* R. *He is now in his forties. He carries a container of coffee.*)

PAUL. (*Referring to her candy.*) Up to your old tricks again, Sylvia? You'll never keep your figure that way.

SYLVIA. Don't worry about my figure; just worry about your own.

PAUL. (*Pulling his stomach in.*) You've got a point there. Here, I brought you some coffee.

SYLVIA. Thanks. (*Gets newspaper.*) How is it outside?

PAUL. A little chilly, but the sun's strong; nice. I took a walk up to the park. You never saw so many characters sitting on the benches and sunning themselves. I sure would like to know how they do it.

SYLVIA. Half of them are probably on relief.

PAUL. We work and they sun themselves.

SYLVIA. You should see the cars some of them have.

PAUL. You don't have to tell me. I know.

SYLVIA. I read in the newspapers that by the year 2000 people will work only three hours a day and have a three-day week.

PAUL. That's not going to help me.

SYLVIA. (*At typewriter, opens newspaper.*) We could try to get into a union.

PAUL. Do you know one that isn't crooked?

SYLVIA. How I wish this day was over.

PAUL. It'll feel good getting these shoes off.

SYLVIA. I'll wash my hair and do a little ironing.

PAUL. No date tonight?

SYLVIA. Don't be funny.

PAUL. (*At typewriter.*) You know, I was thinking, Syl. Ever since I was a kid I always thought I would like to be independent, to live my own life, without getting involved with responsibilities and families. Inside of me I suppose I always was afraid of that. But, you know, everything I've done in my life has taken me away from what I thought I'd like to be when I was a kid. I got married as soon as I could; I had children right away; I made it so tough for myself I couldn't get through law school. I couldn't live the kind of life I thought I wanted. I've been asking myself lately, what is it I really wanted? You know what the answer to that is, Syl? You know what it has to be? What I got. What I am. Maybe all I really wanted was to be sorry for myself.

SYLVIA. Does anyone know what they want, Paul?

PAUL. Don't you?

SYLVIA. Not any more. I thought I knew, just as you did. But if that's what I wanted, why am I where I am today?

PAUL. It doesn't make sense, does it?

SYLVIA. I swore that at the first opportunity I'd break away from my mother and my sister; I'd have nothing more to do with them and that would be happiness for me. But here I am still living with my mother and every day I ask how my sister is, what she's doing, how her husband is, the children . . . And I don't give a damn. Not a damn.

PAUL. The things I don't give a damn about . . . Syl, let's look into it. This is important.

SYLVIA. I've always said there's nothing more important than getting to know yourself. When you realize that people can live their whole lives without knowing themselves, without really getting to understand themselves, it . . . it reaches the ridiculous.

PAUL. (*Rising.*) You're absolutely right.

SYLVIA. (*Rising.*) Let's see what's behind it all. Let's study it a moment.

PAUL. All right, let's get to it. Why?

SYLVIA. Why?

PAUL. Why do you say that leaving your family would make you happy? If that's all there was to it, you could have left them years ago. No, there's something you're hiding.

SYLVIA. You're not telling the truth. If all you wanted was to feel sorry for yourself, all you'd have to do is sit in a corner and feel sorry for yourself; that's all there is to it. But, no; that isn't it.

PAUL. Then what is it?

SYLVIA. What are you hiding? (*As one speaks, wagging a finger, the other paces back and forth, nodding without listening, following a separate train of thought.*)

PAUL. The fact remains that you do care what happens to your family, you care a lot, an awful lot; that's why you phone every day, that's why you're always asking about your sister. You have to keep them together; you need them more than they need you because you never developed emotionally enough to forget the past and start a new life for yourself.

SYLVIA. You deliberately put yourself in situations in which you had to fail. Why is it I never heard you say you loved your wife? What was behind your marriage at such an early age? Why didn't you wait until you finished school so that you'd have a fair chance of getting ahead?

PAUL. Simply because you wanted something from them. It had nothing to do with your father's ring; you use that for a smoke screen.

SYLVIA. Now we're coming closer to the truth. You had to rush into marriage, have children and become burdened with impossible responsibilities, the very things you were afraid of; you had to fail because it wasn't that you wanted to feel sorry for yourself, but you wanted other people to feel sorry for you.

PAUL. That's it! They alone could give you what you wanted; no one else, not even a husband; that's why you never got married. Now we're coming closer to it . . .

SYLVIA. So that they would pity and pamper you like a child; you mistook that for love, which was what you really wanted from them, the love which you couldn't get from your parents. (*They suddenly stand face-to-face.*)

PAUL. There it is! You wanted love!

SYLVIA. You wanted love, of course!

PAUL. Don't you see it now, Syl?

SYLVIA. It's all so clear.

PAUL. When you know something about yourself, then you can start doing something about it. (*They march back to their typewriters.*)

SYLVIA. This has been one of the most pleasant conversations I've ever had, Paul.

PAUL. I enjoyed it myself. (*Glancing at wristwatch.*) And the afternoon's going pretty fast.

SYLVIA. Thank God for that. (*They both type.*)

PAUL. You know, thinking about it. I'm sure a lot better off than you are.

SYLVIA. Why's that?

PAUL. Well, I've got a place of my own; I did marry, have children. You could say I fulfilled a pretty important part of my life.

SYLVIA. That's nonsense. Do you think it requires any special ability to get married and have children?

PAUL. All I'm saying is that there are some people who would be awfully glad if they could have gotten married.

SYLVIA. Are you referring to me, Mr. Cunningham?

PAUL. I didn't mention any names, did I? But if the shoe fits, wear it, Miss Payton!

SYLVIA. (*Grimly.*) Don't make me laugh. If I had to make the choice—and I assure you I don't—I would much prefer being single than being forced to continue an unhappy marriage.

PAUL. An unhappy marriage? Where do you get that from? Did you ever hear me say that?

SYLVIA. I can put one and one together, Mr. Cunningham. We both know that if you had your way about it you would have left her long ago.

PAUL. Is that right?

SYLVIA. That's exactly right.

PAUL. Well, for your information, Miss Payton, my wife is the finest (*Rising.*), do you hear me? The finest, the most decent woman I ever had the good fortune to meet.

SYLVIA. Please, Mr. Cunningham.

PAUL. And for your further information, I wouldn't trade her for a dozen like you.

SYLVIA. You couldn't possibly. (*The buzzer rings; she fixes her hair, etc.*) Thank God, at last I'll have a moment away from you.

PAUL. I bet you think I don't know what goes on in there?

SYLVIA. What is he raving about now?

PAUL. Go ahead in. I can hear your boyfriend panting behind the door.

SYLVIA. Jealous?

PAUL. Of you?

SYLVIA. It's happened before.

PAUL. (*Turning away from her, loud undertone.*) You bitch!

SYLVIA. (*Turning, flaring.*) What did you say? (*No answer.*) You'd better be quiet. (*She exits L. Paul goes to hanger and without unwrapping or removing the whiskey bottle from his coat pocket pours a drink into a water cup, swallows it, then fills the cup again. He dials the phone.*)

PAUL. Barbara. Paul. How're the kids? That's good. Oh, pretty much the same. Listen, Barb, I'm . . . I'm sorry about last night. I had a little too much to drink. No, no, don't go excusing it. I just want you to know I didn't mean any of it. I think an awful . . . an awful lot of you, you know that, and I respect you, I always have. It's when I'm drinking, it's the whiskey that does the talking. I'm going to stop, I promise you. Barb, you forgive me, don't you? Well, say it; I want to hear you say it; please. (*Pause.*) Thank you. I'll try to get home early and we'll do something, we'll do something different, something . . . different, I promise you. All right. Don't forget. So long. (*He finishes his drink, crumples cup and slips it into his pocket. Sylvia enters* L., *carrying several sheets of paper, which she places on Paul's typewriter. She is now in her forties.*)

SYLVIA. He wants you to type copies of these. He's waiting for them.

PAUL. What's that?

SYLVIA. (*At typewriter.*) You heard me.

PAUL. Well, you hear me now. You can go right in there and tell him to go to hell. I'm not his secretary.

SYLVIA. Why don't you tell him yourself?

PAUL. That's a good idea! (*Moves to employer's office, grabbing papers from typewriter, turns.*) That's a damn good idea! (*Exits* L.)

SYLVIA. (*Typing, singsong, as before.*) Mr. Thomas Weaver, of 424 Harley Street, in the Bronx, New York. (*Taking card out, putting card in.*) I hope that you're having a pleasant day, Mr. Thomas Weaver. Now who is this coming along? Oh, it's (*Typing.*) Miss Tina Lee Weaver, of number 78 Monroe Avenue, in the Bronx, New York. How are you . . . (*Paul enters* L. *He shouts at employer's door as he rips papers in half and throws them in the air.*)

PAUL. There, there, that's what I think of you and your job, you old bastard!

SYLVIA. Paul!

PAUL. Why don't you go in and see your boyfriend now? You'll see him hiding behind the desk. If he stayed on his feet like a man I would have punched him right in the nose.

SYLVIA. Did you . . . quit?

PAUL. What the hell do you think I did? Trying to pull that stuff on me. I'm not his secretary and I never was. (*Shouting at employer's door.*) Do you hear me, you old bastard! I'm not your secretary and I never was!

SYLVIA. (*Rising, with concern.*) Please, Paul, be quiet; you're in enough trouble.

PAUL. Trouble? Me? Ha! That's the funniest thing I heard yet. You're looking at a free man, Miss Payton; a free and independent man. Yes, sir, I haven't felt this good in years.

SYLVIA. (*Following him to coat hanger.*) But what will you do?

PAUL. (*Removing whiskey bottle from coat, throwing wrapper away.*) Start living for one thing; start being myself; start being a man again. You know what it means to be a man, Miss Payton? You don't meet men any more; they're all afraid of losing their jobs, afraid of spending a dollar, afraid of their own shadows. But not this man. No, sir. I don't lick anybody's boots. What are you staring at? This? It's an old custom of mine. Care to join me? No, I didn't think so. (*He drinks from bottle.*)

SYLVIA. Paul, don't; this isn't like you.

PAUL. How do you know what I'm like? How does anybody know? We all live alone, Miss Payton; we all live alone in a cruel and lonely world. (*He drinks.*)

SYLVIA. How true that is.

PAUL. You know what I'm going to do? Yes, sir. The hell with it. I'm dropping everything, leaving everything. The first bus heading west tomorrow, you know who's going to be on it? I am. You bet. (*He raises bottle to mouth.*)

SYLVIA. (*Tries to take bottle from him.*) Paul, you've had enough of that.

PAUL. (*Pulls bottle away from her.*) Listen, this is no spur-of-the-minute thing with me, and it's not the whiskey doing the talking either. I've been thinking of it for a long time. This city stinks for my money; there's nothing here but a lot of smoke, noise and corruption. I don't know where that bus is going to take me, but I'm not getting off until I find a place where there's plenty of fresh air, lots of room, that's what I want, lots of room, and mountains, mountains as high as you can see. Yes, sir. When I find that place I'm getting off and that's where I'm staying.

SYLVIA. I always dreamt of going somewhere like that, ever since I was a girl; some place away from everyone and everything I know.

PAUL. Do you mean that?

SYLVIA. I'd give anything.

PAUL. (*Puts bottle on typewriter table.*) Syl.

SYLVIA. Yes, Paul?

PAUL. Listen, we . . . we get along pretty well, don't we?

SYLVIA. We get along extremely well.

PAUL. (*Standing behind her.*) The times I thought of taking you in my arms and holding you . . .

SYLVIA. Oh, if you only had.

PAUL. It's not too late, is it?

SYLVIA. No, no, it's not.

PAUL. The two of us, together. (*He holds her about the waist, she clasps his hands.*)

SYLVIA. Oh, Paul. I'm so happy. I'll call my mother. And you call your wife. I don't want there to be any hard feelings. Let's make it as pleasant as possible for everyone.

PAUL. (*Stunned.*) You want me to call my wife?

SYLVIA. Of course, silly; we're getting married, aren't we?

PAUL. But you don't understand . . .

SYLVIA. We are getting married, aren't we?

PAUL. Aw, what's the use.

SYLVIA. I know; it's my fault; no matter what I do or say it's my fault.

PAUL. No, my fault; it's my fault. I'm no good, Sylvia. I never was. I never had the guts to do anything but feel sorry for myself. I've been a lazy selfish son-of-a-bitch all my life. I never did a damn thing that amounted to a bag of beans. And now . . . Oh, my God! (*Leaning on typewriter, he sobs loudly.*)

SYLVIA. Paul, stop it; what are you doing? What's wrong?

PAUL. I don't care for myself; it's not for me. My life's over. My wife . . . (*Shouting.*) That bitch can go to hell! But the kids, Sylvia. I love those kids. Now what's going to happen to them? I don't have a job; there's no money put away, nothing. What did I do? What was I trying to prove?

SYLVIA. Why don't you go in and speak to him? Apologize, tell him anything. You're one of the best typists he's ever had; don't forget that.

PAUL. Do you think there's a chance? I can type; no one can say I can't. That's one thing I can do. Look, Sylvia. Look. (*He stands with his back to the type-writer and with his hands behind him types.*) Check that. Go ahead. You'll find there isn't a single mistake. And this, look at this. (*He stands between both typewriters, spreads his arms out and types on both machines simultaneously.*)

SYLVIA. I know, Paul; you're very good.

PAUL. There. Perfect. Check it. Check it. And this, Sylvia, look at this.

SYLVIA. That's enough, Paul. I believe you. I know you can . . . (*He stands on the chair at his typewriter, removes one shoe, gives it to Sylvia, and types with his stockinged foot, swings carriage across with his large toe, then slumps down in chair.*) Come down from there. You are good, you're very good.

PAUL. They deserve everything I can give them, Syl. I love those kids. (*He lifts up his foot; Sylvia puts on his shoe.*)

SYLVIA. I know. Now let's get you fixed up so you'll look presentable when you see him. (*Straightens his tie, brushes his jacket, etc.*) Stand still. Stop moving around.

PAUL. He'll never give me another chance, not after what I said to him.

SYLVIA. You just walk in and speak to him. There. Now you look fine. I'll fix things up out here. And we'd better get rid of this bottle. (*She takes it away from him as he raises it to his mouth.*)

PAUL. No more of that for me. I learned my lesson.

SYLVIA. I hope so. Well, go ahead in.

PAUL. Syl, I just want you to know this: if I get my job back, you're going to see some changes. Paul Cunningham has grown up at last.

SYLVIA. Go ahead in.

PAUL. No, not until I thank you for . . . for everything you've done.

SYLVIA. I didn't do a thing.

PAUL. Yes you did; more than I can thank you for. Did you ever think, Syl, what would have happened if the two of us had met before I married Barbara?

SYLVIA. (*Wistfully.*) Yes, I thought of it, many times.

PAUL. (*Moving toward her.*) Syl, listen to me . . .

SYLVIA. (*Raising her hands, moving away from him.*) Not that again. Please. Go in. Go on in. (*Paul exits* L. *to employer's office. Sylvia empties whiskey bottle in drain of water cooler, then drops bottle into basket; she picks papers from floor; sits at typewriter, puts eyeglasses on, and types. Paul enters* L. *He is now in his fifties.*)

PAUL. It's all right; it's all right. He's taken me back.

SYLVIA. I'm so glad for you.

PAUL. He was darn nice about it, too. He just listened to me and then he said, "It's understandable, Mr. Cunningham. We all have our problems."

SYLVIA. He can be nice when he wants to.

PAUL. "We all have our problems." He's not a stupid man.

SYLVIA. On the contrary, he understands a great many things.

PAUL. You know, we should buy him something; a little gift from the staff, something to show our appreciation. (*Rubbing hands, sits at typewriter.*) Well, let's get to it. There's not much left to the day now.

SYLVIA. Yes, soon it'll be over. (*They type in silence. Suddenly Paul breaks out in forced laughter.*) What's so amusing?

PAUL. Miss Supervisor . . . I'll never forget that as long as I live. "Believe me, Mr. Cunningham, I didn't ask him to be made a supervisor. I don't like telling anyone what to do."

SYLVIA. We all have our pretensions, Paul.

PAUL. (*Clearing his throat.*) That's very true. (*They type. Sylvia starts to laugh.*) What is it? What . . . what is it? What?

SYLVIA. I was just thinking of a boy I once went with.

PAUL. The Chinese fellow?

SYLVIA. No, no. I don't know any Chinese fellow. This boy was an entertainer. He could make you laugh by just looking at you.

PAUL. Did I ever tell you, Sylvia, that I used to take singing lessons?

SYLVIA. No?

PAUL. I did. When I was eight, nine . . .

SYLVIA. (*Rises, collects typed cards.*) I didn't know that.

PAUL. (*Sings.*) Way down upon the Swanee River . . . Far, far from home . . .

SYLVIA. You do have a voice.

PAUL. (*Sings monosyllabically.*) Da, *da*, da, da, da, *da*, da . . .

SYLVIA. (*At employer's door.*) Shh, not too loudly. (*Sylvia exits* L., *without tidy-*

ing herself, to employer's office. Paul types and sings monosyllabically, using his typewriter as if it were a musical instrument. On the card he has just typed he notices an error, crumples it and slips it into his pocket; he continues singing. Sylvia enters L. They are now in their middle-sixties, aged, slow-moving, but not gray-wigged, not senile.)

PAUL. (*Looking at his watch.*) Sylvia, it's twelve minutes to five.

SYLVIA. We don't generally stop until ten minutes to, Paul.

PAUL. I know. But I thought . . .

SYLVIA. That wouldn't be fair.

PAUL. You're right, as always. (*They type.*) Now, Sylvia? (*Without looking at timepiece.*)

SYLVIA. There's still . . . I would say a minute. (*They type.*)

PAUL. Now, Sylvia?

SYLVIA. Yes . . . Now.

PAUL. Thank God.

SYLVIA. I am tired. A good hot bath and then to bed with me. (*Rising he inadvertently brushes a card off the table, he picks it up, reads.*)

PAUL. "All wool knickers. From factory to you. At a tremendous saving." Knickers. We've been selling knickers.

SYLVIA. (*Covering typewriters.*) Come, come, let's put everything away.

PAUL. (*Going to coat hanger.*) Not many people wear knickers nowadays, do they? Knickers. They're warm, though; and practical, they're very practical.

SYLVIA. (*As Paul struggles with his coat.*) Here, let me help you with that. Isn't it too early yet?

PAUL. Just getting ready. (*He helps her put on her coat.*)

SYLVIA. What time is it, Paul? It doesn't feel like five.

PAUL. (*Looking at wristwatch.*) Another . . . two minutes. (*They sit down at typewriters, in their coats, immobile, expressionless, waiting for the two minutes to pass. Then Paul looks at his watch. Rising.*) It's time.

SYLVIA. (*As they move toward the employer's office.*) I have such a bad recollection. What is this new man's name, Paul?

PAUL. Smith or Stone or . . . I never could remember names.

SYLVIA. We'll give him a friendly good-bye just the same. (*They stand on the threshold of the office L., wave and cry shrilly.*)

PAUL. Good night. Good night in there.

SYLVIA. Have a pleasant evening. Good night.

PAUL. I'll walk you to the subway, Sylvia.

SYLVIA. That would be very nice. (*Sylvia stands by the door, buttoning her coat. Paul removes some crumpled cards from his pocket, he looks at them, forlornly, lets them fall from his hands to the floor. He starts toward Sylvia but changes his mind, returns, gets down on his haunches and picks up some crumpled cards; he looks around the office for a place to put them; finding none he slips them back into his pockets and exits R. with Sylvia.*)

BIBLIOGRAPHY

These books and articles, dealing with the problems of the actor, will provide informative and interesting reading.

Brook, Peter. *The Empty Space*. New York: Atheneum, 1968.

An influential director and experimentalist discusses what makes theatre vital and what makes it deadly. Throughout there are many penetrating comments about the art and craft of acting.

Brown, Richard P. (ed.). *Actor Training I*. New York: Drama Book Specialists, 1968.

This first issue of an intended series deals with approaches to acting through group improvisation, through placing emphasis upon performer rather than upon character, and through attempts to objectify subjective experience.

Chaikin, Joseph. *The Presence of the Actor*. New York: Atheneum, 1972.

A valuable aid to the understanding of self-exploration as a means of breaking away from convention and cliché.

Chekhov, Michael. *To the Actor*. New York: Harper & Row, 1953.

A creative approach by a student of Stanislavski and a one-time member of the Moscow Art Theatre. The concepts, especially the "psychological gesture," are imaginative. The exercises are stimulating, providing excellent problems in improvisation.

Cole, Toby (ed.). *Acting: A Handbook of the Stanislavski Method*. New York: Lear Publishers, 1947.

A group of articles describing principles and practices derived from Stanislavski. I. Rapoport, "The Work of the Actor," is particularly useful.

————, and Chinoy, Helen Krich (eds.). *Actors on Acting*. New York: Crown Publishers, 1949.

The long subtitle is significant: *The Theories, Techniques, and Practices of the Great Actors of All Times as Told in Their Own Words*. A selection of material by and about actors from Plato to José Ferrer.

Drama Review, The, Volume XVI, Number 1 (March 1972), "Acting Issue."

A collection of articles discussing new approaches to actor training and new concepts of actor-audience relationships.

Duerr, Edwin. *The Length and Depth of Acting*. New York: Holt, Rinehart and Winston, 1962.

An account of acting and actors from the Greeks to the present day. Of value both as history and as analysis of the actor's problems and objectives.

Funke, Lewis, and Booth, John E. *Actors Talk About Acting*. New York: Random House, 1961.

Taped interviews with fourteen "stars of the theatre": John Gielgud, Lynn Fontanne and Alfred Lunt, Helen Hayes, José Ferrer, Maureen Stapleton, Katharine Cornell, Vivien Leigh, Morris Carnovsky, Shelley Winters, Bert Lahr, Sidney Poitier, Paul Muni, and Anne Bancroft. The interviews provide some understanding of the creative processes of these actors.

Grotowski, Jerzy. *Towards a Poor Theatre*. New York: Simon and Schuster, 1968.

Articles by and about the famous Polish innovator. They describe a theatre devoid of commercialism, demanding the ultimate in personal dedication and rigorous physical and vocal training.

Hagen, Uta, with Frankel, Haskel. *Respect for Acting*. New York: Macmillan, 1973.

Distinguished both as actress and teacher, Miss Hagen talks about acting in both conceptual and practical terms. A stimulating and rewarding book for the serious student.

Hethmon, Robert H. (ed.). *Strasberg at the Actors Studio*. New York: Viking Press, 1965.

Tape-recorded sessions at the Actors Studio giving Lee Strasberg's comments and criticisms on scenes and exercises presented by Studio members. The comments reveal remarkable understanding of the actor's problems. They offer much practical help, especially in inducing relaxation and freeing the imagination.

Lewis, Robert. *Method—or Madness?* New York: Samuel French, 1958.

Eight witty and illuminating lectures explaining Stanislavski's principles and describing their use and misuse by American actors.

Magarshack, David. *Stanislavsky on the Art of the Stage*. New York: Hill and Wang, 1961.

Includes a posthumous collection of Stanislavski's lectures under the title "The System and Method of Creative Art." The introduction is a clear summary of the so-called Stanislavski system.

Marowitz, Charles. *Stanislavsky and the Method*. New York: Citadel Press, 1964.

Helpful application of Stanislavski's principles to various acting problems including the playing of Brecht and Shakespeare.

Stanislavski, Constantin. *An Actor Prepares*. Translated by Elizabeth Reynolds Hapgood. New York: Theatre Arts Books, 1936.

The most widely known in England and America of Stanislavski's works. It sets forth the principles of the "inner technique" and describes the concepts of sensory recall, emotion memory, relaxation, concentration, units and objectives, super-objectives, communion, adaption, through line of action.

————. *An Actor's Handbook*. Edited and translated by Elizabeth Reynolds Hapgood. New York: Theatre Arts Books, 1963.

Described accurately on the title page as "an alphabetical arrangement of concise statements on aspects of acting." The statements have been selected from the whole body of Stanislavski's writings.

————. *Building a Character*. Translated by Elizabeth Reynolds Hapgood. New York: Theatre Arts Books, 1949.

Less well known than *An Actor Prepares*, but vital to an understanding of Stanislavski's principles. It is concerned with developing an "outer technique." It is a necessary supplement to the earlier work.

————. *Creating a Role*. Translated by Elizabeth Reynolds Hapgood. New York: Theatre Arts Books, 1961.

How to work on a role from a first reading through various necessary stages of development.

Tulane Drama Review, Volume IX, Numbers 1 and 2 (Fall and Winter 1964).

These issues entitled *Stanislavski and America* marked the hundredth anniverary of Stanislavski's birth. They contain articles and interviews about Stanislavski's principles and their uses by prominent actors, directors, and teachers.

Young, Stark. *Theatre Practice*. New York: Charles Scribner's Sons, 1926.

A series of articles by a perceptive critic of acting.

ADDITIONAL SOURCES

On Acting

Barker, Cliff. *Theatre Games*. New York: Drama Book Specialists, 1977.

Berry, Cicely. *Voice and the Actor*. New York: Macmillan, 1973.

Benedetti, Robert L. *Seeing, Being, and Believing: Acting in our Century*. New York: Drama Book Specialists, 1977.

————. *the Actor at Work*. Englewood Cliffs, N.J.: Prentice-Hall, 1976.

Boleslavsky, Richard. *Acting: The First Six Lessons*. New York: Theatre Arts Books, 1933.

Cohen, Robert. *Acting Power*. Palo Alto, Calif.: Mayfield Publishing Co., 1978.

————. *Acting Professionally: Raw Facts About Careers in Acting* (2nd ed.). Palo Alto, Calif.: Mayfield Publishing Co., 1975.

Dezseran, Louis John. *The Student Actor's Handbook: Theatre Games and Exercises*. Palo Alto, Calif.: Mayfield Publishing Co., 1975.

Gielgud, John. *Early Stages: A Theatrical Reminiscence*. New York: Taplinger, 1976.

Glenn, Stanley L. *The Complete Actor*. Boston: Allyn and Bacon, 1977.

Goldman, Michael. *The Actor's Freedom*. New York: Viking, 1975.

Hornby, Richard. *Script into Performance*. Austin: University of Texas Press, 1978.

Joseph, Bertram. *Acting Shakespeare*. New York: Theatre Arts Books, 1969.

Kahan, Stanley. *An Actor's Workbook*. New York: Harcourt Brace Jovanovich, 1967.

Klein, Maxine. *Time, Space, and Designs for Actors*. New York: Macmillan, 1975.

Lessac, Arthur. *The Use and Training of the Human Voice*. New York: Drama Book Specialists, 1967.

Linklater, Kristin. *Freeing the Natural Voice*. New York: Drama Book Specialists, 1976.

Lyon, Harold C., Jr. *Learning to Feel, Feeling to Learn*. Columbus, Ohio: Charles E. Merrill Co., 1971.

Machlin, Evangeline. *Dialects for the Stage*. New York: Theatre Arts Books, 1975.

Markus, Thomas. *The Professional Actor from Audition to Performance*. New York: Drama Book Specialists, 1978.

Moore, Sonia. *Training an Actor*. New York: Penguin, 1979.

Matson, Katinka. *The Working Actor: A Guide to the Profession*. New York: Viking, 1976.

McGaw, Charles. *Working a Scene: An Actor's Approach*. New York: Holt, Rinehart and Winston, 1977.

Nahas, Rebecca. *Your Acting Career*. New York: Crown, 1976.

Pisk, Litz. *The Actor and His Body*. New York: Theatre Arts Books, 1975.

Redfield, William. *Letter from an Actor*. New York: Viking/Compass, 1969.

Rockwood, Jerome. *The Craftsmen of Dionysus*. Glenview, Ill.: Scott, Foresman, 1966.

Schechner, Richard. *Environmental Theatre*. New York: Hawthorn Books, 1973.

Seyler, Athene, and Haggard, Stephen. *The Craft of Comedy* (2nd ed.). New York: Theatre Arts Books, 1957.

Shurtleff, Michael, and Hunt, Gordon. *Audition: Everything an Actor Needs to Get the Part*. New York: Walker, 1978.

Spolin, Viola. *Improvisation for the Theatre*. Evanston, Ill.: Northwestern University Press, 1963.

White, Edwin, and Battye, Marguerite. *Acting and Stage Movement*. New York: Arco, 1978.

Biographies and Autobiographies

Ashley, Elizabeth. *Actress: Postcards from the Road*. New York: M. Evans, 1978.

Fontaine, Joan. *No Bed of Roses*. New York: William Morrow, 1978.

Forbes, Brian. *Dame Edith Evans: Ned's Girl*. Boston: Little, Brown, 1978.

Heston, Charlton. *The Actor's Life: Journals, 1956–1976*. New York: Dutton, 1978.

Lahr, John. *Notes on a Cowardly Lion*. New York: Knopf, 1969.

Mostel, Kate, and Gilford, Madeline. *170 Years of Show Business*. New York: Random House, 1978.

Seldes, Marian. *The Bright Lights*. Boston: Houghton Mifflin, 1978.

Skinner, Cornelia Otis. *Madam Sarah*. Boston: Houghton Mifflin, 1966.

Taranow, Gerda. *Sarah Bernhardt: The Art Within the Legend*. Princeton, N.J.: Princeton University Press, 1972.

Ullmann, Liv. *Changing*. New York: Knopf, 1977.

THEATRES AND GROUPS

MAJOR RESIDENT THEATRES

Tyrone Guthrie Theatre
Vineland Place
Minneapolis, Minnesota 55403

The Guthrie, which opened its doors in 1963, is one of the leading American resident theatres. Named for its noted British founding director, it is a handsome 1437-seat theatre with a thrust stage.

The American Conservatory Theatre
450 Geary Street
San Francisco, California 94102

Artistic director William Ball has made A.C.T. the nation's largest and most active repertory company. It has presented more than 100 major productions ranging from classics to contemporary works.

Actor's Theatre of Louisville
316 West Main Street
Louisville, Kentucky 40202

The theatre complex, housed partly in a Victorian warehouse and partly in a beautiful Greek revival building that forms the lobby, has been serving its community for more than a dozen years. The 641-seat Pamela Brown Theatre and the upstairs Victor Jory Theatre have seen numerous premieres, among them D. L. Coburn's *The Gin Game* and David Mamet's *Reunion*.

Center Theatre Group
135 N. Grand Avenue
Los Angeles, California 90012

Located in the Music Center, the Mark Taper Forum's 750-seat thrust stage playhouse has offered the premieres of many fine plays, among them *The Trial of the Catonsville Nine, The Shadow Box*, and *Ashes*. For the experimentally minded, the Improvisational Theatre Project and the Forum/Laboratory, under the Mark Taper auspices, present works by new dramatists.

The Long Wharf Theatre
222 Sargent Drive
New Haven, Connecticut 06511

Known for the vitality of its productions, New Haven's Long Wharf has a reputation for spotlighting plays of international importance. It was the first theatre in the United States to present David Storey's *The Changing Room*, the South African drama *Sizwe Banzi Is Dead*, and David Rabe's *Streamers*.

The Arena Stage
6th and M Streets, S.W.
Washington, D.C. 20024

Known for its lively productions of Howard Sackler's *The Great White Hope* and Arthur Kopit's *Indians*.

The Hartford Stage Company
50 Church Street
Hartford, Connecticut 06103

Recent productions include Wilder's *The Matchmaker*, Brecht's *Galileo*, and Alice Childress' *Wedding Band*.

Trinity Square Repertory Company
201 Washington Street
Providence, R.I. 02903

Artistic director Adrian Hall gained national attention with his production of *Feasting with Panthers*, about the life of Oscar Wilde.

Dallas Theatre Center
3636 Turtle Creek Blvd.
Dallas, Texas 75219

Paul Baker is the head of this remarkable theatre, which presented the premiere of *A Texas Trilogy*.

Alley Theatre
615 Texas Avenue
Houston, Texas 77002

The Alley managed to corral international attention with a production of
Echelon, directed by Galina Volchek, the first Soviet director to restage a
Soviet play for an American company.

OTHER SELECTED MAJOR RESIDENT THEATRES

A.C.T.: A Contemporary Theatre (Seattle, Washington)
Alliance Theatre Company (Atlanta, Georgia)
Asolo State Theatre Company (Sarasota, Florida)
Barter Theatre (Abingdon, Virginia)
Center Stage (Baltimore, Maryland)
Cincinnati Playhouse in the Park (Cincinnati, Ohio)
Cleveland Playhouse (Cleveland, Ohio)
Company Theatre (Los Angeles, California)
Detroit Repertory Theatre (Detroit, Michigan)
Goodman Theatre (Chicago, Illinois)
Hartman Theatre Company (Stamford, Connecticut)
Loretta-Hilton Repertory Theatre (St. Louis, Missouri)
McCarter Theatre Company (Princeton, New Jersey)
Meadow Brook Theatre (Rochester, Minnesota)
Milwaukee Repertory Theatre Co. (Milwaukee, Wisconsin)
Negro Ensemble Co. (New York, New York)
New York Shakespeare Festival (New York, New York)
Oklahoma Theatre Center (Oklahoma City, Oklahoma)
Seattle Repertory Theatre Company (Seattle, Washington)
Studio Arena Theatre (Buffalo, New York)
Yale Repertory Theatre (New Haven, Connecticut)

THEATRE ORGANIZATIONS OF INTEREST TO ASPIRING ACTORS

American Theatre Association (Washington, D.C.)
Theatre Communications Group (New York, New York)
University/Resident Theatre Association (New York, New York)
League of Professional Theatre Training Programs (New York, New York)

INDEX